SAGE was founded in 1965 by Sara Miller McCune to support the dissemination of usable knowledge by publishing innovative and high-quality research and teaching content. Today, we publish over 900 journals, including those of more than 400 learned societies, more than 800 new books per year, and a growing range of library products including archives, data, case studies, reports, and video. SAGE remains majority-owned by our founder, and after Sara's lifetime will become owned by a charitable trust that secures our continued independence.

Los Angeles | London | New Delhi | Singapore | Washington DC | Melbourne

URBAN RENEWAL in INDIA

Thank you for choosing a SAGE product!
If you have any comment, observation or feedback,
I would like to personally hear from you.

Please write to me at **contactceo@sagepub.in**

Vivek Mehra, Managing Director and CEO, SAGE India.

Bulk Sales

SAGE India offers special discounts
for purchase of books in bulk.
We also make available special imprints
and excerpts from our books on demand.

For orders and enquiries, write to us at

Marketing Department
SAGE Publications India Pvt Ltd
B1/I-1, Mohan Cooperative Industrial Area
Mathura Road, Post Bag 7
New Delhi 110044, India

E-mail us at **marketing@sagepub.in**

Get to know more about SAGE

Be invited to SAGE events, get on our mailing list.
Write today to **marketing@sagepub.in**

This book is also available as an e-book.

S. K. Kulshrestha

URBAN RENEWAL in INDIA

Theory, Initiatives and Spatial Planning Strategies

Los Angeles | London | New Delhi
Singapore | Washington DC | Melbourne

Copyright © S. K. Kulshrestha, 2018

All rights reserved. No part of this book may be reproduced or utilised in any form or by any means, electronic or mechanical, including photocopying, recording, or by any information storage or retrieval system, without permission in writing from the publisher.

First published in 2018 by

SAGE Publications India Pvt Ltd
B1/I-1 Mohan Cooperative Industrial Area
Mathura Road, New Delhi 110 044, India
www.sagepub.in

SAGE Publications Inc
2455 Teller Road
Thousand Oaks, California 91320, USA

SAGE Publications Ltd
1 Oliver's Yard, 55 City Road
London EC1Y 1SP, United Kingdom

SAGE Publications Asia-Pacific Pte Ltd
3 Church Street
#10-04 Samsung Hub
Singapore 049483

Published by Vivek Mehra for SAGE Publications India Pvt Ltd, typeset in 10.5/13 pt Adobe Caslon Pro by Fidus Design Pvt. Ltd., Chandigarh and printed at Chaman Enterprises, New Delhi.

Library of Congress Cataloging-in-Publication Data
Name: Kulshrestha, S. K., author.
Title: Urban renewal in India: theory, initiatives and spatial planning strategies/
   S. K. Kulshrestha.
Description: New Delhi, India; Thousand Oaks, California: SAGE, 2018. | Includes index.
Identifiers: LCCN 2017058360| ISBN 9789352806379 (hardback) |
   ISBN 9789352806386 (e-pub 2.0) | ISBN 9789352806393 (ebook)
Subjects: LCSH: Urban renewal—India. | City planning—India.
Classification: LCC HT178.I4 K85 2018 | DDC 307.3/4160954—dc23
LC record available at https://lccn.loc.gov/2017058360

ISBN: 978-93-528-0637-9 (HB)

SAGE Team: Abhijit Baroi, Vandana Gupta, Kumar Indra Mishra and Ritu Chopra

Contents

List of Tables	vii
List of Figures	ix
List of Annexures	xi
List of Abbreviations	xiii
Preface	xix
Acknowledgements	xxv

1	Theory of Urban Renewal	1
2	Urban Renewal Initiatives in India	28
3	Spatial Planning Strategies for Urban Renewal	98
4	Reforms as Strategy for Rejuvenating Urban Governance and Promoting Urban Renewal	114
5	Tools and Techniques of Urban Renewal	156
6	Resource Mobilisation for Urban Renewal	216
7	The Future of Urban Renewal	251

Index	272
About the Author	275

List of Tables

2.1	Status of Sector-wise Committed Funds (UIG) (31 December 2012)	35
2.2	Status of Metrorail in Different Cities in India (2016)	37
2.3	Types of Settlements in Delhi and Their Population in the Year 2000	62
2.4	Specialised Market Streets in Shahjahanabad	64
2.5	Percentage of Total Population Living in Slums in Mumbai (1971–2011)	74
2.6	Sabarmati Riverfront Scheme, Proposed Land Use of Reclaimed Land	82
4.1	Reforms under JNNURM	117
4.2	Status of State/UT-level Reform Under JNNURM (31 March 2013)	120
4.3	ULB-level Reforms Committed up to Seven Years Under JNNURM (31 March 2013)	125
4.4	Commitment to Internal Earmarking of Funds in the Budget for Basic Services for Urban Poor (31 December 2013)	127
4.5	Reduced Time Taken for a Variety of Services due to Implementation of CARD in Andhra Pradesh and Karnataka	131
4.6	Implementation of AMRUT Reforms by Eight States (April 2017)	140
4.7	Implementation of AMRUT Reforms and Award of Reform Incentive to States and UTs (30 September 2016)	141

5.1	Statutory Provisions for Urban Renewal in Some of the Town Planning and Development Acts in India	158
5.2	Spatial Norms for Slum Redevelopment in Mumbai and Delhi	174
5.3	Spatial Norms for Relocation of JJ Clusters in Delhi	176
5.4	Spatial Norms for the Regularisation of Unauthorised Colonies in Delhi	177
5.5	Service-level Benchmarks	196
6.1	Central Government Grants Available for Urban Renewal in India	227
6.2	The Central Government Share of Grant Under JNNURM as Percentage of the Total Project Cost	228
7.1	Projected Urban Population, Decadal Increase and Urbanisation in India 2020–2050	252
7.2	Variation of FSI in CBDs of Selected Cities in the World	258

List of Figures

1.1	Cycle of Growth and Decay of Cities and Role of Urban Renewal	2
5.1	Interrelationship Among Various Tools	163
5.2	Steps in the Process of Redevelopment	165
6.1	Concept of Land, Its Potential and Transfer of Land Potential	217
7.1	Growth Rate of Employment in Select Metropolitan Core, Suburban Towns and Villages, 1998–2005	253
7.2	The Spatial Approach for Urban Renewal	255
7.3	FSI Distribution in CBDs of Select Cities	263

List of Annexures

2.1	List of 98 Cities Selected Under Smart Cities Mission	86
2.2	New Projects Sanctioned Under Swadesh Darshan During 2016–2017 (as on 31 December 2016)	89
4.1	Twelfth Schedule (Article 243W) to the Constitution (74th Amendment) Act, 1992	147
4.2	Reforms, Milestones and Timeline Under AMRUT for Mission Cities	148
4.3	Investment Grade Credit Ratings of Urban Local Bodies in India, 2017	153
5.1	Stage-wise Description of Slum Redevelopment Process in Mumbai	197
5.2	Guideline for Area Redevelopment in Mumbai	200
5.3	Guideline for Area Redevelopment in Delhi	202
5.4	Cluster Redevelopment Scheme, Mumbai	203
5.5	Guidelines for Regularisation of Unauthorised Colonies in Delhi	205
5.6	Policy Guidelines for the Scheme for Relocation of JJ Clusters in Delhi	209
6.1	Composition of the Slum Rehabilitation Authority, Mumbai	245
6.2	Structure and Functions of SPV	246

List of Abbreviations

A&OE	administrative and office expenses
ADB	Asian Development Bank
AGNI	Action for Good Governance Network of India
AHP	Affordable Housing in Partnership
AIIMS	All India Institute of Medical Sciences
AKDN	Aga Khan Development Network
AMRUT	Atal Mission for Rejuvenation and Urban Transformation
ASI	Archaeological Survey of India
AusAID	Australian Aid
BLT	Build–Lease–Transfer
BMC	Bombay Municipal Corporation
BMRP	Bombay Metropolitan Region Plan
BOOT	Build–Own–Operate–Transfer
BOT	Build–Operate–Transfer
BRTS	Bus Rapid Transit System
BSUP	Basic Services for Urban Poor
BSY	Balika Samridhi Yojana
CAG	Comptroller and Auditor General
CARD	Computer-aided Administration of Registration Department
CBD	Central Business District
CBO	community-based organisation
CBRI	Central Building Research Institute
CCTV	close circuit television
CDPs	city development plans
CLAP	city-level action plans
CLSS	Credit Linked Subsidy Scheme
CM	chief minister
CMEY	Chief Minister's Empowerment of Youth

CMP	comprehensive mobility plan
CMPO	Calcutta Metropolitan Planning Organisation
CPL	Community Participation Law
CPWD	Central Public Works Department
CRRI	Central Road Research Institute
CSS	Centrally Sponsored Scheme
CST	Chhatrapati Shivaji Terminus
DCB	Demand Collection Book
DCR	Development Control Rules
DDA	Delhi Development Authority
DEAS	double entry accounting system
DFID	Department for International Development
DPR	detailed project report
DRC	Development Rights Certificate
DSIIDC	Delhi State Industrial and Infrastructure Development Corporation
DU	dwelling unit
DUAC	Delhi Urban Art Commission
DUSIB	Delhi Urban Shelter Improvement Board
ECS	equivalent car spaces
E-MAAS	e-Municipality as a Service
EWS	economically weaker sections
FAR	floor area ratio
FSI	floor space index
GIS	geographic information system
GNCTD	Government of National Capital Territory pf Delhi
GPS	global positioning system
GST	goods and services tax
GVMC	Greater Visakhapatnam Municipal Corporation
HIG	high-income group
HPC	High Power Committee
HPSC	High Power Steering Committee
HRHD	high-rise-high-density
HRIDAY	Heritage City Development and Augmentation Yojana

HUDCO	Housing and Urban Development Corporation
ICE	innovative creative excellence
ICT	information communication technology
IDFC	Infrastructure Development Finance Company
IGBC	Indian Green Building Council
IHSDP	Integrated Housing and Slum Development Programme
IIPA	Institute of Public Administration
IIT	Indian Institute of Technology
IL&FS	Infrastructure Leasing and Finance Services
IMC	Indore Municipal Corporation
INTACH	Indian National Trust for Architectural and Cultural Heritage
IRMA	Independent Review and Monitoring Agencies
IRSDC	Indian Railway Station Development Corporation
JBIC	Japan Bank for International Cooperation
JICA	Japan International Cooperation Agency
JJ	*jhuggi jhopri*
JNNURM	Jawaharlal Nehru National Urban Renewal Mission
KMC	Kolkata Municipal Corporation
KMDA	Kolkata Metropolitan Development Authority
LIG	low-income group
MCD	Municipal Corporation of Delhi
MHADA	Maharashtra Housing and Area Development Authority
MIG	middle-income groups
MLA	Member of Legislative Assembly
MoA	Memorandum of Agreement
MoHUPA	Ministry of Housing and Urban Poverty Alleviation
MoUD	Ministry of Urban Development
MP	Member of Parliament
MPC	Metropolitan Planning Committees
MPD	Master Plan for Delhi
MRTS	Mass Rapid Transit System

NAGAR	NGOs' Alliance for Governance and Research
NBCC	National Building Construction Corporation
NDMC	New Delhi Municipal Corporation
NGO	non-governmental organisation
NHB	National Housing Bank
NIIF	National Investment and Infrastructure Fund
NIT	National Institute of Technology
NITI	National Institute for Transforming India
NSDP	National Slum Development Programme
O&M	operation and maintenance
ODF	open-defecation-free
OECD	Organisation for Economic Cooperation and Development
PFDS	Pooled Finance Development Scheme
PM	prime minister
PMAY	PM Awas Yojana
PMAY-HFA (U)	PMAY–Housing for All (Urban)
PMAY-U	Pradhan Mantri Awas Yojana (Urban)
PMDC	project management and development consultant
PMU	programme management unit
PPP	public–private partnership
PRASAD	Pilgrimage Rejuvenation and Spiritual Augmentation Drive
PUDR	Peoples Union for Democratic Rights
RAY	Rajiv Awas Yojana
RCC	reinforced cement concrete
RFCTLARR	Right to Fare Compensation and Transparency in Land Acquisition, Rehabilitation and Resettlement
RIF	Reform Incentive Fund
ROW	right of way
RWAs	Resident Welfare Associations
RWH	rainwater harvesting
SAAP	State Annual Action Plan
SBM	Swachh Bharat Mission
SC	scheduled cast

SCP	smart city proposal
SFC	State Finance Commission
SFCPoA	Slum Free City Plans of Action
SHG	self-help groups
SJSRY	Swarna Jayanti Shahari Rozgar Yojana
SLIP	Service Level Improvement Plan
SLTC	State Level Technical Committee
SMC	Surat Municipal Corporation
SRA	Slum Rehabilitation Authority
ST	Scheduled Tribe
TDR	Transferable Development Right
TOD	transit-oriented development
TSM	Traffic System Management
UIDSSMT	Urban Infrastructure Development Scheme for Small and Medium Towns
UIG	Urban Infrastructure and Governance
ULB	urban local bodies
ULCRA	Urban Land (Ceiling and Regulation) Act
USTDA	US Trade Development Agency
VHIG	very high-income group

Preface

India is changing. Winds of change seem to be spreading everywhere—politics, administration, financial system and planning. In politics, the focus seems to be shifting from social engineering to a development agenda. In administration, the centre–state relationship is heading towards cooperative federalism, where states are equal partners in nation-building, and the prime minister (PM) along with all chief ministers (CMs) forms 'Team India' to realise the vision of 'New India'.

The financial system in India, in the form of the annual budget, has changed where Railway Ministry is not special with a separate slot in the budget session of the Parliament. Now, it is an integral part of the general budget like any other ministry. There is a move to change the financial year from April–March to January–December. The other changes in the financial system include demonetisation, new design of currency notes and introduction of ₹2,000 note. Efforts are on to shift from cash to cashless transactions. Introduction of Goods and Services Tax (GST) is another financial system reform introduced in July 2017, which makes India a unified common market with a slogan: 'One Country, One Tax, One Market'. Acceptance of GST by the state governments is an indication of their support to cooperative federalism and its spirit—one nation, one aspiration and one determination.

The national planning system has been completely transformed. The Planning Commission has been replaced with a think tank known as National Institute for Transforming India (NITI). It is functioning as a commission (*aayog*) and designated as NITI Aayog. Following the approach to cooperative federalism, it is conceived as a collaborative federal body whose strength lies in its ideas rather than in administrative and financial controls. As a procedure now, CMs do not visit NITI Aayog for approval of state five-year plans and annual plans, as was the practice with erstwhile Planning Commission, instead the

Aayog members visit states to identify their developmental challenges and the alternative solutions in consultation with the CMs and their teams. At the central government level, each ministry now prepares and implements its respective development plans.

The era of Five Year Plans ended this year, on 31 March 2017. India's development will be guided by a new planning system based on a long-term, 15-year vision; medium-term, 7-year strategy; and short-term, 3-year action agenda.

Indian cities are also transforming. There seems to be political support to urban transformation. Various ministries have introduced programmes and schemes to promote the transformation of urban centres. Ministry of Urban Development (MoUD), Government of India, has introduced the Smart Cities Mission, which focuses on transforming 100 selected urban centres as smart cities through smart solutions pertaining to urban governance and management of water, solid waste, energy and transport based upon application of information communication technology (ICT). MoUD has initiated another programme, Atal Mission for Rejuvenation and Urban Transformation (AMRUT), which covers 500 cities and focuses on improved service delivery and public transport as well as enhancement of amenity value of city through creating public spaces. AMRUT also includes transformation of urban governance and urban planning through a set of 11 reforms. These two missions have also changed the pattern of work culture where achievement is judged not by money spent but by milestones crossed and targets achieved within a given timeline. For the first time, a healthy competition has also been introduced among cities to perform better. It seems well received by the states and urban local bodies; social transformation is taking place under Swachh Bharat Mission, another programme of MoUD, which aims at changing the social habit of open defecation.

Various ministries have introduced their programmes for transforming India. Ministry of Railway is redeveloping 300 stations to facilitate visitors and present a welcome reception on their arrival. Ministry of Tourism has initiated Pilgrimage Rejuvenation and Spiritual Augmentation Drive (PRASAD) to provide unique experience to visitors on religious tourism in selected 25 places.

In short-term, these efforts to transform urban India are commendable and would provide useful learning experience regarding policies and manner of urban transformation. However, the efforts are piecemeal, fragmented and uncoordinated. I am aware of the mention of convergence of schemes which have similar goals attained through different paths. In the long term, say next two decades, a planned approach is needed for India's urban transformation.

In addition to the policy initiatives discussed in the preceding paragraphs, there are other reasons to renew cities in India. Indian cities are ageing, and about 1,800 cities are more than 100 years old. By 2050, more than 50% of the country's population will be living in urban centres. To accommodate ever-growing urban population, peri-urban areas of large cities are expanding, causing urban sprawl when there are several planned and unplanned areas, within the municipal limit, which are unutilised or underutilised. The core areas of most of the existing cities are generally congested, unplanned and decaying.

Due to the introduction of liberalisation of the economy in 1991 and the resultant flow of foreign direct investment, cities have become centres of attention and preferred destinations for investment. Improving the quality and liveability of cities, therefore, becomes a prime concern.

Considering the previously mentioned scenarios, this book aims at providing all the stakeholders, engaged in the process of urban renewal, the required technical knowledge, including theory, initiatives, spatial planning strategies, tools, techniques and innovative approaches, for the mobilisation of land and fiscal resources and the creation of institutional mechanism for urban renewal.

This book comprises seven chapters. Chapter 1 attempts at discussing the theory of urban renewal, incorporating the process of growth, decay and demise of cities and how, through urban renewal, the urban decay could be mitigated. It defines urban renewal and various terms associated with it and then discusses innovative approaches that provide the driving force to the process of urban renewal. This chapter also attempts at evolving a set of four principles of urban renewal that must be followed in all such programmes.

Chapter 2 focuses on urban renewal initiatives taken in India at national, state and city levels. At the national level, it discusses various missions and programmes such as JNNURM, Slum-free Cities under Rajiv Awas Yojana (RAY), Pradhan Mantri Awas Yojana (Urban), Housing for all by 2022, Smart Cities Mission, AMRUT, HRIDAY, Swadesh Darshan, PRASAD, and redevelopment of railway stations. Since the implementation of national policies, programmes and missions is the responsibility of the states, this chapter discusses the enabling climate created by them in terms of creation of legal and institutional support. At the city level, it presents the urban renewal initiatives taken by various cities, including Delhi, Mumbai, Kolkata, Indore, Ahmedabad, Mysore City, Pune and Hyderabad, and discusses various urban renewal projects proposed/implemented in these cities by the urban local bodies and other agencies.

Observing that 'one-strategy-fits-all' approach cannot be applied to all cities as each place is unique and has specific problems, peculiarities and potentials, Chapters 3 and 4 explore and discuss the various strategies being used in urban renewal and advocate that depending upon the characteristics of the area, a combination of strategies may be applied. Chapter 3 focuses exclusively on spatial planning strategies and covers strategies such as clearance, redevelopment, resettlement, decongestion, redensification, regularisation, in situ upgradation, rehabilitation, revitalisation/retrofitting, conservation, restructuring and creation of underground spaces. Chapter 4 deals with reforms as a non-spatial strategy in the revitalisation of urban governance and urban renewal. This chapter covers reforms advocated by JNNURM, RAY, AMRUT, PMAY-U and Smart Cities Mission.

Chapter 5 discusses the tools and techniques of urban renewal and covers legal as well as the spatial planning tools and techniques for the preparation, implementation, marketing and outcome assessment of urban renewal plans. It discusses various processes, guidelines, spatial planning norms, methods of the promotion of community participation, contents of spatial plans and implementation initiatives taken by various stakeholders including owners, cooperative societies, politicians, government agencies, public–private joint-sector bodies, and private developers. This chapter also discusses implementation actions which could be comprehensive, strategic and/or tactical.

Chapter 6 covers the mobilisation of land, financial and institutional resources for urban renewal. This chapter explains the land and its potentials. It also explains the manner in which the land potential can be transferred to another site for protecting development right of the landowners and also mobilising land or fiscal resource, for the implementation of plans, using spatial planning tool such as Transferable Development Right (TDR). In addition to traditional sources, it discusses the innovative spatial planning techniques for the mobilisation of land and fiscal resources using land potential.

Finally, Chapter 7 presents the future of urban renewal in India. This chapter presents the future scenario of urbanisation and urban spatial growth in India. It discusses the way forward, highlighting the approaches related to accessibility and connectivity; density, the extent of built-up space and infrastructure; mixed land uses pattern, inclusive of urban renewal; urban reforms and implementation actions. The book advocates that to meet the challenges of urbanisation, planned urban extension along with urban renewal will serve as a potent strategy to equip cities to help serve their role as homes for urban population and the centres of economic activates, employment opportunities, innovations and hope. The book concludes that the next 10 years will be the 'decade of urban renewal in India'.

This book will provide useful material and serve the various stakeholders engaged in the process of urban renewal through various missions and programmes in India. These stakeholders include various state and central ministries, municipal corporations of class I cities, development authorities, state government departments, consultants and foreign or multinational consultancy firms engaged in urban renewal in India, NGOs, undergraduate and postgraduate students of urban planning and architecture, practising urban planners, architects, housing experts, urban designers and conservation architects and civil engineers. This book will be of interest to academicians and researchers in India and foreign countries and will provide material on the subject in the Indian context. Since urban renewal affects common man, this book will be of interest to them as well.

Acknowledgements

I started working on this book sometime in 2014. The progress was a bit slow. One fine day, I got a surprise present from my niece Puja and nephew Devesh. It was a book-sized laptop to assist me in writing my book. I appreciate their thought and thank both of them for their timely present.

Mr Abdul Qaiyum, my neighbour, a former Town and Country Planner, Town and Country Planning Organisation, Government of India, who passed away in 2016, always encouraged me in my writing efforts and, like a monitor, enquired about the progress. He is a person I admire and miss, and express my gratitude to.

I am thankful to Mr S. C. Gupta, former Additional Commissioner, Delhi Development Authority, and Mr A. R. Patharkar, Director Town Planning, Government of Maharashtra, Pune, for their constructive comment and suggestions on Chapters 2, 5 and 6.

The work of several authors, organisations and institutions has inspired me, and I express my gratitude to all whose work has been quoted in this book.

In the end, I would like to thank my wife, Saroj, for her constant support.

CHAPTER 1

Theory of Urban Renewal

Process of Growth, Decay and Demise of Cities

Cities are not inert entities. They are like living organisms. They evolve, grow, decay and, in some cases, degenerate as ruins. It is a process. Mumford (1946), very aptly, described this process in six stages: eopolis, polis, metropolis, megalopolis, tyrannopolis and necropolis (Figure 1.1).

Eopolis is the first stage of the process when a village shows signs of transformation from rural to urban. The occupation of a majority of the community continues to be farming and the level of facilities and services is, generally, as per local needs of the village. In Indian context, such an area, as per Constitution (74th Amendment) Act, 1992, is called area in transition from rural to urban which is governed by Nagar Panchayat.

Polis refers to the second stage when eopolis grows and evolves as 'an association of villages' and transforms into a town/city where a majority of people are engaged in non-farm occupations and have industries, markets, colleges, hospitals, socio-cultural and entertainment centres, administrative offices and other higher order facilities and services. It is governed by a municipality.

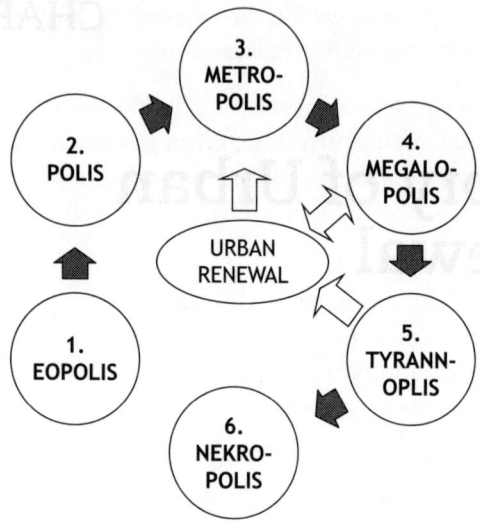

Figure 1.1 Cycle of Growth and Decay of Cities and Role of Urban Renewal
Source: Based on Mumford (1946).

The polis continues to grow and attains, in the third stage, population of more than 1 million and becomes a metropolis—a dominant city in the region, comprising several other urban and rural settlements. A metropolis is a dominant centre of trade, commerce and industry. It is the mirror of socio-economic development in a country. It is a centre of art, culture, innovations, research, political activities and governance. In India, as per Census 2011, there are 53 metropolitan centres.

The growth of metropolis continues with more dominance and it reaches the fourth stage when its population grows to 10 million. Mumford calls such urban centre a megalopolis—the most dominant city in the region, comprising several large cities and even, in some cases, metropolises. In India, as per 2011 Census, there are three megalopolises—Mumbai, Delhi and Kolkata. The National Capital Region comprises 108 cities which include three metropolises—Meerut, Faridabad and Ghaziabad. Due to size of city and the complexities in its management, the megalopolis starts showing signs of decline and the beginning of decay in the city.

With further growth of the megalopolis, there is extensive deterioration of socio-economic structure, urban governance and municipal services, leading to all around chaos. According to Mumford (1946), it is tyranny to live in such a city and he calls the fifth stage tyrannopolis.

With continued deterioration of socio-economic structure, urban governance and municipal services in tyrannopolis, it loses its activities, attractions and population and reaches the last stage, that is, necropolis—an almost dead city.

According to Mumford, these are logical stages of the process of growth and decay of cities 'systematised through intellectual analysis' (1946, p. 292), and in fact, all cities may not necessarily follow all the six stages and, finally, end up as dead cities (Figure 1.1). In fact, in cities that are in the stage 3, 4 or 5 of the process of growth and decay, the physical, social and economic deterioration may be managed through deliberate urban renewal policies and programmes resulting in urban transformation having new ambience, opportunities and improved quality of life of the people. Even, in the case of large-scale destruction due to natural calamities or war, a new city evolves on the debris of old or at another site, and the remains of the old city conserved as heritage and promoted as tourist products.

Delhi is a good example of this phenomenon; Delhi has always been an attractive site for location of capital by the rulers who ruled India. Historically, there are eight cities of Delhi that include Lal Kot, Siri, Tughlaqabad, Jahanpanah, Ferozabad, Purana Qila, Shahjahanabad (Walled City Delhi) and New Delhi (the British Capital). The capital of the independent India, covering the entire National Capital Territory, can be termed as the ninth city of Delhi. Remains of Lal Kot, Siri, Tughlaqabad, Jahanpanah, Ferozabad and Purana Qila are conserved as heritage. Currently, Delhi has crossed the third stage, metropolis, and is a booming megalopolis which is heading toward the fifth stage, tyrannopolis.

The following headline of *The Times of India* (2015a) indicates the state of affairs of Delhi caused by a bus breakdown in Chirag Delhi and malfunctioning of a traffic light at Moolchand flyover:

> *Nightmarish Jams, Helpless Cops, Frayed Tempers:*
> *This City Is Becoming Unliveable*
>
> **Delhi on the road, going nowhere**
>
> *Traffic Gridlock like Bangkok in the 1980s*

Civic services in Delhi appear to be failing. Drainage system is very poor, as a short shower results in water logging of arterial roads; road rage is rampant. Crime is on the increase. Solid waste management is very poor and in a survey conducted by the Ministry of Urban Development, Government of India (*Sunday Times*, 2015), the city is ranked 397 among 476 municipalities. To counter the process of decay of cities, the focus of the Government of India is on urban renewal as indicated by Jawaharlal Nehru National Urban Renewal Mission (JNNURM) and Atal Mission for Rejuvenation and Urban Transformation (AMRUT; see Chapter 2). Here, the basic role of urban renewal is regeneration of existing blighted areas and brownfields, in a city, to check further decay.

Why Do Cities Grow and Decay?

Two questions emerge: (a) Why do cities grow? and (b) What are the factors that cause decay of cities? The answer to the first question is that cities are the physical manifestation of socio-economic activities, needs, aspirations and actions of people who live there. In natural process, with time, people multiply and grow and so the population of settlements increases. With this increase, the nature and extent of socio-economic activities and needs also change and to accommodate these changes, cities provide work places such as industries, commercial centres, wholesale markets and offices. To serve people, housing complexes and social facilities such as educational institutions, healthcare centres and entertainment facilities develop and, thus, cities grow. Cities evolve as centres of employment, innovation, technological advancement and mirrors of change and socio-economic and technological development. Growth continues as more and more people are attracted to come there for better employment opportunities, education, healthcare and better quality of life.

To answer the second question, there are temporal, physical, socio-cultural, economic and technological factors that can be generalised to explain the process of decay of cities. The provisions of different legislations and the manner of city governance, and development controls, norms and standards, given in master plans, also, in specific conditions, cause urban decay.

Cities in India are ageing. According to the 1901 Census, there were 1,830 urban centres in the country. This indicates that more than 1,800 cities in India are more than 100 years old. Kolkata has passed more than 300 years. Delhi, Walled City, is about 375 years old. Many of the metro cities are in existence for over 100 years. This ageing of cities has started showing, in their core areas, in the form of high-density built-up areas, physical deterioration of buildings, congestion, environmental pollution, conflicting land uses and poor accessibility.

Three generations of families are living in the same house, causing higher occupancy ratio, overcrowding, physical decay of buildings and stress on basic services. As a result, the quality of life also gets deteriorated. However, the social bonds are so strong in old city core areas that people prefer to continue living there; it is a kind of social support that binds them together. It provides social identity and security. The *pol*s, *katra*s,[1] *mohallas*[2] are such areas that can be identified in city cores. Way back in 1915, Patrick Geddes, who was invited to India to advise the Governor of Madras on replanning and redevelopment of some towns, advocated that town planning should not be limited to widening of roads and provision of houses, but should also include people, their occupation, social way of life, aspirations and ambitions (Town and Country Planning Organisation, 1962, p. 32).

---

[1] Pols and katras are housing clusters which comprise a group of households of a particular caste, occupation/profession or religion.
[2] A, generally organically grown, neighbourhood.

Old cities are mostly depositories of rich socio-cultural heritage as demonstrated by lifestyle, music, arts, *bazaar*s (markets), monuments and public spaces. In many cases, these heritage sites and buildings are neglected, misused and encroached upon. It is due to changes in lifestyle and economic status, technological advancement, lack of administrative will, ineffective laws and, above all, public apathy towards heritage conservation. The Ancient Monuments and Archaeological Sites and Remains Act, 1958 (updated in 2010) provides for protection of heritage, but it covers only those monuments that are protected under this Act. Other such thousands of places are left unattended, which adds to theirs as well as the decay of surrounding areas.

Old city or the city core generally provides a strong well-networked and convenient relationship between workplace (commerce or household industry) and residence and also among various work-related activities. Most of the things/services are available within a short distance. As a result, there is a mixed-use pattern which is convenient in some cases and generates conflicts in others, especially, when the uses are not compatible and causing noise and air pollution, traffic congestion and delays.

Urban poverty and its implications in the form of growth of slums and informal economic activities is another socio-economic reason that, in the absence of careful handling, adds to urban blight. Development plans of cities do not generally provide designated areas for economically weaker sections (EWS) of the society or low-income group (LIG) people. There are some rules where 15% of the area/dwelling in a residential area must be reserved for EWS/LIG. Such rules, however, remain on paper/plans only, and poor people are left to fend themselves. As a result, the urban poor are deprived of the access to affordable land for shelter. The outcome of this is growth of slums and unauthorised colonies. More than 54% of the population of Mumbai and about a third of population of Kolkata live in slums where there is poverty, inadequate basic services, deteriorating living environment and deplorable quality of life.

Introduction of automobile has tremendously affected the old city core. The narrow roads and the volume of traffic create traffic congestion and delays. Parking is another big issue that compounds the problems of such areas. There is congestion on roads as shown by the fact that in case of Mumbai, the average speed is only 6–8 km/h (NIPEF, 2006).

Rent Control Act is one of the main factors of urban decay in old area. This Act protects the tenants and controls the rent charged by the owner. As a result of this Act, the rent paid by the tenants in the city core is generally very low. For example, as reported by Chattopadhyay (2014), in Old China Bazar Street, located in core of Kolkata, the rent of a 150 sq. ft shop is as low as less than ₹100 per month. The rate of the space, which is utilised for office-cum-residence, comes to less than one rupee per sq. ft per month. Market rent cannot be charged and low rent makes it practically impossible for the owner to maintain the building and carry out annual maintenance works. The tenants also do not care to maintain the building. As a result, the buildings are neglected, and, with time, they get dilapidated and the city decays.

Another main factor of urban decay is poor urban governance, especially, provision and maintenance of sewerage system and collection and disposal of solid waste. Drains are blocked by polythene bags and solid waste can be seen littered on roadsides, vacant plots and open spaces.

Old parts of cities are congested and in spite of their renewal incorporated in the master plans, no action actually takes place as the development control rules normally suggest reduction of density and hence, lower floor space index/floor area ratio (FSI/FAR).[3] The property owners prefer repairs rather than redevelopment, as repair will allow the existing space while renewal will be with reduced FAR.

As a strategy to decongest the core areas and reduce pollution, master plans provide for closure of large-scale polluting and goods and passenger traffic generating industries. But, generally, they do not

---

[3] FAR/FSI is the ratio of the total built-up area to the plot area. FAR is expressed as percentage and FSI is expressed as ratio. Accordingly, 100 FAR is the same as 1 FSI.

provide clear policy and scheme for redevelopment of the site so vacated. The abundant mill areas, therefore, remain unattended vacant lands or unauthorised slum areas.

Popular and politically motivated policies also, sometimes, add to urban deterioration. The mixed land use policy of Delhi that allows commercial activity in residential areas is a good example in this context. It has facilitated invasion of residential areas by commercial activities and resulted in congestion, encroachment and other problems such as parking, inconvenience for the residents and quarrels among people. This policy has also made the planned commercial areas, such as, community centres in Delhi, unattractive, and they are losing business and are in poor physical conditions due to falling business, ageing and poor maintenance.

To accommodate future growth of the population, the planning area of master plans invariably extends beyond the current boundary of the municipality. As a result, several neighbouring villages are merged within the municipal limit. The *abadi*[4] area of these villages continues to be undisturbed and provides a convenient and affordable place for accommodating workers engaged in construction activities in surrounding new areas. These places, known as urban villages, also provide convenient location for hardware and building material shops and warehouses. There is no control on building activities, and these urban villages continue as blighted islands of unplanned growth in the planned urban landscape around them. Their condition is generally chaotic with haphazard and high-density development lacking facilities and services.

Natural and manmade catastrophes such as severe earthquake, floods and act of war also cause destruction of cities. Earliest example of a dead city is Mohenjo-daro, the ancient Indian city (now in Pakistan after partition in 1947) also known as the ancient Indus Valley Metropolis, which declined due to severe floods in river Indus. Fatehpur Sikri is another dead city, abandoned due to the shortage of

---

[4] *Abadi* is the habitation area of a village defined by *lal dora* which is the red line drawn on a cadastral map of a village which separates the *abadi* area from the nearby agriculture area.

water. Shahjahanabad was destroyed completely by Nadir Shah who massacred citizens and looted the city. It was again destroyed by the British soldiers after the First War of Independence in 1857. Mohenjo-daro was rebuilt several times after being inundated by floods and so was Shahjahanabad. In a recent incident, Uttarakhand faced a catastrophe due to cloudburst, flash floods and landslide on the night of 16–17 June 2013 and Kedarnath Town was completely wiped off. It is being redeveloped.

Sometimes politics plays a major role in the growth of unauthorised building clusters. To reap the harvest of votes, politicians encourage people to encroach land and build shelters, and later on they (the politicians) are the ones who make all possible efforts to regularise these slums (*Dainik Jagran*, 2015). As a result of such political patronage, slums continue to grow, adding to city decay. For example, in Dehradun, the banks of Rispna and Bindal rivers are encroached by squatters for decades. Under the river front policy, they were to be rehabilitated (a political move before election). Dehradun Municipal Corporation built 150 flats to rehabilitate these squatters; however, no one is willing to move to flats as the political bosses have promised 'ownership rights wherever they live' (*The Times of India*, 2015b). Due to encroachment, the river is polluted; there is a danger of floods and loss of property and life of slum dwellers, but it seems politically incorrect to save river and people by right action to rehabilitate them at a safer place. The slums along the rivers continue to grow.

The situation in other cities is not different. In Delhi, unauthorised colonies have been growing under political patronage. During the elections, the manifestos of political parties promise their regularisation to attract voters. Unplanned and unauthorised development continues and city suffers. Politics is strange. Politicians exploit both the rich and the poor in their political interest. In a case of to reap the rich, in Island City Mumbai, people were deprived of much needed open spaces and housing for poor. According to the Development Control Rules (DCR) 1991, the area of closed-down textile mills was to be shared equally among the owner, Bombay Municipal Corporation (BMC) and Maharashtra Housing and Area Development Authority (MHADA) with the provision that BMC will develop open spaces and recreational facilities in its share of land; MHADA will construct housing for poor and the owner was free to use his portion for any permissible land use. It was opposed by the rich owners. Later on, under political pressure, Section 58 of DCR 1991 was modified and the combined share of BMC and MHADA was reduced to mere 5%, remaining 95% being the share of the owner (Apte, 2014).

According to Patharkar (2014), in 1995, political parties in Maharashtra, pronounced an agenda of providing *pucca* (made of permanent material) reinforced cement concrete (RCC) structure to each slum dweller free of cost, and the slogan almost created political turmoil. The subsequent governments not only continued with the policy but also liberalised the schemes by increasing the size of free dwelling unit from 225 sq. ft to 350 sq. ft by allowing still higher FAR/FSI. Number of slum pockets continued to grow and as a result, more than half of the population of Mumbai lives in slum area.

Are Slums Parts of Urban Fabric?

About half a century back, we were taught in planning technique class that slums are like cancer in city and should be treated as such. There was Slum Clearance Act which provided for demolition of notified slums with no resettlement or rehabilitation. Many slum pockets were demolished under this Act. Slums, however, continue to grow in number and size. Looking objectively, it is highlighted that slums grow because they provide affordable shelter to poor urban migrants. Slums also grow because people living there perform a useful function in the city by providing service to industry, trade, commerce, transport and households. Their contribution in running the city affairs is enormous. Informal sector provides more than 50% jobs, and it cannot be neglected and should not be ignored in planning and development. Without them, the city will come to a grinding halt. Patharkar (2014) says that slums were there, slums are there and slums will be there.

Slum conditions are part of urban life cycle (Figure 1.1). The parameters in defining the slum, however, change with socio-economic and physical development in the city. In poor countries, slum condition is defined by makeshift structures, narrow pathways, no sanitation and lack of amenities such as toilets and bathrooms. With development, the parameters defining slums change to *pucca* structures with poor maintenance, poor roads, inadequate sanitation and amenities. With further development, factors such as high density, high occupancy ratio, and poor level of services are added. Then are added parameters such as the household possessions—electronics, automobile, and communication and entertainment gadgets. The slum condition is comparative. Both, developing and developed countries have slums; however, definitions change. Slums are part of urban fabric performing very useful service to the city development, and they should be recognised as such and treated with appropriate urban renewal strategies (Chapters 3 and 4).

What Is Urban Renewal?

Woodbury (1953) defines urban renewal as 'a tool or set of tools to help provide an environment that meets the social, psychological as well as physical needs of the people'. Sachithanandan (2014) describes it as the 'process of rebuilding areas of cities that have become obsolete and abandoned, or are in a state of considerable decay'.

> Urban regeneration puts together physical, economic and social restructuring of the city ... It addresses social dynamics, economic diversification, and environmental degeneration. (Khobragade, 2014, p. 207)

According to Roberts and Sykes (2000) urban renewal can be defined as a comprehensive and integrated vision and action which leads to the resolution of urban problems and which seeks to bring about a lasting improvement in the economic, physical, social and environmental conditions of an area that has been subject to change.

According to the *Dictionary of Urban and Regional Planning* (Kulshrestha, 2006), urban renewal is a process of rejuvenation of a dilapidated area in a city having physical decay and economic stagnation, caused by age-old buildings, poor accessibility, loss of real estate value and changes in technology, transportation systems, land use and activity patterns. This rejuvenation may be achieved through improvement of buildings, accessibility and circulation system; augmentation of facilities and services; and reassignment of compatible land uses that promote economic activities and improve quality of life.

These definitions of urban renewal, however, cover generally the physical and economic aspects. The urban renewal, in fact, is a wider concept and in addition to physical and economic aspects, it also covers socio-cultural, environmental, and heritage conservation and urban governance concerns. It brings economic vibrancy, physical quality improvement, functional efficiency of facilities and services and a pleasing quality of socio-cultural life having regard for conservation of environment and heritage. It improves the performance and urban design qualities of an otherwise decaying area; enhances the living conditions of communities with better services, access to facilities, reduced water, air and sound pollution; conserves heritage; augments property value and employment opportunities and checks urban decay.

Urban Renewal as Perceived by Different Stakeholders

The various stakeholders in urban renewal are the slum dwellers, the residents neighbouring a slum area, the politicians, the builders, the spatial planners and the local bodies/authorities.

The unauthorised slum dwellers, who are eligible under the renewal scheme, see it as an opportunity to own a house/plot where they can live with their families without the fear of eviction. It provides them access to facilities, services and finances that improve their quality of life. For those who are not covered under the scheme, it is a nightmare, as they will be uprooted without any compensation. Such people are forced to go back to the place of migration or squat at another place in the city and continue the life of uncertainty and live in unhealthy conditions.

Residents of the areas neighbouring a slum see it (slum) as an eyesore affecting the ambience of the surroundings and quality of living. Nearness to such areas reduces the property value and returns from rents. They want slums removed or renewed and, in many cases, pressurise the local authorities to take concrete actions. In some cases, they resort to legal actions, particularly in cases where the slums are located on public land and community open spaces. If the area is redeveloped, both the neighbouring residents and the slum dwellers feel benefited from renewal exercise.

The politicians see slum dwellers as dedicated vote bank and exploit the wishes of people to have better shelter, better quality of services and facilities. Invariably, just a few months before elections, the politicians of the ruling party take action to renew the area by improving roads, constructing drains, providing street lighting and such other facilities or services. Sometimes, such action gets converted into votes, benefiting the politicians. The slum dwellers also get benefited from the renewed services. National schemes, such as slum-free city under Rajiv Awas Yojana (RAY), are politically motivated. RAY, an urban renewal programme at national level to improve the living conditions of urban poor, was initiated in 2009 and launched for implementation in 2013 with the general elections in 2014 in mind.

Builders look at the slum areas as great opportunities for real estate development and making huge profits. There are a large number of incidents when the builders have coerced poor slum dwellers of *chawls*[5] of Mumbai to sell their dwelling so that they (builders) can redevelop the area as high-end residential or commercial property and earn huge profits. The slum dwellers are partial gainers as they do get a price of their house but lose their home, job linkages and social contacts due to forced displacement.

Urban renewal for the spatial planners is an opportunity to provide a good quality of life to the people living in blighted areas through planned development and urban design; conserving heritage buildings and sites; promoting compatible land uses and economic activities; and creating an ambience that attracts socio-economic development and enhances the image of the city. This wish list of spatial planners appears utopian and fails to attract the owners of properties in blighted old core areas as the benefits are abstract and losses are real. For

---

[5] Chawl is a residential area typically housing poor workers employed in mills and other places. This term is common in Mumbai.

example, by reducing congestion, all residents will get benefits of light, ventilation, parking, wider roads and pleasing atmosphere; however, to achieve this, reduced density, FAR and increased setbacks have to be followed which will reduce the usable built space or saleable area. It is this factor that makes the renewal exercise unattractive, and status quo continues. It requires innovative and practical approaches as discussed later in this book.

The local bodies get more revenue from the redeveloped properties and look at renewal as a beneficial proposition. The law enforcement authorities consider slums as den of all sorts of social crimes. They support renewal of such areas as a right step in crime reduction. In the process, both the authorities and the community get benefited.

Considering the interests of all stakeholders, urban renewal generally appears to gain support from all stakeholders. There is, however, a need to evolve strategies that make urban renewal a win-win situation for all stakeholders where conflicts are minimised, gains are enhanced and losses are sufficiently compensated.

Understanding Terms Associated with Urban Renewal

There are several terms used in literature to discuss urban renewal as a subject. These include renewal, rejuvenation, regeneration, redevelopment, relocation, rehabilitation, in situ development, restoration, conservation and reforms. These terms are currently being used interchangeably or as synonyms. In some other cases, they are used to describe strategies to tackle specific problems or issues pertaining to urban renewal. For better understanding, it will be desirable to differentiate among these terms that are general and represent urban renewal as subject and those terms that are specific and correspond to a renewal strategy. Accordingly, it is suggested that the terms such as renewal, rejuvenation and regeneration may be taken to represent the urban renewal as a subject. These terms may be used interchangeably. On the other hand, terms such as conservation, restoration, redevelopment, relocation, rehabilitation, in situ upgradation/development and reforms may represent strategies pertaining to urban renewal considering different situations, approaches and issues.

They are specific and may not be used interchangeably. In the following sections, an effort is made to describe and differentiate these terms.

- *Conservation* refers to judicious and sustainable use and management of natural or manmade heritage in such a manner that their natural, ecological, architectural, historical, socio-cultural significance, as applicable, is maintained.
- *Restoration* is a process of bringing an object, building, social custom, art form, etc., in its original state.
- *Redevelopment* is the strategy of renewal applicable to dilapidated area, with crumbling structures, declared unfit for human habitation or any other function (commercial, industrial, etc.) that needs to be demolished and rebuild.
- *Relocation* strategy is applicable in two situations: (a) redevelopment and (b) slum clearance. In case of redevelopment, it refers to temporary or permanent housing of affected people on the same site or at another site. In the case of slum clearance, it refers to shifting of eligible families to a designated place, on a plot or in built tenements as per relocation scheme.
- *Rehabilitation* in housing and urban development is a process of improving the quality of a blighted area by one or more of the following actions: partial rebuilding, repair, remodelling, renovating, conserving, providing educational, healthcare and recreational facilities or augmenting utilities and services. In case of large projects requiring displacement of people, it is a process of providing the project-affected-people housing, job opportunities, training to enable them to take up new jobs and necessary financial and technical assistance. Rehabilitation strategy is also applicable in two situations: (a) physical, which deals with rejuvenation or regeneration of a blighted area and (b) socio-economic, which caters to capacity-building of the affected and providing them job opportunities so as to enable them to cope with the new challenges caused by their displacement.
- *Reform* is a strategy that aims at making an otherwise deteriorated system of urban governance/management better by introducing

changes necessary to improve its performance, accountability and effectiveness.

Urban Renewal Zones

Historically, urban renewal refers to rejuvenation of the inner city or core areas. This is true for mono-centred cities. There are cases when cities have multi-nodal structures, several urban villages, slum clusters, heritage sites and monuments, environmentally sensitive areas, water bodies, natural landscaped areas, heavily polluted industrial areas or abandoned mill sites showing signs of decay and needing renewal. A city, thus, may have several urban renewal zones with different nature and extent of decay requiring different strategies for their rejuvenation.

In a city, these urban renewal zones may be the old city core; old commercial, residential or industrial areas located within or outside the city core; slum pockets/jhuggi[6] clusters; unauthorised colonies; urban villages and heritage areas. The influence area along Mass Rapid Transit System (MRTS) and major transport nodes and corridors, such as railway stations, city bus stands, metro rail stations, is another zone that is under transformation and needs renewal.

Urban renewal is also needed in areas of low-density development that require re-densification to accommodate more population and desired activities as guided by the market forces and provisions of the master plans.

An area designated for urban renewal may have more than one renewal zone. For example, the city core may have heritage zone, slum pockets and commercial streets and vacated industrial areas. In such cases, through a diagnostic survey, the extent of each of these zones needs to be identified and strategies for their renewal should evolve in an integrated manner.

---

[6] *Jhuggi* is a shelter housing urban poor.

Innovative Approaches to Urban Renewal

Place-based Approach

As mentioned in the previous section, urban renewal area may have more than one renewal zone with different characteristics requiring different strategies. To achieve this, the urban renewal approach has to be place-based where strategies are evolved out of local issues, potentials, community aspirations and their spatial variations and implemented through local organisations with agency support. In essence, place-based approach focuses on three questions: (a) What to do? (b) Where to do? (c) Who will do it? These questions refer to the identification of actions, places where actions will be taken and local community organisations who will take action with active support of agencies and developers. For example, if an area designated for urban renewal has a heritage site, slum pockets and low density-high-income residential plots, strategy for each zone will be different depending upon the issues and community aspirations, and organisations for taking action will also be different. This indicates the spatial variation of actions/strategies and institutional support in the place-based urban renewal approach.

The basic objective of place-based urban renewal approach is to ensure equity, social justice, conservation of socio-cultural values, heritage and environment; to ensure good quality of life for all the sections of society; and to promote sustainable socio-economic development. It avoids gentrification, a criticism generally targeted to urban renewal programmes. It encourages community participation and improves organisational capacity of the community.

JNNURM is a place-based urban renewal programme which targets selected 63 cities and builds local capacity through reforms (see Chapters 2 and 3). Current missions such as Smart Cities Mission and Atal Mission for Rejuvenation and Urban Transformation (AMRUT) and also Heritage City Development and Augmentation Yojana (HRIDAY) also have a place-based approach (see Chapter 2). Depending upon the characteristics, problems and potentials of places, they promote urban renewal strategy with equity, community participation and efficient institutional structure planning and implementation.

Tourism-based Approach

The tourism sector is one of the topmost promoters of economic development and generators of employment. According to World Travel and Tourism Council (2017), the total contribution of tourism to the National GDP (Gross Domestic Product) in 2016 was 9.6%. In monetary terms, tourism contributed ₹140,185 crore to Indian economy in 2016 and generated 4.03 crore jobs, which is 9.3% of the total employment. In spite of having a rich and varied heritage, cultural resources, natural features, sun, sand and snow and traditional hospitality (*atithi devo bhava*, meaning 'guest is god') India ranked 24th in the world ranking in terms of international tourists as per UNWTO Barometer 2017 (Government of India 2017). It should also be noted that the share of domestic tourist is about 60–70% of total tourists. The physical condition of several tourist products is bad. Waste management is pathetic and sometimes repulsive to the tourists. Observing this status and with a view of making cities attractive to the tourists, a few new programmes such as Swachh Bharat Abhiyan and HRIDAY have been introduced recently (see Chapter 2 for details). It may be termed as tourism-based urban renewal. As an entry point to the places of tourist interests, all the major airports have been redeveloped. About 400 railway stations are being redeveloped to make them clean convenient and passenger-friendly. Ministry of Tourism, Government of India, has launched two programmes to rejuvenate tourist centres visited by pilgrims and tourists. These include Swadesh Darshan Initiative and Pilgrimage Rejuvenation and Spiritual Augmentation Drive (PRASAD; see Chapter 2 for details).

EWS Housing-based Approach

This approach focuses on both the social and economic concerns. The social focus aims at providing housing and good quality of life to urban poor. The economic focus is the by-product of housing which generates employment for all skilled and unskilled workers. The EWS housing-based approach also provides answer to the criticism that urban renewal is elitist and results gentrification. This criticism is based on the facts that in the traditional 'slum clearance and urban design' approach to urban renewal, the urban poor was displaced, deprived of his shelter and livelihood and was further marginalised.

About 21.7% of the total urban population lives in slum (Ministry of Urban Employment and Poverty Alleviation, 2005). In 2012, the housing shortage in India was 1.878 crore where more than 95% shortage was for EWS and LIG sectors. Observing this, the government has launched the National Mission for Urban Housing (also known as Housing for All by 2022 or Pradhan Mantri Awas Yojana, i.e., PMAY; see Chapter 2 for details). It has two components that deal with urban renewal. These are slum rehabilitation and subsidy for house enhancement (repair/renewal).

Reform-based Approach

Reform-based urban renewal aims at rejuvenating institutions, through introduction of reforms, to improve their performance in urban governance and service delivery as well as citizen services. JNNURM was the pioneering programme in this direction, which introduced reform-linked release of funds for urban renewal. A reform-based approach is also being followed by the AMRUT to improve service delivery, mobilise resources and make functioning of ULBs more efficient, transparent and accountable (see Chapter 3).

Urban Renewal Principles

Based upon discussion so far in this chapter and field experience, it is my considered opinion that all the urban renewal efforts should pursue the following four principles which state that urban renewal should

1. be humane and provide social justice;
2. strike balance among physical, economic and environmental concerns;

3. conserve socio-cultural values, public spaces and heritage monuments, buildings and sites and
4. involve stakeholders at all stages of the renewal process.

Principle 1. Urban Renewal Should Be Humane and Provide Social Justice

Urban renewal directly affects the people. The effect is good if the process is people-friendly and the result is in their favour. People should be in the centre of such actions. Chattopadhyay (2014) observes that in actual practice, urban renewal is considered as opportunity to freeing space for more profitable development of commercial and office spaces and luxury residential apartments by displacing urban slums from prime lands. Thus, urban renewal programmes have worked in gentrification of residential neighbourhoods alienating urban poor. The argument put forward is that appropriate compensation has been given to the affected people.

In a drive to cleanse Delhi slums and to resettle them at outskirts of the city, houses of residents of Turkman Gate, in walled city of Delhi, were demolished in 1976, and residents were allotted flats, located more than 10 km away in the outskirts of the city. Mostly people refused to move as they would have to commute for job every day paying heavy bus fares and also loose social and economic links established due to long period of living in the area. There was unrest, police firing and even causalities (Chapter 2).

In many cases, especially in case of clearance of slums, the attitude of the agencies is rude and sometimes inhumane. According to the facts contained in a report by Peoples Union for Democratic Rights (PUDR, 2004) on demolition of slum at Yamuna Pushta and resettlement of eligible families in Bawana in outer Delhi, the approach of the enforcement agencies was harsh. A woman committed suicide when her house was razed by the agencies. There were demonstrations by people and use of force by law enforcement agencies. Two incidences of fire occurred, several jhuggis were gutted and a child and an old person died. There was a lot of mismanagement in transporting the eligible families to Bawana for resettlement. At Bawana, the resettlement site was not developed, several plots needed levelling, there were mobile pay-and-use toilets which added a daily burden of ₹20 to a family of 5 (₹1 each for toilet, ₹2 each for bathing and ₹5 for washing clothes). There was mismanagement in allocation of sites to eligible families and people were forced to stay in open for a few days.

In this case, the strategy was right. Theoretically, it followed social justice as slum clearance was followed by resettlement of those who were eligible, based upon a cut-off date and ownership of jhuggi. All the tenants and the owners who built their jhuggi after the cut-off date were not eligible for resettlement. In a study (PUDR, 2004), out of 1,346 households surveyed, only 635 (47%) were eligible. In another case, out of 2,390 only 500 (21%) were eligible for resettlement. This indicates that more than 50% jhuggi dwellers were not eligible for a 12.5–18 sq. m plot as per resettlement deal. They were forced to vacate the site and find place for living by themselves. Probably this was the cause of unrest among the people displaced by demolition. But the situation should have been tackled in a humane manner. There is no excuse for the mismanagement and hardship to the people at the resettlement site. Had the agency been sensitive and humane, site should have been prepared in advance. The transport arrangement and also allocation of plot to the eligible household should have been done in a more efficient, orderly and people-friendly manner.

The eligibility criterion for resettlement invariably causes exclusion. Both groups of people—the eligible and the ineligible—face exclusion. For example, both groups were excluded from their right to vote due to demolition of their place of living and subsequent relocation of eligible families or migration of non-eligible families to a place where they are not registered voters. They also face temporary exclusion from jobs as they mostly lose their job in the old area and the new area may not absorb them immediately. Children of both groups of people also face exclusion from education.

In another case at Delhi, as mentioned as 'Facts', in the Judgement of Delhi High Court (2010), the Gadia Lohar Basti, occupied by the dwellers for more than 40 years, was 'demolished by the Municipal

Corporation of Delhi (MCD) on 12.01.2009, without prior notice and irresponsibly displaced more than 200 people without giving them a chance to take their belongings at safe place'. Demolition without prior notice and not allowing the affected persons to collect and take with them their belongings is simply inhuman. It is not social justice. They were encroachers, right, but they were human beings also. They should have been treated with a humane touch. The Delhi High Court questioned on the state government's policy for relocation and rehabilitation: 'Whether the manner in which the alleged policy is being implemented by the respondents (state government) is arbitrary, discriminatory and in violation of Articles 14 and 21 of the Constitution and various international covenants to which India is signatory?'

Delhi High Court (2010) further observed:

- United Nations General Assembly, in 1948, made explicit reference to housing as a fundamental human right. Article 25(1) states: 'Everyone has the right to a standard of living adequate for the health and well-being of himself and his family, including food, clothing, housing and medical care, and necessary social services.'
- Article 11 of the International Covenant on Economic, Social and Cultural Rights expanded on UN General Assembly Article 25(1) of the Universal Declaration and stated: 'The State Parties to the present Covenant recognize the right of everyone to an adequate standard of living for himself and his family, including adequate food, clothing, and housing, and to the continuous improvement of living conditions.'
- In 1987, the International Year of Shelter for the Homeless, the United Nations spoke of the right of all individuals to: 'a real home ... one which provides protection from the elements; has access to safe water and sanitation; provides for secure tenure and personal safety; and within easy reach of centres for employment, education and healthcare; and is at a cost which people and society can afford'.
- India has signed and ratified this Covenant and the State is under an obligation to give effect to its provisions.

The urban renewal process, particularly while dealing with slum pockets, should respect human dignity and human right. It should be humane and ensure social justice.

Principle 2. Urban Renewal Should Strike Balance among Physical, Economic and Environmental Concerns

Urban renewal is a process that addresses the complex interplay of physical, economic, socio-cultural, environmental and political concerns. These concerns, sometimes, are conflicting and require careful handling. A blighted area physically is one that is characterised by physical decay caused by old age of buildings, high density, poor light and ventilation, insanitary conditions, overcrowding, narrow lanes, poor accessibility, traffic congestion, poor transport systems, low rent, loss of real estate value and non-compatible pattern of land use and activities. In spite of all these shortcomings, the same area may have a booming economy due to locational advantages, linkages and agglomeration of supporting activities. For example, Walled City Delhi, designated as redevelopment area since the First Master Plan for Delhi 1962, is booming with wholesale trade, warehousing, household industries and shops penetrating deep into lanes and by-lanes. It continues to be the trading centre of northern India. This is the conflict. What do we do? Do we disturb/dislocate the economic activities for redevelopment? Or allow the status quo?

The strategy followed in most of the master plans is decongestion/dispersal, that is, reduction in density, FAR/FSI, closure of large-scale and hazardous industries, wholesale markets and such other activities. These measures have invariably remained on paper as they did not find favour with the owners and business-as-usual continues.

These deteriorating physical and booming economic characteristics of the blighted areas result in pollution (air, water, noise and visual) and fire hazards, and generate another conflict—a conflict with environment. Non-compliance of the master plan provisions further deteriorates the conditions. If compliance of master plan provisions, such as closure of polluting industries in residential areas, is insisted through legal actions or other measures, there is a mass resistance, and mass-politics comes into play which attracts politicians who, in the name of the people, make it a political issue and even enact a new law to counter dislocation. Physical and environmental deterioration continues, business and those engaged in industries feel a relief but other residents of the area, children and elderly, continue to suffer. Are objectives of planned development faulty? Is there a communication gap between people and planners? Is good quality of life, achieved through planned urban renewal, not saleable? Can the conflict among the physical, economic, environmental and political concerns not be minimised? If yes, then how?

This is a conflict of interest among traders, residents, businessmen and those running household industries, warehousing and other economic activities. Urban renewal will be successful if there is a harmony among the interests of all stakeholders in the process of preparation and implementation of renewal plans and projects. Urban renewal should, therefore, strike a balance among physical, economic and environmental concerns. Innovative and negotiated solutions need to be evolved in this respect.

Principle 3. Conserve Socio-cultural Values, Public Spaces, and Heritage Monuments, Buildings and Sites

Socio-cultural characteristics, specialised markets, natural features, monuments and landmarks make cities unique. It is this uniqueness of the area that needs to be conserved under this principle of urban renewal. Conservation of historical monuments, building and places is becoming more and more difficult with the exorbitant increase in land price and optimum utilisation of every square centimetre of space. There also appears to be a general lack of concern among people and authorities on heritage conservation. As a result, such places are heavily encroached upon, misused and abused. Commercialisation appears to be invading heritage buildings and sites. Landmarks, monuments and public squares are lost to commerce and cars (for parking). For example, in Mussoorie, the famous hill town of British Period in Uttarakhand, landmarks such as Clock Tower and Town Hall, the main cultural centres are lost forever. In 2009, Town Hall was demolished to make way for parking (*The Times of India*, 2016, p. 4). In 2010, the Clock Tower was removed and the site was left vacant. Now it is used for parking. In 2016, the Jhula Ghar, a popular amusement park with a giant wheel, was converted into a shopping complex. Gopal Bhardwaj, a historian, questions, 'How is Mussoorie different from any city now?' 'We have killed heritage, what next?' (Quoted from *The Times of India*, 2016, p. 4).

The national monuments are protected by Archaeological Survey of India (ASI) but other such places are to be taken care of by the state government and the local authorities. Urban renewal plan must recognise the heritage value of the area and conserve the heritage through innovative solutions.

The contemporary heritage which could be a good layout—an impressive building, a public square, an avenue or a landmark—should also be conserved. In April 2017, for redevelopment of Pragati Maidan in New Delhi, the iconic Hall of Nations, a contemporary building and an imposing landmark with design and structural excellence, was demolished. The argument was that it is only 45-year-old and cannot be categorised as a heritage building. Should age be the only criterion to determine the heritage value of a structure?

This principal of urban renewal should also cater to socio-cultural activities such as fairs, festivals, music, dance, arts and crafts, handloom works, etc., and opportunities be created to preserve and promote them for future generations.

Principle 4. Involve Stakeholders at All Stages of the Renewal Process

Urban renewal directly affects people living in the area being rejuvenated. Success of renewal efforts depends upon the support of the affected people and this can only be gained through their active involvement at all stages of the renewal process which includes identification of issues, priorities, solutions and strategies, sharing of benefits, monitoring, evaluation and maintenance. Stakeholder consultation is also effective and desirable in resolving conflicts, if any. The objective of this principle is to involve people in the decision-making in such a manner and extent that they feel ownership of the project: 'It is our efforts; we have brought this change in our area'.

There is generally no platform where all stakeholders involved in the urban renewal process can participate and contribute. Renewal introduces changes based on local issues and their solution as guided by technological advancement, market forces, policies, and site potentials. Any change, before it is adapted, is first resisted, and it needs sincere effort to convince people to accept the change. Recognising this, efforts should be made to create mechanisms, opportunities and legal support to attract stakeholders' participation in the urban renewal process and beyond.

References

Apte, Prakash M. (2014, January). *An urban renewal option for mill lands: Mumbai*. Paper presented in the 62nd NTCP Congress at Pune, ITPI, New Delhi.

Chattopadhyay, Barnika. (2014, January). *Urban renewal of CBD and its adjacent areas of Kolkata: Past initiatives and present strategies*. Paper presented in the 62nd NTCP Congress at Pune, ITPI, New Delhi.

Dainik Jagran. (2015, 27 June). Editorial: Smart city *ki chunotian*. *Dainik Jagran*, Dehradun.

Delhi High Court. (2010, 11 February). Judgement on combined writ petitions WP(C) nos. 8904/2009, 7735/2007, 7317/2009 and 9246/2009. Delhi High Court.

Government of India. (2017). Rank of India improves in international tourist arrivals, Ministry of Tourism, New Delhi Press Release, 19 May 2017. Retrieved 31 December 2017, from http://pib.nic.in/newsite/PrintRelease.aspx?relid=161959

Khobragade, Sonal. (2014, January). *Urban regeneration: A continuous healing of urban metabolism*. Paper presented in the NTCP Congress at Pune, ITPI, New Delhi.

Kulshrestha, S. K. (Ed.). (2006). *Dictionary of urban and regional planning*. New Delhi: Kalpaz Publications.

Ministry of Urban Employment and Poverty Alleviation. (2005). *National urban housing and habitat policy 2005*. New Delhi: Government of India.

Mumford, Lewis. (1946, reprint). *The culture of cities*. London: Secker and Warburg.

NIPEF. (2006). *Mumbai CDP an appraisal report*. New Delhi: Ministry of Urban Development.

Patharkar, A. R. (2014, January). *Metabolism of human settlements and urban regeneration*. Paper presented in the 62nd NTCP Congress at Pune, ITPI, New Delhi.

PUDR. (2004). *India shining: A report on demolition and resettlement of Yamuna Pushta Basti*. New Delhi: Peoples Union for Democratic Right.

Roberts, P., & Sykes, H. (2000). *Urban regeneration: A handbook*. London: SAGE.

Sachithanandan, A. N. (2014, January). *Urban aesthetics in the context of continuity and change*. Paper presented in the 62nd NTCP Congress at Pune, ITPI, New Delhi.

Sunday Times. (2015, 9 August). Dirty Delhi flunks swachh test. *Sunday Times*, New Delhi, p. 1.

The Times of India. (2015a, 7 August). Delhi on the road, going nowhere. *The Times of India*, New Delhi, p. 1.

———. (2015b, 30 June). Doon DM orders squatters on Bindal and Rispana banks to shift. *The Times of India*, Dehradun.

———. (2016, 15 June). Mussoorie's landmarks fall prey to commercialisation, town hall, clock tower razed to make way for new structures. *The Times of India*, Delhi and Dehradun.

Town and Country Planning Organisation. (1962). *Town and country planning in India*. New Delhi: Government of India.

Woodbury, Coleman. (Ed.). (1953). *The future of cities and urban redevelopment*. Chicago, IL: The University of Chicago Press.

World Travel and Tourism Council. (2017). *Travel and tourism economic impact 2017, India*. London. Retrieved 1 May 2017, from www.wttc.org.

CHAPTER 2

Urban Renewal Initiatives in India

Introduction

Urban renewal in India is not a new subject. As mentioned in Chapter 1, Patrick Geddes, as early as 1915, redeveloped some of the old towns (Government of India, 1962, p. 32). His redevelopment plan for Bara Bazar, Kolkata, prepared in 1919, is preserved in the archives of the Kolkata Municipal Corporation (KMC; Dutta, 2014).

Even before Geddes, examples of renewing cities are available in India. In 1870s, efforts were made to revitalise Mysore. The fort was decongested by relocating the inhabitants outside the fort and Sayyaji Rao Road was constructed after partially filling up the Purnaiah Nala. The moat surrounding the palace was covered and the existing Curzon Park was developed. The sewage and underground drainage works were also developed around the same time (Kumara, 2014).

More than 300-year-old Shahjahanabad (Old Delhi) built by Shahjahan was the capital of Mughal empire in India. It had a beautiful wide boulevard with a central canal, connecting the Red Fort and Fatehpuri Mosque. It had a large garden known as Begum ka Bagh. The city was the centre of poetry, music, literature, culture and trade. Its beauty, wealth and fame attracted Nadir Shah, who invaded the city and, on 11 March 1739, ordered 'general slaughter of citizens of Shahjahanabad' and looted all its wealth. The city was rejuvenated and its social and cultural fabric was restored by the efforts of some well-meaning people (Jagmohan, 1994).

In 1803, British took control of the Shahjahanabad. The social and cultural life in the city continued as is. Trading became brisk. The First War of Independence in 1857, which was crushed by the British rulers, again resulted in large-scale killing and destruction in the city caused by the British soldiers. As a part of political agenda to demonstrate the dominance of the British, there were fanatic proposals. One group proposed that the old city should be razed to the ground. City Magistrate Philip Edgerton proposed the conversion of Jama Masjid to a church. Another proposal was to demolish it! But, due to the efforts of Sir John Lawrence, Chief Commissioner of Punjab, the mosque was saved. All buildings within 448 yards around the Red Fort were demolished. The main artery of Chandni Chowk was widened, the central canal was filled and roadside trees were cut. The road became wide but its uniqueness and oriental atmosphere was destroyed (Jagmohan, 1994). Several parts of the city were restructured, making British power more visible. Traditional neighbourhoods were destroyed and Edgerton Street (now Nai Sarak) was introduced. Royal *sarai* was demolished to give way for the Town Hall. Roads were realigned for isolating the Red Fort from the city and tram was introduced (Dutta and Bandyopadhyay, 2014).

In 1867, Shahjahanabad was connected to Calcutta (Howrah) by a broad-gauge railway line and a portion of Begum ka Bagh (Queen's Garden) was redeveloped as Delhi Railway Station and its yard. As a result, there was a tremendous increase in trade, commerce and business. Large buildings near railway station were converted into warehouses and commercial activities invaded lanes and by-lanes of the city. Shahjahanabad evolved as a major wholesale trade centre for the North India. This status still continues.

In Lutyens' New Delhi plan, there was a green buffer between Connaught Place and Shahjahanabad, the Walled City, which is now reduced to Ramlila Maidan.

During 1930s, Delhi Improvement Trust demolished a portion of the dilapidated city wall for building Asaf Ali Road and planned commercial strip between Delhi Gate and Ajmeri Gate. It provided a visual and functional transition from the organic Shahjahanabad Walled City to well-planned Lutyens' New Delhi. The project was criticised as blocking the old city skyline (Mohan, 1992, p. 40). Shahjahanabad in the past three centuries has transformed from a capital city of mighty Mughal emperors to a major wholesale market of northern India. The Walled City has 42 of the 170 protected monuments in Delhi. The Indian National Trust for Architectural and Cultural Heritage (INTACH) has documented 800 buildings within Walled City that have heritage significance.

Urban renewal, in Post-Independence India, was generally limited to slum improvement and clearance. The Government of India passed Slum Areas (Improvement and Clearance) Act in 1956. Most of the states implemented slum improvement projects. There was no national or state urban renewal policy. Various master plans of cities did highlight the need for renewal of the respective core area. These plans generally suggested a policy of decongestion of core area through reduction of density. As an implication of this policy, no action has actually been taken because the reduction in the intensity of development did not attract the property owners and most of them relied on repairs rather than renewal with the reduced density which was not economically viable (Patharkar, 2014).

During 1975–1977, state of emergency was declared by the ruling Congress Party due to 'internal law and order situation in the country' (Nayar, 2013). During this period, some renewal programmes were to improve the conditions around major tourist spots. In Agra, the roads leading to the Taj Mahal were widened. Another example of urban renewal during this period included the clearance of Turkman Gate, Delhi, which included the resettlement of about 700 families. The original proposal was to build a 50-storey building which would accommodate the wholesale market of the Walled City (Old Delhi) in 13 floors and the rest would be residential flats to accommodate the affected families. There was a very strong opposition and non-acceptance to this proposal, and it was rejected. Finally, four-storey flats were constructed to accommodate the affected families. It, however, disturbed their living, employment and social links (Mohan, 1992, p. 39). Most of the households had 250 sq. ft area and after redevelopment, they were given flats of just 80 sq. ft, which was inadequate to accommodate a household of eight or more persons. Other initiatives include the redevelopment of slums along rivers Khan and Sarasvati in Indore and riverfront development along Sabarmati River in Ahmedabad.

Because of greater political attention given to the rural sector, the urban sector was on low priority. The flow of funds to this sector was low. The magnitude of the number of people living in slums became an asset that attracted political parties as vote banks. It became a practice to regularise unauthorised areas and improve slums just a few months before the municipal, state or federal elections to attract votes. This practice still continues.

Due to the liberalisation in 1991 and as a consequence of foreign direct investment and economic development, cities became a focus of attention. The number of million-plus cities increased from 23 in 1991 to 35 in 2001 and now, as per 2011 Census, their number is 53. The pace of urbanisation became faster as in 1991 the rate of urbanisation was 23 which increased to 28 in 2001 and 31 in 2011.

Since the preparation and implementation of urban renewal plans is the function of the urban local bodies (ULBs), the role of central and state governments is limited to the enactment of laws to provide legal support to the urban renewal and the formulation of enabling policies and programmes. To provide a clear picture of the urban renewal in India, this chapter, therefore, discusses the initiatives at national, state and individual city levels.

National-level Initiatives

To provide legal support to the urban renewal, the central government passed The Slum Areas (Improvement and Clearance) Act in 1956, which is applicable to union territories. It came into force in Delhi in 1957.

The National Urban Housing and Habitat Policy, 2007, advocated the improvement of housing stock through the urban renewal and in situ upgradation of slums (MoHUPA, 2007, p. 6) and endorsed:

- Specially designed slum improvement programmes, which focus on upgrading of basic services and environment improvement of urban slums with a participative, in situ slum rehabilitation approach.
- Inner-city slum redevelopment with cross-subsidisation and special incentives.
- Land pooling and sharing arrangements to facilitate land development.
- Release of Transferable Development Rights (TDRs) and additional FAR for accelerating private investment and involving private sector, in partnership with community-based organisations (CBOs), non-governmental organisations (NGOs) and self-help groups (SHGs).
- Primacy to provision of shelter to the urban poor at their present location or near their workplace.
- Restriction of relocation of slums and allow it only on account of severe water pollution, safety problems, proximity to rail track or other critical concerns and with condition that reliable transportation to work sites shall be ensured.
- Mixed land use pattern, in slum renewal schemes, with non-polluting income-generating activities.
- Integration/convergence of slum renewal schemes with other existing schemes related to housing, basic services, environmental improvement, etc. (MoHUPA, 2007, pp. 31–33).

The various urban renewal programmes initiated by the central government include JNNURM, slum-free cities under RAY, Smart Cities Mission and AMRUT. The following sections present brief details of these programmes.

Jawaharlal Nehru National Urban Renewal Mission

For the first time, after independence, cities got political attention when JNNURM, supported by the central government funds of

₹50,000 crore with equal share of the state governments (total ₹100,000 crore), was launched in December 2005. In his address to the nation, on the Independence Day (15 August 2006), Manmohan Singh, the then prime minister of India, highlighted:

> Our cities need to have a new look for which they need massive investment and renewal. They need basic amenities like sanitation, drinking water and proper housing for the poor.[1]

He declared, from the ramparts of the Red Fort in Delhi, the formal launch of JNNURM to ensure better infrastructure and better living conditions, the Mission covered 63 cities, including mega and metro cities, all state capitals and cities of historical and religious importance.

Focus and Scope

The focus of JNNURM was on upgradation of urban infrastructure, creation of housing stock and provision of basic services to the urban poor, community participation and accountability of ULBs. There were four components. The following two components were implemented in 65 mission cities:

- Sub-Mission for Urban Infrastructure and Governance (UIG)
- Sub-Mission for Basic Services to the Urban Poor (BSUP)

The remaining two components were implemented in all other cities and included:

- Urban Infrastructure Development Scheme for Small and Medium Towns (UIDSSMT)
- Integrated Housing and Slum Development Programme (IHSDP)

These components were distributed between the Ministry of Housing and Urban Poverty Alleviation (MoHUPA) and Ministry of Urban Development (MoUD). MoHUPA was the nodal ministry for

---

[1] Retrieved from archivepmo.nic.in

implementing BSUP and IHSDP components, and the MoUD was in charge of implementing the UIG and UIDSSMT components.

The Mission aimed at creating cities that are economically productive, efficient, equitable and responsive. It covered the renewal and redevelopment of inner city areas to reduce congestion and included the integrated development of slums; provision of basic services for the poor; and the planned transformation of villages, located in the peri-urban areas, outgrowths and urban corridors that are in process of change from rural to the urban character. The thrust areas included water supply, sanitation, roads, urban transport, renewal of inner city and heritage areas, preservation of water bodies and integrated development of infrastructure in slum areas.

It was a 7-year (2005–2012) reform-oriented, fast-track, mega-urban renewal programme where the introduction of reforms was mandatory by the state government (six reforms) and ULBs (seven reforms). There were, however, 10 additional reforms that were optional. The objective of these reforms was to improve efficiency and accountability of ULBs to deliver infrastructure and services to the people and encourage private sector participation (see Chapter 4 for details).

On completion of seven years, JNNURM was extended for further two years up to 31 March 2014. With a view to complete the projects sanctioned up to 31 March 2012, the BSUP and IHSDP components were extended further up to 31 March 2015.

At the end of the Mission period in 2012, the performance of JNNURM was less than average as evident from the fact that out of 1,358 sanctioned projects only 36% could be completed by 31 December 2012 (DMU-JNNURM, 2013).

The Government of India, up to 31 December 2012, committed a total amount of ₹28,586.07 crore on all UIG projects (Table 2.1). An analysis of Table 2.1 reveals that out of this amount, a sum of about ₹18,703.8 crore (65%) was released, indicating the inability of agencies to complete requirements for the draw of next instalment. It also indicates that the Mission gave insignificant attention to urban renewal and heritage conservation as only less than 1% of the total

Table 2.1 Status of Sector-wise Committed Funds (UIG) (31 December 2012)

Sectors	Amount Committed (₹Crore)	Amount Released (₹Crore)	Percentage of Amount Released to Committed	Percentage of Amount Released to Total	Summary of % Amount Released to Total
Water supply	10,085.64	6,935.59	69	37.08	
Sanitation (sewerage/solid waste management)	8,164.04	4,969.12	61	26.57	76.12
Drainage (drainage/storm water drains)	3,460.57	2,331.68	67	12.47	
Transport (roads/flyovers/ RoB/other urban transport/ MRTS)	6,122.26	4,175.51	68	22.32	22.32
Urban renewal	203.54	97.65	48	0.52	0.86
Heritage	144.13	62.86	44	0.34	
Others	405.89	131.39	32	0.70	0.70
Total	28,586.07	18,703.80	65	100.00	100.00

Source: Author; based upon DMU-JNNURM (2013) Format 3.

released amount was spent on such projects. Most of the money (76%) was spent on water supply, sewerage and drainage. The visible success of JNNURM can only be seen in the improvement of mass transportation, including the provision of buses and introduction of Bus Rapid Transit System (BRTS) and Metro Rail System. The share of this sector in the total amount released was 22.32%. BRTS was introduced in Ahmedabad and Delhi. It was a success in Ahmedabad but failed in Delhi. BRTS in Ahmedabad was introduced in 2009 on a stretch of 12 km, serving about 18,000 passengers per day, which was further extended to 90 km by 2014, serving 175,000 passengers per day. This project has saved almost 200,000 vehicle-kilometres per day as 20–22% commuters using motorcycles have moved to BRTS (World Bank, 2013, p. 121).

MRTS has been successfully implemented in Bangalore, Jaipur, Chennai, Hyderabad and Kochi. According to a study (Sharma, 2013), introduction of MRTS has impacted the city in the form of transformation of residential land use to commercial, increase in property values and reduction in volume of traffic conditions of the areas along the corridor in cities where this has been provided. Table 2.2 presents the latest status of metrorail projects in different cities in India.

An evaluation of achievements of JNNURM by Kshirsagar and Srinivas (2014) found that it has managed to provide a strong impetus to investments in mission cities; made people, administration and politicians aware of the problems of urban growth and management; created favourable governance and institutional framework for private sector participation under people–private–public partnerships (PPPPs) mode; and improved public services and public transportation.

In spite of preparation of city development plans (CDPs) of practically all mission cities, JNNURM ended up as an *ad hoc*, piecemeal and project-oriented financing mechanism for urban renewal that lacked integration with projects of other sectors. Mehta and Mehta (2010) observe that though this programme has significant infusion of capital investments into urban infrastructure, 'it has not always translated into better services, especially for the poor'. According to Ahluwalia (n.d., p. 6), the CDPs typically were reduced

Table 2.2 Status of Metrorail in Different Cities in India (2016)

Already Operational Metro Rail	Under Consideration Metro Rail
• Delhi & NCR (213 km) • Bangalore (32 km) • Kolkata Metro (27 km) • Chennai (18 km) • Jaipur (9 km) • Mumbai Metro Line 1 (11km) • Rapid Metro Gurgaon (5 km) • Mumbai Monorail Phase 1 (9 km) Total Length: 324 km	• Delhi Metro Phase IV (103.93 km) • Delhi & NCR (55.3 km) • Pune (31.25 km) • Vijayawada (26.03 km) • Visakhapatnam (42.55 km) • Bhopal (27.81 km) • Indore (31.55 km) • Kochi Ext.(11.2 km) • Thiruvananthapuram (21.82 Km) • Kozikode (13.3 km) • Patna (27.88 km) • Chandigarh (37.56 km) • Guwahati (61 km) • Kanpur (32.38 km) • Varanasi (29.24 km) Total Length: 553 km
Under Construction Metro/MRTS Projects	**Under Consideration—RRTS Phase 1**
• Delhi and NCR (115 km) • Bangalore (82 km) • Chennai (36 km) • Kochi (26 km) • Jaipur (2.5 km) • Hyderabad (71 km) • Mumbai Line 3 (33.5 km) • Nagpur (38 km) • Ahmedabad (36 km) • Lucknow (23 km) • Kolkata East West Metro (16.55 km) • Mumbai Monorail (11 km)—State initiative • Chennai Monorail (20 km)—State initiative • Rapid Metro Gurgaon (7 km)—Private initiative Total Length: 517 km	• Delhi-Sonipat-Panipat (111 km) • Delhi-Gurgaon-Alwar (180 km) • Delhi-Ghaziabad-Meerut (90 km) Total Length: 381 km

Source: MoUD (2016).

to a list of projects for funding under JNNURM and failed to serve as a holistic strategy document for development of the city.

The objectives and intended reforms under JNNURM are laudable. However, their impact is unclear. The self-evaluation process tends to focus on inputs and processes rather than outcome and impact (World Bank, 2013). An appraisal by the Planning Commission in 2011, as quoted from the World Bank (2013, p. 17), concludes that the performance of JNNURM was lacklustre on reforms and lacked integration with urban planning while preparing the CDPs. The only positive outcome of JNNURM is that it has generated interest of decision-maker in urban issues and huge public investment in the urban sector.

As per the Annual Report 2014–2015 (MoHUPA, 2015), after extension of JNNURM, the progress as on 31 December 2014 improved, and under the BSUP scheme, 481 projects in 32 cities were approved with the total project cost of ₹22,346.38 crore for the construction of 781,402 dwelling units (DUs). Under IHSDP scheme, 1,037 projects in 887 cities were approved with a total project cost of ₹9,382.42 crore for the construction of 445,149 DUs. As shown hereunder, 70% of the total approved numbers of DUs were constructed and 76% of those constructed were occupied by the beneficiaries. The Annual Report also mentions that 223,996 DUs were dropped as they remained non-started during this period.

Progress of Dwelling Units Sanctioned under JNNURM as on 31 December 2014

Description	Number	Percentage
DUs constructed under BSUP	781,402	–
DUs constructed under IHSDP	445,149	–
Total DUs	1,226,551	–
DUs completed	871,818	70
DUs occupied by beneficiaries	664,882	76
DUs under progress	354,733	30

Source: Based upon MoHUPA (2015, p. 19).

Rajiv Awas Yojana

Slum-free India

Addressing to the nation on 15 August 2009, Manmohan Singh, the then prime minister of India, said,

> We had started the Jawaharlal Nehru National Urban Renewal Mission for the urban areas. We will accelerate this programme also. Today, lakhs of our citizens live in slums which lack basic amenities. We wish to make our country slum-free as early as possible. In the next five years, we will provide housing facilities to slum dwellers through a new scheme, Rajiv Awas Yojana. (MoHUPA, 2013, p. 3)

To fulfil this vision of 'slum-free India', RAY was launched in 2011 in two phases: the preparatory phase of two years (2011–2013) followed by implementation phase covering the period 2013–2022.

The objective of RAY was to create 'slum-free India' with inclusive and equitable cities where every citizen has access to basic civic infrastructure, social amenities and decent shelter (MoHUPA, 2013). It covered all cities and priority was given to those that had large slum population or concentration of scheduled cast (SC)/scheduled tribe (ST) population and other vulnerable groups.

Based upon the lessons learnt from the implementation of JNNURM, the approach followed under RAY was holistic which included preparation of Slum-free City Plans of Action (SFCPoA), covering *the whole city, all slums and whole slum* which may be notified, non-notified, recognised or identified. At the structural level, therefore, RAY moved away from an ad hoc and project-based approach of JNNURM. To ensure that renewal of slums does not lead to the loss of livelihood linkages of the residents, the approaches such as in situ development and upgradation were promoted. RAY also supported redevelopment of the entire slum after the demolition of the existing built structures and providing adequate housing and infrastructure (civic and social) to the slum dwellers. It also supported temporary transit housing to accommodate the displaced slum dwellers in such redevelopment scheme (for further details, see MoHUPA, 2013).

The SFCPoA, prepared at state and city levels, provided the road map for the planning and implementation of the programme. It advocated strong community involvement in planning, decision-making, implementation and monitoring followed by asset maintenance. It provided community ownership to the project and its sustainability. RAY also emphasised the integration of housing with employment through the convergence of Swarna Jayanti Shahari Rozgar Yojana (SJSRY), the only employment scheme aimed at urban poor.

According to the Annual Report 2014–2015 of the MoHUPA (2015, p. 21), the progress in respect of RAY, as on 31 December 2014, can be summarised as follows:

- The number of cities included in RAY was 228.
- Number of states that had signed the Memorandum of Agreement (MoA) was 25. These states included Andhra Pradesh, Assam, Bihar, Chhattisgarh, Goa, Gujarat, Haryana, Himachal Pradesh, Jammu and Kashmir, Jharkhand, Karnataka, Kerala, Manipur, Odisha, Rajasthan, Tamil Nadu, Uttarakhand, Uttar Pradesh, West Bengal, Telangana, Mizoram, Madhya Pradesh, Punjab, Tripura and Arunachal Pradesh.
- Out of 228 cities, 70 had submitted their Slum Free City Plans of Action (SFCPoA) to the Ministry and out of these plans, 47 were accepted so far. It was reported that 110 cities were at various stages of preparing SFCPoA.
- A total of 233 projects with a total project cost of ₹8,661.78 crore involving central share of ₹4,807.64 crore for construction/upgradation of 164,806 DUs had been approved and ₹1,758.80 crore was released.
- A total of 67 detailed project reports (DPRs) with a total project cost of ₹2,189.72 crore, involving central share of ₹1,297.27 crore for construction/upgradation of 43,894 DUs, were approved during June 2014 and December 2014 and ₹336.90 crore was released as the first instalment.

The impact of RAY could not be seen on the ground as only 30% cities could prepare the required SFCPoA. The proposals remained on paper as only 67 DPRs for construction/upgradation of 43,894 DUs were approved which insignificant considering the number of slums. Probably due to lack of enough time for implementation of the scheme, the slum-free city vision remains a utopian idea.

Affordable Housing in Partnership

To tackle the incidence of slum formation in the future by increasing affordable housing stock, the Government of India introduced, in 2013, the Affordable Housing in Partnership (AHP) scheme which was incorporated in RAY for the implementation as a central support. Accordingly, an amount of ₹75,000 was granted per DU of 21–40 sq. m size, built for EWS/LIG in an affordable housing scheme taken up under various types of partnerships, including private partnership. Such partnerships could be between the communities, industry, financing institutions, cities, state governments and the Government of India.

The minimum size of project to avail the central support was the one having at least 250 DUs, comprising a mix of EWS/LIG as well as higher income categories. Commercial use was also permitted. The only restriction was that at least 60% of the FAR/FSI must be used for DUs of carpet area of not more than 60 sq. m.

Under AHP Scheme, as on 31 December 2014, a total of 21 projects from 3 states (Karnataka, Gujarat and Rajasthan) for the construction of 24,141 DUs were sanctioned. The first instalment of ₹44.19 crore was released. Construction of 4,968 DUs was completed, of which 2,432 DUs had been occupied. Construction of 15,504 DUs was under progress. During 2014–2015, a total of 10 projects of Gujarat were sanctioned for the construction of 17,373 DUs, and the first instalment of ₹41.11 crore was released (MoHUPA, 2015, p. 21).

Progress, as on 31 January 2017, in respect of AHP—a component of RAY—includes a total of 21 projects for 3 states (Karnataka, Gujarat and Rajasthan) with a total project cost of ₹1,398 crore, involving central share of ₹140 crore that has been approved, and ₹69 crore that has been released for the construction of 24,141 DUs. During the period, April 2016 to December 2016, some 8,797 DUs were completed and 10,275 DUs, including unoccupied DUs of preceding years, were occupied (MoHUPA, 2017, p. 31).

RAY has been discontinued with the launch of the PMAY–Housing for All (Urban) or PMAY-HFA (U) in June 2016 and the liabilities of its 183 projects (including AHP scheme) which had started on the ground in various states have been subsumed in the new PMAY-HFA (U) (MoHUPA, 2016a, p. 25). RAY was also a reform-oriented scheme (see Chapter 4 for details).

Pradhan Mantri Awas Yojana (Urban): Housing for All by 2022

The prime minister, on 9 June 2014, announced that 'by the time the Nation completes 75 years of its independence, every family will have a *pucca* house with water connection, toilet facilities, 24×7 electricity supply and access' (MoHUPA, 2016b, p. i). Pradhan Mantri Awas Yojana (Urban) (PMAY-U) is a way to achieve this vision to ensure housing for all during 2015–2022. It covers all urban centres in the country and supports DUs for EWS/LIG[2] for the construction of houses with a carpet area of 30 sq. m, which may be changed by the state governments, if so needed, in consultation with the central government. The basic focus of PMAY (U) (MoHUPA, 2016b) is to promote slum rehabilitation with participation of private developers using land as resource; AHP with public and private sectors; and affordable housing through credit-linked subsidy. The PMAY (U), therefore, has the following four components:

1. In situ slum redevelopment with participation of private developers using land as resource for providing housing to eligible slum dwellers

[2] EWS: A family with annual income up to ₹3 lakh. LIG: A family with annual income of ₹3–6 lakh.

2. Credit Linked Subsidy Scheme (CLSS) for providing interest rate rebate to EWS/LIG beneficiaries
3. AHP with public and private sectors
4. Beneficiary-led individual house construction/enhancements

In situ Slum Redevelopment

This component provides a grant of ₹1 lakh per house built for eligible slum dwellers in an in situ slum redevelopment scheme, using land as a resource, with the participation of private developers. This grant can be utilised by states/UTs for any of the slum redevelopment projects.

Credit-linked Subsidy Scheme

Under the CLSS beneficiaries of EWS and LIG, seeking housing loans from banks, housing finance companies and other such financial institutions is eligible for an interest subsidy of 6.5% on such loan amount up to ₹6 lakh. This loan can be utilised for the acquisition, construction and addition of rooms, kitchen, toilet, etc., to existing dwellings as incremental housing for EWS houses with carpet area of 30 sq. m. For LIG housing, the carpet area is up to 60 sq. m. This scheme is also available for the middle-income groups (MIG) as CLSS-II.

Affordable Housing in Partnership

Central assistance of ₹1.5 lakh per EWS house is provided by Government of India in projects where at least 35% of the total houses are for EWS category and a single project has at least 250 houses. The remaining houses may have any mix of dwellings. This caters to the housing supply side and PMAY (U) encourages EWS houses being built with different partnerships by states/UTs/cities so that the availability of such housing at an affordable cost is increased. The partnership by states/UTs/cities may be with private sector including industries.

Beneficiary-led Individual House Construction/Enhancements

Under this component, central assistance of ₹1.5 lakh is available for individual eligible families belonging to EWS categories for construction or repairs.

The programme recognises a housing shortage of ₹1.878 crore where 95% is for the EWS and LIG people. A majority (80%) of this shortage is due to congestion; additional 12% is because of obsolescence and the remaining is due to homelessness (3%) and *kachha* nature of buildings (5%).

The programme takes a very practical approach to the provision of housing for all and incorporates various strategies for various groups of people—slum dwellers, urban poor people living in non-slum areas, prospective migrants to cities and those who are homeless and destitute. The urban renewal strategies for slum dwellers vary according to the nature, location and legal status of slums which have been classified as (a) tenable, (b) untenable, (c) located on government land and (d) unauthorised colonies. For tenable slums, the strategy is in situ redevelopment or upgradation. Relocation strategy is to be followed for non-tenable slums, as they are located on sites, such as floodplains, that are not fit for residential purposes. In case of slums located on government lands, two strategies are suggested as the land-owning agencies are generally reluctant to release their land for housing. The programme advocates in situ relocation of slums on non-essential land that the land owning agency can release. For other lands, relocation strategy will be followed. For unauthorised colonies, the strategy of regularisation is to be followed (see Chapter 3 for details of various strategies). For other urban poor and migrants, AHP with public and private sectors is being promoted. For homeless people, it proposes a strategy of subsidised rental housing and night shelters.

Implementation of PMAY (U)

As on 31 December 2016, some 34 MoAs have been signed with 29 states and 5 UTs. The number of cities selected under the mission is 3,888. The Government of India has approved 3,031 projects for the construction of 1,401,097 houses of EWS category in 1,792 cities of 29 states/UTs. These projects are supported by the central assistance of ₹20,724.61 crore, and ₹4,686.82 crore been released as the part of first instalment (MoHUPA, 2017, p. 24).

During the year 2016, a total of 17,634 claims for subsidy amounting to ₹316.20 crore were processed under the CLSS.

Smart City Mission

In June 2015, the Government of India launched the Smart City Mission for transforming urban India. It is a five-year mission covering the period 2015–2020.

Objective

The objective of Smart Cities Mission is to create futuristic cities that provide clean and sustainable urban spaces and a decent quality of life to all its citizens using smart solutions for provision, use and maintenance of utilities facilities and services.

The Smart City Mission includes the development of 100 urban centres as smart cities during the mission period (2015–2020). These cities are distributed among all the states and UTs based on their urban population and number of statutory towns (Annexure 2.1). The formula gives equal weightage (50:50) to urban population and the number of statutory towns. This ensures equity in the distribution of cities under the Mission. This is for the first time that a competitive approach has been introduced in any programme of the MoUD. Smart cities, for funding under the Mission, are selected through a competition, among ULBs, called the 'city challenge'. This approach follows the spirit of 'competitive and cooperative federalism' (MoUD, 2015a, p. 18) where the states and ULBs will play a key supportive role in the development of smart cities. It is a place-based approach (see Chapter 1), as it focuses on the selected 100 cities and promotes smart leadership and vision by the state governments and ULBs, and it also focuses on their ability to act decisively.

With a view to achieve urban transformation, the Smart City Mission focuses upon two strategies: (a) area-based strategy and (b) a pan-city initiative. On one hand, the area-based strategy has three components: (a) city improvement (retrofitting), (b) city renewal (redevelopment) and (c) city extension (greenfield development). The pan-city initiative, on the other hand, promotes application of smart solutions covering larger parts of the city or the entire city so that all the citizens are benefited and they feel being served by the initiatives. In this case, the smart solutions could be e-governance and services, waste management, intelligent traffic management and such others.

As a reform and in the true spirit of cooperative federalism, the central government has, virtually, withdrawn from the earlier practice of appraising and sanctioning individual projects, thereby ending the scope for subjectivity and discretion as the Smart Cities Mission provides full liberty and flexibility to states in the formulation, approval and execution of projects.

Considering the minimum area norms for retrofitting (covering 500 acre/200 ha), redevelopment (50 acre/20 ha) and greenfield development (250 acre/100 ha), smart city approach seems to be piecemeal where different parts of an existing city may be showcased as a smart city under different strategies—retrofitting, redevelopment and greenfield development. Probably, the intention of the Mission is that these projects, when successfully completed, will attract more similar projects and initiate a continuous process of urban renewal to make the city smarter and smarter as the time goes by.

The Smart City Mission is a centrally sponsored scheme (CSS) and the central government will give financial support to the Mission to the extent of ₹48,000 crore over five years. An equal amount, on a matching basis, will have to be contributed by the state/ULB; therefore, nearly ₹100,000 crore will be available for triggering development in 100 smart cities. This amount, about ₹1,000 crore per city, will meet only a part of the project cost and the balance funds would expected to be mobilised by the state and the local bodies (MoUD, 2015a).

The Smart Cities Mission strongly advocates convergence of various schemes and programmes connected to the provision of social infrastructures such as health, education and culture. These programmes include AMRUT, Swachh Bharat Mission (SBM), HRIDAY, Digital India, Skill Development, Housing for All and others. The objective of this convergence is to integrate and maximise the physical, institutional, social and economic infrastructure being developed through such initiatives and make the city smart.

As indicated below, till December 2016, a total of 60 cities had been selected for this Mission, covering a total of 9,152 sq. km of urban area. The total area proposed for area-based development in the selected smart cities is 28,032 ha. These cities will serve an urban population of 7.23 crore (MoUD, 2017, pp. 42–43). Special purpose vehicles (SPVs) of 20 smart cities have been constituted. A grant of ₹2 crore per city has been released to prepare the Smart City Plan. Actual implementation will start when all SPVs are in place.

Progress of Smart City Mission till December 2016

Cities Selected	Total
Total number of winning cities	60
Total population impacted	72,266,232
Total households covered	15,682,638
Total area covered under area-based development (acres/hectare)	70,078/28,031
Total urban area impacted (sq. km)	9,152

Source: Based upon Government of India (2017a, pp. 42–43).

Atal Mission for Rejuvenation and Urban Transformation

Launched in 2015, AMRUT focuses on transforming quality of life of cities through (a) provision of access to basic services, including water supply, sewerage facility, seepage management and storm water drains to every household; (b) increasing the amenity value of city by developing and maintaining parks, children play areas, open spaces and greenery and (c) reducing pollution by switching to public transport and constructing walkways and cycle tracks and providing parking.

The approach of the Mission is to follow the process of 'incrementalism' and gradually progress towards achieving the service-level benchmarks set by the MoUD (see Table 5.5), which, *inter alia*, include 100% coverage of basic services, 24×7 water supply, recycle and reuse of waste water, cost recovery and operational efficiency. Following the spirit of 'cooperative federalism', the Mission makes the state governments equal partners in the planning and implementation of the projects. Accordingly, each state prepares State Annual Action Plan (SAAP) based upon the Service Level Improvement Plans (SLIPs) prepared by the various ULBs in the state. The SAAP gives the current status of services, priorities, manner of bridging the gaps and requirement of resources and indicates the year-wise improvements in the level of services. The MoUD approves the SAAP every year and based on the SAAP, the state government approves the projects through the State Level Technical Committee (SLTC), which are implemented by the ULBs. This clearly defines the role of centre, state and local bodies in the set-up of 'cooperative federalism'.

The Mission covers 500 cities and the total allocation is ₹50,000 crore spread over five years up to 2020 (MoUD, 2015b). As on 15 December 2015, the MoUD, Government of India, had approved City-Level Action Plans (CLAPs) of 474 out of a total 497 cities for improving the basic urban infrastructure under AMRUT with an investment of ₹19,170 crore for the year 2015–2016 (MoUD, 2015c).

An analysis of the review of four SAAPs (Andhra Pradesh, Telangana, Haryana and Karnataka) for the year 2015–2016, as presented to the Apex Committee of MoUD, Government of India, on 3 August 2016 (see the table on the next page), indicates that the first year of the implementation of the Mission was basically limited to the identification and approval of projects and the preparation and approval of DPRs. No implementation had actually taken place during 2015–2016.

An Analysis of Review of Four SAAPs (2015–2016)

Number of	Andhra Pradesh SAAP	Telangana SAAP	Haryana SAAP	Karnataka SAAP
AMRUT cities	31	12	18	27
Projects	56	22	74	85
DPRs prepared	56	22	9	81
DPRs approved	56	22	9	80
Tenders floated	29	1	0	0
Contract awarded	3	0	0	0
Projects completed	0	0	0	0
Share of approved funds				
% of total approved fund for basic services	98	98	91	97
% of total approved fund for parks	2	2	4	2
% of total approved fund for urban transport	0	0	5	1
Total	100	100	100	100

Source: Based upon various SAAPs available at http://amrut.gov.in/Presentations.aspx

If the distribution of the total approved fund for various components of the Mission is considered, it reveals that this exercise is basically focused on the provision of basic services (water supply, sewerage and drainage) which accounts for more than 91% funds in all the four states. Urban transport is not considered by Andhra and Telangana at all, and Haryana and Karnataka had earmarked only 5% and 1% funds, respectively. Similarly, the development and maintenance of parks, children play areas, open spaces and greenery seem to be the last priority among all the four states where the provision of funds for this component was only 2–4%. It is to be agreed that water is essential for sustaining life and should be the top priority. However, to reduce pollution, to increase the amenity value of city and to improve the quality of life of people, urban transport and parks, playfields and open spaces are necessary and must be given the due emphasis while planning. These are essential components of AMRUT for urban transformation. It would be desirable to highlight here that the provision of basic services should not be limited to the achievement of the set benchmark. It should, in fact, aim at augmenting the services in accordance with the carrying capacity of the area.

In July 2014, the National Declaration on Urban Governance and Housing for All was adopted by a Conclave of Ministers of Housing and Urban Development of states and UTs. According to this declaration, the state governments/UTs agreed to join hand to work together to achieve the target of Housing for All by 2022 and actively consider implementing the 25-point reform agenda (MoUD, 2015b; SDR News, 2014). Taking the spirit of this Declaration, AMRUT mandated a set of 11 reforms to be implemented by the states/UTs and 500 Mission cities. These comprise five reforms that were introduced by JNNURM and include (a) e-governance; (b) augmentation of double entry accounting system (DEAS) in ULBs; (c) devolution of power and functions as per 12th schedule (Annexure 4.1); (d) review of building bylaws and (e) improvement in municipal taxes/fees and in levy and collection of user charges. The difference, however, is that AMRUT reforms cover 500 cities while the JNNURM reforms covered only 63 cities. The rest of the reforms are new and cover constitution of municipal cadre, urban planning, setting up of financial intermediary at state level, credit rating of ULBs, energy and water audit and SBM. These are target-oriented and incentive-driven reforms where compliance of the reforms, as per annual targets, will attract an incentive of 10% of the annual budgeted amount (see Chapter 4 for details of reforms and Chapter 6 for funding).

AMRUT has a much wider coverage (500 cities). JNNURM was centralised, while AMRUT follows the principle of 'cooperative federalism' and a decentralised process where states are equal partners in planning and implementation of projects. SAAPs of 18 states—Jharkhand, Chhattisgarh, Odisha, Mizoram, Madhya Pradesh, Kerala, Tamil Nadu, Gujarat, Andhra Pradesh, Rajasthan, Telangana, West Bengal, Haryana, Bihar, Maharashtra, Himachal Pradesh, Uttar Pradesh and Karnataka—have been approved by the Apex Committee (MoHUPA, 2016a).

Up to December 2016, SAAPs of 36 states/UTs had been approved by the Apex Committee, involving total investment of about ₹24,916 crore which includes the central assistance of ₹11,848 crore. First instalment of this central assistance amounting ₹2,316 crore has been released to the states/UTs.

Heritage City Development and Augmentation Yojana

Recognising that the full potential of the heritage of India has not been explored fully for the benefit of the tourists, the Government of India introduced a programme known as the HRIDAY in 2015. The focus of this programme is to reinvigorate the selected heritage cities and make them aesthetically appealing for tourists taking a comprehensive approach which includes urban planning, conservation of heritage, retaining city's cultural identity, economic development, and provision of infrastructure, security and improvement in quality of life of the community.

HRIDAY covers 12 cities including Ajmer, Amravati, Amritsar, Badami, Dwarka, Gaya, Kanchipuram, Mathura, Puri, Varanasi, Velankanni and Warangal. The scope of this programme is heritage documentation and mapping leading to heritage management plan, heritage revitalisation linked to service provision and city information/ knowledge management and skill development. It is a fully funded CSS that will end by 2018 (MoUD, 2015d).

According to the Guidelines (MoUD, 2015e), the main vision of HRIDAY is to preserve and revitalise the unique character and the soul of heritage city and facilitate inclusive heritage-linked urban development with specific focus on heritage revitalization, tourism, sanitation, security and livelihoods retaining the city's cultural identity. To fulfil this vision, the objectives include the following:

- To document and develop heritage asset inventory of cities covering natural, cultural, living and built heritage zones and the core areas
- To preserve/conserve, retrofit, rehabilitate, revitalise and maintain the heritage in the city

- To establish and manage effective public–private partnership for adaptive urban rehabilitation
- To create effective linkages between tourism, culture and heritage wherein tourists can connect directly with city's unique character
- To develop and promote core tangible economic activities to enhance avenues of livelihoods amongst stakeholders
- To make cities informative with use of modern information communication technology (ICT) tools and making cities secure with modern surveillance and security apparatus like close circuit television (CCTV)
- To increase physical and intellectual accessibility in the heritage city
- To promote planning, development and implementation of heritage-sensitive infrastructure

The expected outcomes of HRIDAY include the following:

- Properly conserved, revitalised and beautified heritage monuments
- Heritage resources mainstreamed with city systems and city economy and improved sanitised environment
- Increase in the inflow of the tourist to cities
- Increase in the duration of stay of the tourist in the town
- Substantial improvement in local economy and quality of life of its communities
- Improvement in social safety and reduction in crime
- Improved basic urban infrastructure at existing and emerging tourist destinations and gateways
- Improved sanitation standards at natural and cultural tourist attractions with convenience and safety for visitors
- Greater participation by local communities in tourism-related economic and livelihood activities
- Improvement in the service level benchmark indicators for urban service delivery

Swadesh Darshan

Ministry of Tourism, Government of India, had launched the Swadesh Darshan initiative for an integrated development of 13 theme-based tourist circuits in the country in 2014–2015. These circuits include Northeast India Circuit, Buddhist Circuit, Himalayan Circuit, Coastal Circuit, Krishna Circuit, Desert Circuit, Tribal Circuit, Eco Circuit, Wildlife Circuit, Rural Circuit, Spiritual Circuit, Ramayana Circuit and Heritage Circuit. The basic objective is to promote local arts, culture, handicrafts and cuisine to generate livelihoods in the identified regions, improve infrastructure to make the tourist sites, along the circuit, attractive for visitors and harness tourism potential for its direct and multiplier effects in employment generation and economic development (SDR News, 2016, p. 156).

The objectives of the Swadesh Darshan initiative are as follows:

- To promote cultural and heritage value of the country and provide complete tourism experience with varied thematic circuits
- To develop circuits, having tourist potential, in a planned and prioritised manner and harness tourism potential for its direct and multiplier effects in employment generation and economic development
- To create awareness among the local communities about the importance of tourism for them in terms of diversification in sources of income, improved living standards and overall development of the area
- To enhance the tourist attractiveness in a sustainable manner through integrated development of world class infrastructure in the identified theme based circuits
- To promote local arts, cultural, handicrafts, cuisine, etc., to generate livelihoods in the identified regions by leverage public capital and expertise

According to this initiative, heritage circuit will be developed in Madhya Pradesh and Uttarakhand. Tourist sites such as Jageshwar–Devidhura–Katarmal–Baijnath circuit in Uttarakhand will be rejuvenated to attract tourists. In Madhya Pradesh, tourism infrastructure will be augmented along Gwalior–Orchha–Khajuraho–Chanderi–Bhimbetka–Mandu Circuit. Chennai–Mamallapuram–Rameshwaram–Manapad–Kanyakumari circuit will be developed as the Coastal Circuit in Tamil Nadu. Chitrakoot and Shringverpur will form part of the Ramayana Circuit in Uttar Pradesh.

This Scheme is proposed to be implemented in a mission mode. During 2016–2017 (up to 31 December 2016), Ministry of Tourism, Government of India, sanctioned 31 projects under Swadesh Darshan Scheme (Annexure 2.2) with central financial assistance of ₹2,601.76 crore and ₹506.47 crore had been released (Ministry of Tourism, 2017).

As detailed in Annexure 2.2, out of the total 31 projects, there are 7 projects under Spiritual Circuit and 6 under Himalayan Circuit. Coastal Circuit covers 5 projects. There are 4 projects under the Heritage Circuit and 2 projects each have been approved under the Tribal, Northeastern India, Buddhist and Krishna Circuits. There is a single project from Uttar Pradesh on the Ramayana Circuit.

Pilgrimage Rejuvenation and Spiritual Augmentation Drive

PRASAD is also an initiative of the Ministry of Tourism, Government of India, for the redevelopment of infrastructure in cities that are visited by pilgrims and tourists. It was launched in the year 2014–2015. The basic objectives of PRASAD are as follows:

- To promote integrated development of pilgrimage destinations in a planned, prioritised and sustainable manner to provide unique experience to visitors on religious tourism
- To harness pilgrimage tourism for employment generation and economic development
- Follow community-based development and pro-poor tourism concepts in development of the pilgrimage destinations
- To leveraging public capital and expertise
- To enhance the tourist attractiveness of the pilgrimage destinations in a sustainable manner by developing world class infrastructure
- To make the local communities aware about the importance of tourism in providing job opportunities and improving their living standards
- To promote local arts, cultural, handicrafts, cuisine, etc., to generate livelihoods in the identified places

The Mission strategy is to (a) identify religious destinations that have potential to be showcased as world-class tourism products in consultation with the stakeholders; (b) ensure that the development of these destinations adheres to the sustainability and carrying capacities of the destinations; (c) identify infrastructure gaps in the identified destinations, which have been major roadblocks in unlocking the potentials of these places and (d) plan, in an integrated manner, the development of these destinations in a specific timeframe ensuring full convergence of state and central government schemes as well as private sector investments.

Under this drive, 25 sites have been identified for rejuvenation which include Amaravati (Andhra Pradesh), Amritsar (Punjab), Ajmer (Rajasthan), Ayodhya (Uttar Pradesh), Badrinath (Uttarakhand), Dwarka (Gujarat), Deoghar (Jharkhand), Belur (West Bengal), Gaya (Bihar), Guruvayoor (Kerala), Hazratbal (Jammu and Kashmir), Kamakhya (Assam), Kanchipuram (Tamil Nadu), Katra (Jammu), Kedarnath (Uttarakhand), Mathura (Uttar Pradesh), Patna (Bihar), Puri (Odisha), Srisailam (Andhra Pradesh), Somnath (Gujarat), Tirupati (Andhra Pradesh), Trimbakeshwar (Maharashtra), Ujjain (Madhya Pradesh), Varanasi (Uttar Pradesh) and Velankanni (Tamil Nadu) (Ministry of Tourism, 2017).

As on 31 December 2016, the Ministry of Tourism had approved five projects in Gujarat, Tamil Nadu, West Bengal and Jammu and Kashmir as under:

Gujarat	Development of Dwarka
Tamil Nadu	(1) Development of Kanchipuram
	(2) Development of Velankanni
West Bengal	Development of Belur
Jammu and Kashmir	Development of Hazratbal

The Ministry of Tourism has also sanctioned a sum of ₹120.36 crore for these projects (Ministry of Tourism, 2017).

Redevelopment of Railway Stations

The railway ministry has initiated redevelopment of about 400 railway stations in the country. The objective is to redevelop railway stations by upgrading to better standards the level of passenger amenities including platform surfaces, circulation area and station buildings so as to serve the need of the passengers. The under-utilised railway land will be commercially exploited to finance the project on models such as Build–Operate–Transfer (BOT), Build–Own–Operate–Transfer (BOOT) and Build–Lease–Transfer (BLT). A special purpose vehicle—Indian Railway Station Development Corporation Limited (IRSDC)—has been set up to implement the project. According to Railway Ministry, countries such as France, Japan, Germany, the United Kingdom, South Korea and Belgium have expressed interest in redevelopment projects.

The railway ministry is also collaborating with MoUD to redevelop railway stations in all 100 smart cities. A Memorandum of Understanding (MoU) was signed between the two ministries. National Building Construction Corporation (NBCC) will redevelop 10 stations under this programme. These stations include Varanasi, Jaipur, Kota, Sarai Rohilla (Delhi), Thane, Margao (Goa), Bhubaneswar, Lucknow, Tirupati and Puducherry.

Redevelopment work at Habibganj railway station has already been awarded and plans for Anand Vihar (Delhi), Surat, Bijwasan and Gandhinagar are in advanced stage of preparation. This redevelopment of railway stations later on will be integrated with the cities covered under AMRUT and HRIDAY (Ministry of Railways, 2016a).

Swachh Bharat Mission

Addressing to the Joint Session of Parliament on 9 June 2014, the president of India said,

> We must not tolerate the indignity of homes without toilets and public spaces littered with garbage. For ensuring hygiene, waste management and sanitation across the nation, a '*Swachh Bharat Mission*' will be launched. This will be our tribute to Mahatma Gandhi on his 150th birth anniversary to be celebrated in the year 2019. (MoUD, 2014, p. 3)

Inspired by the president's observation and with prime minister's initiative, the SBM was launched to prepare the nation for giving a very unique present—clean India—to the Father of Nation on his 150th birthday on 2 October 2019. A clean India was one of the desires of Mahatma Gandhi.

Cleanliness is one of the most basic needs of any urban renewal effort. It is the first thing that visitors note and make their impression about the city. Cleanliness is one of the prime factors in the creation of an image of a city. Open defecation along railway lines is a sight a visitor experiences in the morning while entering a city by train. Entry to beautiful monuments is often through dirty roads full of litter, stray animals and defaced walls with posters of all kinds.

The basic objective of SBM is elimination of open defecation, manual scavenging and introduction of scientific solid waste management. This Mission also aims at changing the mind-set of people for healthy sanitation practices. It is a time-bound Mission that ends on 2 October 2019.

The Mission components include environmental upgradation of public places, such as railway stations, bus stands, markets, tourist places and office complexes, by efficient solid waste management and provision of public toilets to be used by the floating population. For slum areas and *jhuggi jhopri* (JJ) clusters, the Mission supports construction of community toilets.

Central government share of ₹14,623 crore is available for the Mission. The state/ULBs share is ₹4,874 crore. The balance fund is to be generated from other sources such as private sector participation, beneficiary's own contribution, user charges, land leveraging, corporate social responsibility, market borrowing and external assistance (MoUD, 2014).

The achievement of the mission includes construction of 115,786 community toilets, 100% door-to-door collection of waste in 42,948 wards and 626 open-defecation-free (ODF) cities.[3] Social behavioural transformation and injecting awareness regarding sanitation is one of the key strategies of SBM (Urban) because it brings health and happiness to the community. In order to foster healthy competition among cities for improving cleanliness standards, MoUD started in

---

[3] www.swachhbharaturban.in/sbm/home/#/SBM

2016 a Swachh Survekshan (survey) and ranked the cities accordingly. The Quality Control Council of India conducted the survey. Some 73 cities were ranked in 2016. In 2017 survey, 434 cities were covered. Indore (Madhya Pradesh) tops the list and Gonda (Uttar Pradesh) is at the bottom.

The methodology of the survey included the following three steps where points were awarded on the basis of the performance.

Methodology of the Survey (Swachh Survekshan)

Step	Description	Points
Step 1	Self-declaration by ULBs on: • Door-to-door collection of waste, sweeping and transportation (40%) • Processing and disposal of waste (20%) • Open-defecation-free toilets (30%) • Innovative creative excellence (ICE) and behaviour change (5%) • Capacity-building (5%)	900 points
Step 2	Independent validation by citizen and 421 third party assessors	500 points
Step 3	Citizen feedback using phone-based Swachh App (18 lakh responses)	600 points
	Total points	2,000 points

Source: The Times of India (2017a).

The five best and worst cities in India as per Swachh Survekshan 2017 are mentioned below:

Best and Worst Cities in India (as per Swachh Survekshan 2017)

Five Best Cities (points scored)	Five Worst Cities (points scored)
1. Indore (1,808)	1. Banda (305)
2. Bhopal (1,800)	2. Bhusawal (345)
3. Visakhapatnam (1,797)	3. Bagaha (367)
4. Surat (1,762)	4. Hardoi (377)
5. Mysuru (Mysore) (1,743)	5. Katihar (383)

Source: The Times of India (2017a).

Ranking of cities appears to be working in motivating ULBs and state governments to improve their performance in achieving cleanliness standards. Indore was ranked 25th in the 2016 survey. Indore Municipal Corporation (IMC) was not happy and worked hard to improve the city. IMC staff was advised to avoid taking leaves. Children and women groups were motivated to check open defecation by blowing whistles and sounding other objects. A total of 12,549 individual toilets, over 200 urinals, 190 public restrooms, 400 modular toilets and 16 mobile loos were constructed in the city, and, in January 2017, the city got ODF tag from the PMO. This motivated IMC to take further initiatives. A mass awareness drive was launched. Surprise inspections and spot fines ranging from ₹250 to ₹20,000 were introduced which worked. People gradually stopped dumping on the roads. Even IMC employees faced expulsion or suspension if they failed to keep a Swachh date. IMC then made it mandatory for 'townships' in the city to install centralised waste treatment plants and segregate waste at source. IMC also launched an App called 'Indore 311' (*The Times of India*, 2017b). Top ranking of Indore is well deserved and IMC deserves hearty congratulations.

At the state level, the chief minister of Uttar Pradesh noted the last position of Gonda and most of its cities performing very poorly on the national cleanliness ranking and promised, in a press conference, to take action and improve performance. He declared that by December 2018, the entire state should be open defecation-free. He stressed on making people aware of not littering on roads and instructed municipal authorities to give clear directions on cleanliness in all wards (*The Statesman*, 2017).

State-level Initiatives

As mentioned earlier, preparation and implementation of urban renewal plans is the function of the ULBs, the role of the state governments is therefore limited facilitate implementation of central government policies and programmes and to enactment of laws to provide legal support to urban renewal efforts of ULBs and formulation of policies and programmes pertaining to rejuvenation of urban areas including state-level reforms which are discussed in Chapter 4.

Provision of Legal Support

The Town Planning Acts or Development Acts of 14 states/UTs have made provisions for the urban renewal (see Table 5.1). These states/UTs are Gujarat, Maharashtra, Delhi, Mizoram, Arunachal Pradesh, Odisha, Goa, Himachal Pradesh, Uttar Pradesh, Tamil Nadu, Andhra Pradesh, Madhya Pradesh, Punjab and Rajasthan. Some states have passed acts pertaining to renewal of slums. Some of these include Maharashtra Slum Areas (Improvement, Clearance and Redevelopment) Act, 1971, and Punjab Slum Areas (Improvement and Clearance) Act, 1961.

State Schemes for Redevelopment

In Maharashtra, urban renewal has been in a piecemeal manner covering slum pockets, tenanted buildings or housing schemes of MHADA. A comprehensive city-level renewal approach has not been attempted till 2009, when regulation was made for urban renewal in a cluster approach (Chapter 5) covering all types of houses—public, private slum and buildings of government and semi-government authorities (Nallathiga 2014).

Maharashtra state initiative for renewal of slum areas includes promotion of the strategy of in situ development through private participation with full involvement of community. A nodal authority—Slum Rehabilitation Authority (SRA)—has been constituted under Maharashtra Slum Areas Act, 1971, for this purpose. The Slum Rehabilitation Scheme of SRA provides for community participation, through formation of a Cooperative Housing Society of slum dwellers in the redevelopment process. It also provides attractive incentives (increased FSI and also TDR) for private participation in slum redevelopment process.

Based upon the Maharashtra SRA scheme, Gujarat has notified Regulations for Rehabilitation and Redevelopment of Slums, 2010, where the government regulates and provides incentives, and the private sector invests and provides housing to slum dwellers at no cost to them. Rajasthan state has also incorporated the Maharashtra SRA model for slum redevelopment with private sector participation in its

Affordable Housing Policy 2009 (Department of Urban Development, Housing and Local Self Government, 2009).

City-level Initiatives

As mentioned earlier, urban renewal is the function of the ULBs. The 12th Schedule of Constitution (74th Amendment) Act, 1992 (74th CAA) includes slum improvement and upgradation at entry no. 10 (see Annexure 4.1). This section discusses the urban renewal initiatives taken by different cities in India and covers Delhi, Mumbai, Kolkata, Indore, Ahmedabad, Mysore, Pune and Hyderabad.

Delhi Initiatives

Delhi, being the national capital and the most pampered city in the country, should have demonstrated a high level of planned development; however, in reality, only 24% of population of the city lives in planned colonies and the balance (76%) gets accommodated in seven types of settlements such as JJ clusters, slum designated areas, unauthorised colonies, resettlement colonies, regularised unauthorised colonies and old villages engulfed by urban extension or other located in urbanizable areas (Table 2.3). Dealing with such a complex system of settlement types occurring in Delhi is a challenge to spatial planners and city administrators.

As early as 1961, some 3,560 households were resettled under a scheme for resettlement of population living in JJ clusters. Each household was provided a serviced plot of 80 sq. yd (66.89 sq. m). The objective of resettlement could not be achieved as the people resold their allotted plots and squatted on other areas in the city. The size of plots was reduced to 40 sq. m in subsequent schemes and was further reduced to 25 sq. m. During 1975– 1977, a massive resettlement programme was introduced by Delhi Development Authority (DDA) and 197,000 households living in JJ clusters were accommodated in 26 resettlement colonies. By the year 1979–1980, the number of resettlement colonies increased to 44, accommodating about 240,000 households (Government of Delhi, 2002).

Table 2.3 *Types of Settlements in Delhi and Their Population in the Year 2000*

S. No.	Type of Settlement	Approx. Population (Lakh) (2000)		Percentage	
A	Planned colonies	33.08	33.08	24	24
B	Unplanned settlements	106.56		76	
1	JJ clusters		20.72		15
2	Slum designated areas		26.64		19
3	Unauthorised colonies		7.40		5
4	Resettlement colonies		17.76		13
5	Rural villages		7.40		5
6	Regularised unauthorised colonies		17.76		13
7	Urban villages		8.88		6
	Total	139.64	139.64	100	100

Source: Government of Delhi (2002).

With a view to resettle the then inhabitants of jhuggis in the city, the MCD, in 1990, made a three-pronged strategy to solve the problem of eligible jhuggi dwellers on encroached land which, *inter alia*, included (a) relocation/resettlement, (b) in situ upgradation and (c) environmental improvement (Chapter 3). This policy is still applicable in Delhi.

Historically, the first Master Plan for Delhi, 1962 (MPD-62) introduced the concept of urban renewal and suggested to follow the strategy of decongestion of Walled City by reducing the density from existing 1,500 pph (persons per hectare) to 100–150 pph. The Walled City was further divided into pockets, depending upon their level of deterioration and cause of blight and three strategies were suggested, which included (a) conservation, (b) rehabilitation and (c) redevelopment (Chapter 3). To protect the spread of slum conditions, areas such as Katra Neel, Ballimaran, Dariba Kalan and New Darya Ganj were earmarked for conservation. Areas, such as Phatak Habash Khan, Chandni Chowk, Naya Bans, Farash Khana Churiwalan and Kucha Pati Ram, where the cause of blight was neglect in maintenance were zoned for rehabilitation. The zones for redevelopment included areas that were in very dilapidated conditions and needed radical development. These areas included Jamuna Basti, Lal Darwaza, parts of Matia Mahal and Suiwalan. However, it remained as a mere proposal as no further action was taken to implement the MPD-62 proposals.

In the Master Plan for Delhi 2001 (MPD-2001), the Walled City was designated as a 'special area'. The main objective for the development of Walled city was to clean the area from noxious and hazardous industries and trades to check further commercialisation and industrialisation of the area and to revitalise the same to its glory of the past. This was impractical in nature and no urban renewal projects/schemes were made (Dutta and Bandyopadhyay, 2014).

The Master Plan for Delhi 2021 (MPD-2021) presents a comprehensive urban renewal approach for the city. It provides for 'restructuring and upgrading' of both planned and unplanned blighted areas and gives detailed procedures, norms, standards and incentives for redevelopment. The various urban renewal zones identified in the city are as follows:

1. Special areas comprising the traditional inner-city area which includes Shahjahanabad Walled City, its extensions and Karol Bagh. These areas are fast changing from their basic residential to commercial character.
2. Unplanned/unauthorised areas which include urban villages, unauthorised colonies, regularised unauthorised colonies, and slums and JJ clusters.
3. Planned blighted areas such as group housing and DDA flats; community and local shopping centres and industrial areas.
4. Heritage areas located in the Walled City Shahjahanabad; Lutyens Bungalow Zone; Nizamuddin and Humayun's Tomb Complex; Mehrauli; Chirag Delhi; and Vijay Mandal–Begumpur–Sarai Shahji–Lal Gumbad complex.

Special Areas

Shahjahanabad, the traditional inner-city area: Shahjahanabad is a unique example of Walled City with its rich heritage, organic street pattern, low-rise-high-density built form, mixed land use pattern, traditional lifestyle and a variety of activities. It is a heritage city with Red Fort, declared as a world heritage site, majestically dominating the area. It has 40 protected monuments as declared by the ASI (DDA, 2010, Annex III) and 3,500 *katras*. It serves as the distribution centre for the North India, accommodates about 20% establishments in the entire city that is engaged in wholesale trade and employs 12% workers. The magnitude of wholesale activities can be judged from the fact that 58% of wholesale shops are located in Shahjahanabad alone. These include 70% textile shops, 74% auto parts shops, 80% hardware shops and 74% food grain shops (Virmani, 1994). There are 37 commercial streets (DDA, 2010, Annex VI); 42 commercial–industrial–residential mixed land use streets (DDA, 2010, Annex VIII); 166 pedestrian shopping streets, some of which are only about 1 m wide (DDA, 2010, Annex VII).

There are at least 10 specialised market streets in Shahjahanabad exclusively dealing with jewellery, paper, rexine and leather work, electrical/electronic items, food and eatable, dry fruits/food grains and spices (Table 2.4).

Table 2.4 *Specialised Market Streets in Shahjahanabad*

S. No.	Name of Street	Specialised Trade
1.	Dariba Kalan	Jewellery
2.	Kinari Bazar	Golden & silver items related to textile
3.	Chawri Bazar	Paper & sanitary fittings
4.	Lal Kuan Tilak Bazar	Sanitary works chemical market
5.	Nai Sarak	Books/stationery
6.	Ballimaran	Rexene & leather work
7.	Lajpat Rai Market Bhagirath Palace	Electrical/electronic items
8.	Naya Bazar & Lahori Gate	Wholesale shops for rice
9.	Khari Baoli	Wholesale shops for dry fruits, food grains and spices
10.	Gali Paranthe Wali	Food & eatables

Source: Bugga (2014).

Introduction of underground MRTS in the area has further enhanced the connectivity and increased economic activities in Walled City. As a result of these economic activities, large compounds and katras have been converted to commercial use. Near Jama Masjid, a part of open space has been redeveloped to recreate the traditional Meena Bazar. The objective of renewal of Walled City Delhi is heritage conservation and revitalisation. The strategy in heritage zone is conservation; for other traditional zones, it is in situ upgradation; and redevelopment for severely dilapidated areas. The existing character of Walled City as the commercial hub will continue. However, storage of hazardous material such as paper, plastics, etc., will be banned. All hazardous industries will be closed down. A second entry to Delhi railway station shall be provided. All katras will be redeveloped. To support informal sector, haats, informal bazaars and weekly markets will be developed (DDA, 2010).

There are several constraints in the renewal of the Walled City which include multiple ownerships in buildings; inadequate properties records; large concentration of population hence large-scale relocation in redevelopment; practically no control on building activities as the enforcement is weak and penalties not effective and, in spite of several directions from courts, there is no control on unauthorised construction and conversion of land use. There is resistance by traders for redevelopment plans of Chandni Chowk. Similarly, in case of redevelopment of Jama Masjid, in spite of plans prepared and approved by Delhi High Court in 2006 by Delhi Urban Art Commission (DUAC) in 2009 and full support of Shahjahanabad Redevelopment Corporation, nothing substantial has happened on the ground (Bugga, 2014). This is due to the reason that the prescribed FAR does not satisfy the owners as the existing built-up area has a higher FAR, and for any reconstruction, they have to lose some percentage of covered area. It is difficult in most of the cases to produce any document of approval in support of the concerned area because the buildings are too old to be conforming to any approved layout plan. It is difficult to find an approved layout for the areas of the Walled City, except for the Wilson Survey conducted sometime in the 19th century. The concept of minimum road width also comes as a constraint in the approval of buildings plans, when the owner has to forego a part of his plot for road widening at the time of sanction of building plans. The Local Area Plan for this zone has been prepared and is awaiting approval of the authorities.

Unplanned Areas

Urban villages: Urban villages are old *abadi* (population) areas within *lal dora* of villages which have been engulfed under the urban expansion of Delhi and are in the process of transformation. In 1957, the MCD issued a notification which exempted *lal dora* area of urban villages from building bylaws. Accordingly, all buildings in the area can be constructed without getting the sanction of the plans by the local authorities. In 1963, the Delhi Administration Notification extended this provision to extended *lal dora* areas also and no building permission is needed for construction in *lal dora* or extended *lal dora* of urban villages (Raina, 2012). These provisions made urban villages 'free for all' areas. There is 100% plot coverage; buildings are G+5 and above; commercial activities have invaded all streets and industrial activities can be seen in several places conflicting with residential activities. As per MPD-2001, there are about 106 such villages in Delhi. Many of these are more than 100 years old and have traditional houses having heritage value. The approach of the MPD-2001 (DDA, 1990, p. 122) was to conserve the village predominantly as residential area, and hence to give a 'sensitive treatment in their planning and development process'. The present condition, however, is chaotic and the market forces have overpowered the traditional values. There is indiscriminate building activity. There is mixed land use pattern with industries, warehouses and commerce mixing with residential buildings. Roads are narrow and sanitary conditions are poor. A plan scheme to improve the civic services in these urban villages is being implemented. Approach of MPD-2021 (DDA, 2007) is to treat these villages as special areas and prepare redevelopment plans ensuring that 'mixed land use zones are compatible to the predominantly residential areas'.

Slum and JJ clusters: In the year 2000, about 2,072,000 people or 15% of total population of Delhi lived in slums and JJ Clusters (Table 2.5). The Delhi Urban Shelter Improvement Board (DUSIB) in 2010 has identified 643 JJ clusters accommodating four lakh households (Government of Delhi, 2013, p. 196). The DDA initiative for the renewal of slums and JJ clusters is a two-fold approach—relocation from areas required for public purposes and in situ upgradation of selected slum pockets identified by the Government of Delhi based on cut-off date and other parameters. The policy of relocation of squatter slum and JJ clusters, with site and services approach, was followed during 1981–2001 (MPD-2001). Each eligible slum household was given a serviced plot of 18 sq. m or 12.5 sq. m. This scheme was grossly misused and the impression was that if you can't get land in Delhi, squat on a public land, wait for next election, you will have your own plot!

The resettlement areas ended up in 'planned slums'. On getting possession, many of the plots were resold at a heavy premium and the allottees shifted and encroached other areas or slum pocket in the city. This phenomenon resulted in the invasion of resettlement areas by low-income and lower-middle income households. Sets of four plots (two adjacent and two on their immediate back with combined area of 50–72 sq. m) were freely available in the market through property dealers. Taneja (1996), through her study of four resettlement colonies in Delhi, has shown that the resettlement policy did not bring about planned development and improvement in the living conditions of urban poor. The location policy did not consider linkage to employment centres or creation of local employment. To earn money from rent, people built more space and each plot accommodated 2–3 households which increased the density of DUs per hectare (DU/ha). To create self-employment, many allottees started commercial or household industrial activities. As a result, there were large-scale changes in land use, from residential to either commercial or industrial. For example, in Naraina resettlement colony, the planned density of 200–240 DU/ha changed to 1,280 DU/ha. The infrastructure was not augmented to support the increase in density. There was pollution, congestion and bad sanitation. The problem of squatting and growth of slums is still there in Delhi; however, there is a shift in the policy and now, instead of serviced plots, built space of 25 sq. m with common area and facilities is provided with conditions (DDA, 2007). Under JNNURM Sub-mission II (Basic Services for Urban Poor, i.e., BSUP), eight projects were approved until March 2012 for the construction of a total of 67,800 DUs for relocating eligible JJ cluster households (Government of Delhi, 2013, p. 196). In 2009, the Minister of State for Urban Development inaugurated, just before elections, four in situ redevelopment DDA schemes. These schemes included Kathputli Colony and JJ colonies at Ashok Vihar, Kalkaji Extension and Vasant Kunj.

Slum redevelopment at Kalkaji Extension, New Delhi: Kalkaji Extension has about 8,000 JJ families. In the first phase, 3,000 families will be accommodated in multi-storey DUs under RAY programme following in situ upgradation strategy. Each flat will comprise a drawing room, one bedroom, kitchen, toilet and a balcony. The complex will have education and health facilities, parks and places for religious congregation. The remaining 5,000 slum families in the area will be accommodated similarly in the second phase of the project (Mehra, 2014).

Kalkaji Slum Redevelopment project is being implemented by DDA, using its resources, in three phases. As of December 2017 (*Hindustan Times*, 2017), a tower of 14 floors, located on a nearby plot, is under construction and it will be ready by June 2018. The first batch of 3,024 slum-families will then be shifted in this building. The area made available by shifting of these families will be used for construction of the next tower which will accommodate another batch of 3,000 slum families. This process will continue and at the end of the third phase the area made available will be used for construction of remunerative buildings for resource generation to recover the finances incurred in this in situ redevelopment project. It should be noted that because of availability of land for construction of the first tower, there is no temporary relocation of slum families in the first phase and, therefore, such a model has a better chance of success.

Slum redevelopment at Kathputli Colony: Migrated from Rajasthan, Maharashtra, Uttar Pradesh, Bihar and Gujarat, about 2,800 families of performing artists, such as puppeteers, magicians, folk singers, painters, traditional dancers, acrobats, jugglers and storytellers, have been living in Kathputli colony for the past 40 years. Some of them are engaged in handicraft businesses and also working as support to the adjoining affluent colonies. This colony is being redeveloped, for the first time in Delhi under PPP mode, by DDA and a private real estate developer. The private real estate developer will build 2,800 flats to accommodate all families on a portion of the site itself and also construct 2,800 independent houses at a transit camp to temporarily accommodate the slum families and vacate the plot for construction. The developer will also provide required educational, healthcare and recreational facilities, and construct an amphitheatre for performance and space for display and sale of artefacts.

The developer will hand over all the 2,800 flats to DDA free of cost for allotment to the slum families living in transit accommodation. The developer will, then, construct high-end multi-storey residential and commercial complex on the remaining portion of the site and recover the cost.

In March 2014, the plans were approved, the temporary accommodation was constructed and the eligible resident of Kathputli Colony had, temporarily, shifted. Some controversy was however created by a group of people, who claimed to be the residents of the colony but were not eligible for the allocation of new flats under the scheme. They also opposed the project and demanded 'in situ plots in exchange of resting their claim on land on which DDA wants to build a residential project with private developer' (*The Times of India*, 2014a). The Delhi High Court has cleared the project and asked the DDA to consider and decide the issue within four weeks. Media is also critical about the development of high-end residential and commercial complex and cramping 10 crowded 15-storey towers in a fraction of land and stuffing about 3,000 families into a 'vertical slum' ... urban transformation cannot be at the expense of the disempowerment of the voiceless people (Sethi, 2014). In the general elections of 2014, politics has entered into the fray. A political party has 'hinted at a land scam' in this scheme and made it an issue to woo voters living in this area. The party wanted a CBI inquiry and relocation of residents to be discontinued until the probe was complete (*The Times of India*, 2014b). Finally, shifting of households to the transit camp started on 20 December 2016 which paved the way for redevelopment work to start (*The Times of India*, 2016).

Unauthorised colonies: Unauthorised colonies are those that are located on government (DDA or *gram sabha*) land or on private lands that are not designated as residential areas in the master plan. Such colonies accommodated about 740,000 persons in the year 2000 (Table 2.5). In 1969, there were 202 such colonies that increased to 518 colonies in 1977 occupying about 4,500 ha land. According to a list prepared by the Urban Development Department of the Government of Delhi in 1993, the number of unauthorised colonies was 1,071.

A scheme of providing minimum civic services was initiated in 1997–1998. Under this scheme, construction of roads, roadside drains and filling of low lying areas were taken up to ensure hygienic conditions in such areas. The policy of the Government of Delhi is to regularise these colonies, periodically. Such regularisation generally takes place before elections. In 1969, the number of colonies that were regularised was 68. By 1993, some 567 colonies out of 607 listed unauthorised colonies were regularised (DDA, 2007, p. 36). In 2008, some 1,639 applications were received and provisional certificate for regularisation was issued to 1,218 unauthorised colonies. By a notification issued in September 2012, the Government of Delhi has regularised 895 colonies and the process of regularising the others was in progress (Government of Delhi, 2013, p. 195). The repercussion of periodic regularisation is not very encouraging for the planned development of a city. It encourages unauthorised growth of residential areas by encroaching government lands, especially the gram sabha/panchayat land, open spaces, flood plains and green belts. This kind of growth and subsequent regularisation defeat the basic purpose of providing green belts and availability of government lands for public purposes. Normally a set of conditions are required to be followed for regularisation of unauthorised colonies in Delhi (Chapter 5).

Industries: As per MPD-2021 (DDA, 2007, p. 71), there are 20 non-conforming clusters of industrial concentration having industrial activities on more than 70% plots in the cluster. The Government of Delhi has notified these clusters, since 2012, for redevelopment with wide roads, basic services, open spaces, parking and improvement of environment through measures that reduce pollution.

Planned Blighted Areas

Government employees housing: Quite a large portion of housing stock in Delhi is for the employees of the central government. Such housing colonies are generally a low-density low-rise development and some of these are more than 4–6 decades old. To meet the increased housing demand for government employees, a proposal has been approved for the redevelopment of low-rise low-density government colonies into multi-storey residential towers equipped with all modern facilities and services. Some of such redevelopment projects include East Kidwai Nagar, Sarojini Nagar, Srinivaspuri, Ramakrishna Puram, Netaji Nagar and Mohammadpur. In July 2016, the Union Cabinet approved the redevelopment of three colonies—Sarojini Nagar, Netaji Nagar and Nauroji Nagar—to be redeveloped by the National Building Construction Corporation, New Delhi. To finance this project, a part of these projects has been allowed to be sold as a commercial area (see Chapter 6 for details).

Redevelopment of East Kidwai Nagar: It is first of the redevelopment of government employees' housing projects, located in the heart of the city adjoining All India Institute of Medical Sciences (AIIMS), Dilli Haat and INA Market. It covers an area of 34.4 ha (86 acre) and will comprise 4,609 residential flats in 7–14-storey towers and 1.7 lakh sq. m (13 lakh sq. ft) of commercial space. It will be a self-contained housing complex with facilities such as schools, shopping centres, ATMs, cycling and jogging tracks, open spaces and power back-up (Kumar, 2013). The plans have been approved by the DUAC. The construction was in progress in March 2016. Deadline for the completion of this project is December 2019.

Redevelopment of commercial areas: The MPD-2021 (DDA, 2007, p. 54) provides for the redevelopment, with enhanced FAR, of the planned community and local shopping centres in Delhi which are old and dilapidated (see Chapter 5 for details). The MoUD has asked DDA to renew the commercial centres in Delhi, including Nehru Place, Bhikaji Cama Place and Basant Lok Market. The South Delhi Corporation has prepared redevelopment plans for Nehru Place and submitted the same to the MoUD for the approval, which has been approved (*The Times of India* 2017c).

Redevelopment of industrial areas: There are more than 30 planned industrial areas in Delhi. Most of these were developed during 1970s. In some cases, the activities have closed down or changed. Introduction of MRTS has changed the market forces and there is a demand for optimisation of land use through redevelopment in industrial areas located near MRTS corridor. All these required redevelopment of these industrial areas (DDA, 2007, p. 70) have provided for a redevelopment scheme for such areas which covers modernisation and upgradation with regard to optimisation of land use and environmental considerations. To attract industrial plot owners to redevelop, DDA Notification dated 1 April 2011 on Regulation and Guidelines for Redevelopment of Existing Planned Industrial Areas has provided an incentive FAR and also permitted amalgamation of plots for effective and functional renewal projects.

Conservation of Heritage Areas

As mentioned earlier, Delhi is a historic city which tells the tale of the rise and fall of various rulers and dynasties. Its monuments are scattered all over the city. The built heritage of Delhi is an irreplaceable and non-renewable cultural resource of immense educational and tourism value. Recognising this, DDA (2007, p. 102) advocates a strategy of conservation. Since the monuments are scattered, the master plan has identified six heritage zones which have concentration, linkage and continuity of buildings, structures or complexes united by history. Such zones include Shahjahanabad, Lutyens Bungalow Zone, Humayun's Tomb Complex, Mehrauli and Chirag Delhi. MPD-2021 has also identified three areas as archaeological parks for conservation. These include Mehrauli, Tughlaqabad and Sultan Garhi. A special conservation plan is to be prepared for each of the heritage zones and archaeological parks.

Lutyens Bungalow Zone: Built between 1912 and 1930 by the British, it is a residential area for government officials. It is now the residential area of the vice president, ministers, members of parliament, senior judges, bureaucrats and other dignitaries. It is characterised by aesthetic qualities and planning; low-density development with wide roads, houses having specious gardens and servant quarters with separate entry. Most of these bungalows have outlived their economic life of about 60 years; structures are unsafe and annual maintenance is also expensive. Accordingly, the central government has decided to conserve the area. According to Das Gupta (2014), Sunehari Bagh area is being taken up in the first phase. It covers an area of 29.89 ha. The approach is to re-densify the area by accommodating 32 bungalows (density: 1.1 DU/ha), thereby adding 11 more to the 21 bungalows already present (density: 0.7 DU/ha). This approach is expected to conserve the basic character of the area—low density, specious gardens and architectural style.

Connaught Place: Conservation of Connaught Place, New Delhi, was taken up to showcase the British-period city centre during the Commonwealth Games in 2010. The project was conceived in 2004 and could not be completed by 2010 due to inefficient project management. The work was completed in 2014 by New Delhi Municipal Corporation (NDMC). It includes removing encroachments, restoring the original architecture and urban design qualities, improving circulation, parking and street furniture; providing a unique system of utilities through a dedicated tunnel; and retrofitting building to make them earthquake resistant. As a part of the New Delhi Smart City Plan, the inner circle of Connaught Place is proposed to be pedestrianised but, as usual, it is facing a stiff resistance from the shopkeepers.

Humayun's Tomb Complex: Humayun's Tomb Complex has been conserved to its pristine glory under Aga Khan Development Network (AKDN). It is, probably, the first project that combines conservation with environmental and socio-economic development with active participation of local communities and stakeholders.

Delhi Metro Heritage Line: As a contribution of Delhi Metro Rail Corporation in conserving heritage of Delhi along with providing accessibility to the Walled City, an underground heritage line has been completed recently (March 2017). It will add to the transformation of the city core. The line connects heritage structures such as Delhi Gate, Jama Masjid, Red Fort and Kashmiri Gate.

Mumbai Initiative

Mumbai has been the city of hope for employment and a preferred destination for migrants from states such as Uttar Pradesh and Bihar. It is a city where skyscrapers and slums exist side by side. The city has the largest slum in Asia (see Dharavi). Probably, that is why more than 50% of the population of Mumbai lives in slum areas (Table 2.5). Mumbai is about 150 years old and has pockets that have dangerously dilapidated buildings due to the lack of maintenance and general neglect by their owners. The main reason of this neglect is exorbitantly low rent structure which cannot be increased due to the provisions of the Rent Control Act that protects the tenants from eviction and also keeps a check on the rent. The owners of such properties find it difficult to maintain the building and deterioration continues.

The Bombay Metropolitan Region Plan 1970–1991 (BMRP, 1991) followed two strategies of urban renewal: (a) decentralisation/dispersal of population and economic activities and (b) restructuring of the city. As a result of the restructuring strategy, Navi Mumbai was created to serve as a counter magnet to the city. Industries and commercial activities were decentralised/dispersed. A new alternative commercial was created at Bandra Kurla to accommodate further expansion of

Table 2.5 *Percentage of Total Population Living in Slums in Mumbai (1971–2011)*

Year	Percentage of Slum Areas' Population to Total Population
1971	46.90
1981	52.16
1991	51.38
2001	54.06
2011	52.33

Source: Census of India (2011).

commercial activities. Crawford Market, the oldest wholesale vegetable and fruit market, was relocated to Navi Mumbai which served as a catalytic agent in the growth of the new town. Crawford Market (renamed as Phule Market) still continues at the original site as a retail outlet of fruits and vegetables.

Development Control Regulations for Greater Mumbai provide redevelopment of existing clusters of old structures in the city and creating space for the development of the infrastructures and provision of public amenities. The experience of implementation of redevelopment schemes has not been encouraging as the approach was piecemeal, leading to fractured development and inadequate provision of public amenities and infrastructure (Isore, 2014). Considering these experiences, the Government of Maharashtra introduced the cluster redevelopment approach in 2007 (see Chapter 5). Renewal of Bhendi Bazaar is a good example of the cluster redevelopment approach.

Redevelopment of Bhendi Bazaar

Bhendi Bazaar is one of the biggest redevelopment projects in Mumbai. It is located 5 km away from Chhatrapati Shivaji Terminus (CST) on the main island of Mumbai. It is about 100-year-old mixed commercial–residential area. It has low-rise (G+2 and G+3) structures on 200 sq. m plots. Ground coverage is 100%. The carpet area of tenements is 150–200 sq. ft (13.94–15.58 sq. m). There are no organised open spaces and no trees. The buildings are in a dilapidated state and are unsafe. There is traffic congestion and the area does not have any parking space.

Since renewal by an individual on his 200 sq. m plot cannot be done within the framework of the DCRs, a cluster approach has been followed. According to the cluster approach, some 280 plot holders agreed to renew the area under this scheme. The site area is 16.5 acre (6.7 ha) and the project provides for rehabilitation of 4,500 stakeholders (3,200 households and 1,300 shopkeepers). It provides new tenements of 350 sq. ft carpet area in high-rise towers with shops on ground floor; wide road; 4,500 parking spaces and all infrastructures (Isore, 2014). The project is divided into nine clusters for implementation. The total cost of the project is estimated to be ₹4,000 crore.

Redevelopment of Bhendi Bazaar presents a win-win situation for all stakeholders in the project. For existing tenants/occupants of dwellings in the cluster, this project provides bigger tenement size (350 sq. ft); change in social status from tenant to owner of new tenement; better physical infrastructure—15 m wide roads with footpath on either sides, dedicated and well organised parking spaces; recreational and community facilities: and safety as all buildings will be earthquake- and wind pressure-resistant, with advanced fire-fighting arrangement and waste disposal.

The benefits for the Planning Authority include (a) transfer of reservations for public amenities such as recreation ground, primary school and other built-up amenities, as per development plan; (b) onsite development of roads and infrastructure; (c) collection of development charges from project promoter for the provision of offsite infrastructure; (d) saving of recurring expenditure to repair and maintenance in the area every year and (f) earning from taxes on the new premises.

For Mumbai City Bhendi Bazar redevelopment presents a good example which can be replicated at other places also. It will improve the visual quality of the area and introduce a culture of good building practices—use of energy saving, materials and conservation of water. The project has received precertification from Indian Green Building Council (IGBC) for Gold Rated Green Buildings.

Textile Mill Area Redevelopment

Mumbai was the hub of textile mills before 1980s; however, due to several factors such as high rate of octroi, extensive power cuts and above all, the mega strike of mill workers in more than 50 textile mills lasting 18 months crippled the industries and they closed down. In the absence of a policy, they remained undeveloped until 1991 when the DCRs (1991 DCR 58) permitted redevelopment of mill sites with the condition that the site area will be equally shared among the owner of land, BMC and MHADA. This provision was not acceptable to the mill land owners. The DCR was amended in 2001 which relaxed the rule and provided that only open land where there was no constriction will be required to be distributed as per 1991 DCR 58. As a result of this amendment, redevelopment of closed-down textile mills started. Such sites have been redeveloped as commercial areas, residential apartments and as mixed-use development.

Dharavi Redevelopment

Dharavi is the oldest slum in Mumbai. Located mostly on government land, it is one of the largest slums in Asia. However, there are pockets of private lands. It is a glaring example of people's action for survival in adverse circumstances. Migrants to Mumbai settled here in groups and made makeshift arrangements as workshop-cum-home. There are potters, tanners, recyclers, blacksmiths and others living and working in Dharavi. With time, it evolved as a massive (239 ha) informal area with high density, mixed residential–commercial or residential–industrial uses, and organic pattern growth. The lanes are narrow (some of them being just one metre wide). The area is facing shortage of water, pollution and insanitary conditions. In spite of all this, the area is booming with economic activities in informal sector and the annual production of goods is worth $500 million (₹3,385 crore at ₹67.70/$; *The Economist*, 2005). With further developments such as airport and Bandra Kurla Business complex, Dharavi attained a central location which attracted the attention of local authorities. Accordingly, SRA declared it for redevelopment under PPP mode. The area was divided into five sectors. A global tender was floated and several national and international consultants submitted their proposals. A controversy cropped in. The issues ranged from the minimum area of the tenement to be given to each household, local people's participation in the redevelopment process, choice of contractors and others. In January 2012, finally, sector 5, which is located on government land, was approved for redevelopment under MHADA. The tenement size to be given free to eligible households was 300 sq. ft with the provision that an additional 100 sq. ft area can be given, if so required, on payment. The Mumbai DCR was amended to provide global FSI of 4 (Ghoge and Kamath, 2012).

Bombay First: Private Sector Initiative

Conceived on the lines of London First, Bombay First (now Mumbai First) is a non-profit initiative of the Bombay Chamber of Commerce and Industry with a vision of transforming Mumbai into globally competitive city through improvements in economic growth, infrastructure and the quality of life (Nallathiga, 2014).

The approach adopted by Bombay First is to build partnerships with government, business and civil society and use research, catalysis, advocacy and networking as the means of achieving the mission. The Bombay First demonstrated it through implementing pilot projects such as medical waste management, design and management of public spaces, creating road signage system and initiatives for maintaining cleanliness and hygiene. It was a tactical action (see Chapter 5) which inspired several NGOs, such as Clean Mumbai Foundation, Action for Good Governance Network of India (AGNI) and NGOs' Alliance for Governance and Research (NAGAR). Bombay First, under the guidance of Bombay City Policy Research Foundation, diagnosed the economic and social structure of the city; found the causes of decline of certain activities and infrastructure and identified the possible solutions which culminated as the Vision Mumbai (40 Years Concept Plan for MMR; Bombay First 2003).

Kolkata Initiative

As mentioned earlier in this chapter, probably the first urban renewal initiative in Kolkata started about a century back when Patrick Geddes prepared a plan for the redevelopment of Bara Bazar (also Burrabazar), the oldest and richest market, functioning in the city even before the arrival of the British which attracted them to establish trading post in the city. He suggested wider roads, large and small open spaces and closure of Mint (Beattie, 2003). Geddes is remembered for his humane approach towards the renewal of old city cores, which places people of the area in the centre of the renewal process and evolves holistic strategies that are socially, physically, environmentally and economically sustainable, and his plan for redevelopment was humane. However, his plan had limited success and the reason was the 'clash between the interests of the market and the interests of the people' (Meller, 1997).

In 1966, Calcutta Metropolitan Planning Organisation (CMPO) prepared Bustee Improvement Programme. In the early 1970s, Kolkata Metropolitan Development Authority (KMDA) also conceived the idea of improving the physical environment of slums and worked out various alternative models which included slum relocation, slum modernisation and slum improvement. The actual implementation of the relocation model has been resisted by the slum dwellers as the relocated site was mostly away from the cleared site which affected their employment opportunities and resulted in the loss of income and increase on hardship.

Kolkata City Core Area Redevelopment

The core area has a large number of warehouses of Kolkata Port Trust. Several attempts have been made for adaptive reuse of these warehouses into commercial, cultural and recreational use. However, due to the lack of political will and litigations, the efforts have failed so far. The area has a great potential that could trigger regeneration of the city and its riverfront.

Dalhousie Square is the central area of Kolkata. During British period, it served as the seat of the imperial secretariat and as the major commercial centre where a majority of British mercantile establishments, shipping corporations and financial institutions were located. After independence, it continues to be the most prestigious destination in the city with sprawling Raj Bhavan, West Bengal State Secretariat, Kolkata High Court, Town Hall, several commercial establishments and offices of insurance companies and banks (Chattopadhyay, 2014).

Piecemeal renewal of the central area has taken place. Custom's House, Railway Office Building on Fairlie Place and Reserve Bank Building came up at the place of godown and bonded warehouses after the shift of port function from the Central Business District (CBD) area. Some multi-storey buildings have come up at Old Court House Street and Netaji Subhas Chandra Road which do not appear to be in harmony with the ambiance of the area. The renewal efforts made in this area, after independence, include New Secretariat Building, office building of Shipping Corporation of India, Eastern Railway Building and quarters of United Bank of India. Other buildings that changed the face of Kolkata city core include the new Ranji Stadium and Netaji Indoor Stadium in the Eden Gardens. Chattopadhyay (2014) observes that the construction of Telephone Bhavan has destroyed the vista of Writer' Buildings with the Raj Bhavan.

Renewal of Kumartuli Area

Extended over an area of 14.8 acre land, Kumortuli, the hub of clay modellers and image makers, located in the northern part of Kolkata, was declared as a slum. The inhabitants are engaged in home-based occupation of making clay images used during the festive season in Kolkata. The families of the artists live on about 20% floor space and the rest is used as work-space. The living conditions and work environment of the area is deplorable and needs urgent renewal. There are 522 families comprising 135 Mrit Shilpi, 42 Sola/Saj Shilpi and 345 others. There are 21 godowns and 39 other structures.

It is proposed to redevelop this area on workplace-cum-residence concept. Each house will have a 25 sq. m carpet area. Ground floor will be used as workplace and other activities, first floor will be used as godown and residence will be on the top floor. Common facilities such as training centre and exhibition-cum-sales counter with seminar hall as well as community facilities such as health centre will be provided as a part of the renewal project (for more details, see Chattopadhyay, 2014).

Indore Initiative

Slum Networking Indore City

About 28% of the population of Indore City lives in slums. The sewerage system of the city was built in 1936 and it serves only about 10% of the population. All sewage was discharged into the two rivers—Khan and Sarasvati. As a result, these rivers were severely polluted.

Most of the slums in the city were located along the banks of these rivers, which further polluted the rivers. Following a holistic urban renewal approach to solve the problem, Indore Development Authority initiated the programme of redevelopment in 1987. The main sewerage artery of the city was so designed that it utilised the natural slope and passed along the banks of the rivers and also connected 183 slum pockets. In situ upgradation of slums was also done which improved the housing, social and environmental conditions and physical and social infrastructure which included the roads, drains, waste disposal system, landscaping and rehabilitation. About 100 NGOs were involved in improving health, education, social welfare and income generation of slum dwellers. The common spaces and services are being maintained through active participation by people. By discharging treated clean water into the river system, the Khan and Sarasvati rivers have been rejuvenated and water now flows throughout the year. The city is clean and revitalised. This project was given the Aga Khan Award for Architecture in 1989. The slum networking idea was improved and replicated in Ahmedabad and Vadodra as well (Ekram, 1989).

Ahmedabad Initiative

Sabarmati Riverfront Development

Initiated by the Ahmedabad Municipal Corporation, Sabarmati Riverfront Development covers 10.06 km long section of the river between Subhash Bridge and Vasna Barrage. Round the year, water in the river was made available from inter-basin transfer of Narmada water into Sabarmati. The objectives of this project cover flood protection to deal with climatic change in a sustainable manner; to create better hygienic conditions and river water protection through new sewage system; to recharge ground water through storage of water within the riverbed; to relocate about 10,000 slum households and provide them better conditions. This created opportunities for the development of recreational and hospitality facilities.

The project includes channelising present 300–600 m wide river into a fixed 275 m wide channel and reclaiming 202.79 ha land for

Table 2.6 *Sabarmati Riverfront Scheme, Proposed Land Use of Reclaimed Land*

Land Use	Area (ha)	Percentage
Roads on both embankments	39.30	19.38
Gardens	76.78	37.86
Promenades	32.40	15.98
Informal market	3.51	1.73
Residential and commercial	29.40	14.50
Public utilities and facilities	18.96	9.35
Residential Unallocated	2.44	1.20
Total	202.79	100

Source: Sabarmati Riverfront Development Corporation Limited (2009) quoted from Modi (2011, p. 94).

the creation of promenades, construction of interceptor sewers and sewage treatment plants, dredging of river bed, relocation of slum dwellers, and use reclaimed land as shown in Table 2.6.

The financing of the project is from JNNURM funds and through the sale of land (15%) devoted to residential and commercial uses to private sector. The implementation of the project has been the responsibility of Sabarmati Riverfront Development Corporation Limited. As reported by Pessina (2011), the flood control claims of the project and channelisation of the river have been criticised by hydrologists and environmentalists.

The project has political support. Work is progressing well. Reclamation work is over. The interceptor sewer lines and sewage pumping stations have started working. The 22 km long lower promenade is complete and since 2012, some parts of this are open for public use. Since 2014, riverfront market is functioning and boating in the river has started from three new jetties.

This project is being replicated for rejuvenation of two rivers—Rispana and Bindal—in Dehradun and rehabilitation of slums located along them. Mussoorie Dehradun Development Authority finally launched the project in October 2015 (*The Times of India*, 2015, p. 2).

Redevelopment of CBD

The Ahmedabad Urban Development Authority is redeveloping the CBD of Ahmedabad. The existing CBD is a low-density development. The FSI for the area is 1.8 but the FSI utilised by the existing CBD is only 0.7%. It is a mixed land use development, accommodating commercial (40%), public and semi-public (17%) and residential (about 8%) activities. The parking is haphazard, there is no provision of cycle track and pedestrian paths are occupied by informal trade activities. The objective is to develop the CBD with higher density (see Chapter 7) and mixed land use development; provide efficient transit connectivity, pedestrian and cycle tracks, and zones for informal commercial activities (Munshi and Dave, n.d.).

Mysore City Initiative

Renewal of Core Heritage Zone

The Dussehra celebrations of Mysore are world famous. It is one of the major tourist attractions of the city. About 5.5 km stretch of road between Harding Circle and Millennium Circle via Albert Victor Road, Sayyaji Rao Road and Nelson Mandela Road was redeveloped as the Dussehra procession route (Raja Marg or Rajapatha) under the JNNURM. For easy and safe movement of tourists, without being disturbed by the major traffic in and around the Mysore Palace, a pedestrian walkway was also developed. The Mysore City Corporation has taken the initiatives to renew some of the old market places in the core city of Mysore and DPRs for the renewal of markets such as Devaraj Market, Mandi Market and Vani Vilas Market have been prepared. The legal support to this initiative has been drawn from the Mysore Master Plan 2031 which has made the provision for the conservation of the heritage of Mysore (Kumara, 2014).

Pune Initiative

Old city Pune evolved as a traditional city with *wada*s and traditional way of living where streets and squares were serving as public spaces and social interaction areas. It has more than 100 heritage structures. The area became blighted due to low rents and the lack of maintenance as a result of the Rent Control Act and invasion of automobile which resulted in traffic congestion and parking problems. The social fabric of the old city was lost and heritage was neglected. Now, old wadas are being redeveloped by private builders who acquire rights to redevelop a wada with an understanding that each owner and tenant living in the wada will get a free tenement and the builder will recover the cost by selling additional flats that are permitted due to increased FSI. The impact of this redevelopment, according to Bhave (2011), is decrease in the area under open spaces (58% to now 33%), increase in density as the structures are now G+4 instead of earlier G+2. There is increase in traffic congestion (v/c ratio increased from earlier 1.67 to 3.37). To conserve heritage structures, Maharashtra Government has introduced the Maharashtra Smarak Vikas Yojana, where heritage buildings are leased for the purpose of their maintenance to private parties who, in turn, are permitted to use the pictures of the heritage structure in their publicity materials and campaigns.

Hyderabad Initiative

Pedestrianisation of Charminar Area

Charminar is the landmark that gives a unique identity to Hyderabad. This area is the core of the historic city. It is the commercial hub of the city and faces inherent problems such as congestion, encroachment, heavy traffic, shortage of parking and inadequate basic services. The Municipal Corporation of Hyderabad has proposed pedestrianisation of the immediate area around the Charminar; introduction of heritage walks; pedestrianisation and beautification of Laad Bazaar; restoration of Pathergatti facades; a comprehensive signage system for Charminar precincts and restoration of Char Kamans.

The objective of conservation of Musi River, which passes through the city of Hyderabad, is to make it pollution-free, improve the river banks and other environmentally degraded areas, and relocate markets to decongest the surroundings (NIUA, 2009).

Summing Up

Urban renewal in India is not a new subject and has been in practice since the 18th Century. Shahjahanabad, the Walled City Delhi, was rejuvenated after its destruction by Nadir Shah (1739). The British soldiers destroyed Shahjahanabad after the 1857 mutiny (the First War of Independence) and city was redeveloped, and the historical monument Jama Masjid was conserved with great difficulty. In the early 20th century (1919), Patrick Geddes redeveloped Bara Bazar in Kolkata.

Urban renewal in the post-independence period has been generally limited to slum clearance and improvement. The Slum Areas (Improvement and Clearance) Act was passed by the Government of India in 1956. Various master plans incorporated urban renewal policies and programmes which included upgradation of slums and decongestion of city core area. These policies were implemented in piecemeal manner with hardly any impact. Large and polluting industries were closed down in Delhi and Mumbai but nothing was done at the vacated mill sites for decades.

Towards the end of the 20th century, with the introduction of economic reforms in 1991 and subsequent improvement in the investment climate in the country, the large cities gained prominence and attracted political attention. Large number of people living in slums became vote bank and renewal of slums became a regular and popular exercise before elections. This trend continues in 21st century as well.

The land, land use and land management are state subjects and fall in the functional domain of the state governments. Accordingly, the national initiatives remained limited to the preparation of model acts, policies, programmes and guidelines.

JNNURM was the first programme of the Government of India that established the political tilt towards the urban sector. It was again the first time when a large sum of ₹100,000 crore was earmarked for the urban renewal. It was, once again, the first time that fund-linked-reforms in urban governance and development were introduced. Promotion of Smart Cities Mission and AMRUT by the NDA Government indicates continued political interest in the urban sector in general and urban renewal in particular.

As state initiatives, more urbanised states such as Maharashtra and Gujarat introduced various acts, rules, procedures and institutional mechanism pertaining to urban renewal. They also introduced innovative methods for urban renewal efforts.

Among cities, Delhi appears to be the most comprehensive in terms of addressing the issue of urban blight. The MPD-2021 covers the entire city and has identified four types of urban renewal areas which includes (a) special areas comprising the traditional inner-city area, (b) unplanned/unauthorised areas which include urban villages; unauthorised colonies; regularised–unauthorised colonies and slums and JJ clusters, (c) planned blighted areas such as group housing and DDA flats; community and local shopping centres; industrial areas and (d) heritage areas located in the City. Theoretically, it is impressive but Delhi failed to implement most of the proposals. Mumbai initiative appears to be a good example where urban renewal has been implemented with innovative approaches, tools and techniques. Initiatives of other cities were limited to one or two areas of concerns which could be renewal of slums, riverfront development, renewal of core area of city or heritage conservation. Networking of slums for their redevelopment is a good initiative of Indore. Conservation of core areas has been attempted by Kolkata, Mysore and Pune. Ahmedabad is a good example of riverfront development.

Annexure 2.1 List of 98 Cities Selected Under Smart Cities Mission

S. No.	Name of State/UT	No. of Cities Shortlisted	Names of Selected Cities	Population of Cities
1.	Andaman & Nicobar Islands	1	Port Blair	140,572
2.	Andhra Pradesh	3	1. Vishakhapatnam 2. Tirupati 3. Kakinada	1,878,980 374,260 350,986
3.	Arunachal Pradesh	1	1. Pasighat	24,656
4.	Assam	1	1. Guwahati	962,334

S. No.	Name of State/UT	No. of Cities Shortlisted	Names of Selected Cities	Population of Cities
5.	Bihar	3	1. Muzaffarpur 2. Bhagalpur 3. Biharsharif	393,724 410,210 296,889
6.	Chandigarh	1	1. Chandigarh	1,055,450
7.	Chhattisgarh	2	1. Raipur 2. Bilaspur	1,047,389 365,579
8.	Daman & Diu	1	1. Diu	23,991
9.	Dadra & Nagar Haveli	1	1. Silvassa	98,032
10.	Delhi	1	1. New Delhi Municipal Council	249,998
11.	Goa	1	1. Panaji	100,000
12.	Gujarat	6	1. Gandhinagar 2. Ahmedabad 3. Surat 4. Vadodara 5. Rajkot 6. Dahod	292,797 5,577,940 4,467,797 1,752,371 1,323,363 130,530
13.	Haryana	2	1. Karnal 2. Faridabad	302,140 1,414,050
14.	Himachal Pradesh	1	1. Dharamshala	22,580
15.	Jharkhand	1	1. Ranchi	1,073,427
16.	Karnataka	6	1. Mangaluru 2. Belagavi 3. Shimoga 4. Hubballi-Dharwad 5. Tumakuru 6. Davanagere	484,785 488,292 322,428 943,857 305,821 435,128
17.	Kerala	1	1. Kochi	601,574
18.	Lakshadweep	1	1. Kavaratti	11,210
19.	Madhya Pradesh	7	1. Bhopal 2. Indore 3. Jabalpur 4. Gwalior 5. Sagar 6. Satna 7. Ujjain	1,922,130 2,195,274 1,216,445 1,159,032 273,296 280,222 515,215

(continued)

(continued)

S. No.	Name of State/UT	No. of Cities Shortlisted	Names of Selected Cities	Population of Cities
20.	Maharashtra	10	1. Navi Mumbai	1,119,000
			2. Nashik	1,486,000
			3. Thane	1,841,000
			4. Greater Mumbai	12,400,000
			5. Amravati	745,000
			6. Solapur	952,000
			7. Nagpur	2,460,000
			8. Kalyan-Dombivali	1,518,000
			9. Aurangabad	1,165,000
			10. Pune	3,124,000
21.	Manipur	1	1. Imphal	268,243
22.	Meghalaya	1	1. Shillong	354,325
23.	Mizoram	1	1. Aizawl	291,000
24.	Nagaland	1	1. Kohima	107,000
25.	Odisha	2	1. Bhubaneshwar	840,834
			2. Raurkela	310,976
26.	Puducherry	1	1. Oulgaret	300,104
27.	Punjab	3	1. Ludhiana	1,618,879
			2. Jalandhar	868,181
			3. Amritsar	1,155,664
28.	Rajasthan	4	1. Jaipur	3,073,350
			2. Udaipur	475,150
			3. Kota	1,001,365
			4. Ajmer	551,360
29.	Sikkim	1	1. Namchi	12,190
30.	Tamil Nadu	12	1. Tiruchirappalli	916,674
			2. Tirunelveli	474,838
			3. Dindigul	207,327
			4. Thanjavur	222,943
			5. Tiruppur	877,778
			6. Salem	831,038
			7. Vellore	504,079
			8. Coimbatore	1,601,438
			9. Madurai	1,561,129
			10. Erode	498,129
			11. Thoothukudi	370,896
			12. Chennai	6,727,000
31.	Telangana	2	1. Greater Hyderabad	6,731,790
			2. Greater Warangal	819,406

S. No.	Name of State/UT	No. of Cities Shortlisted	Names of Selected Cities	Population of Cities
32.	Tripura	1	1. Agartala	400,004
33.	Uttar Pradesh**	12	1. Moradabad	887,871
			2. Aligarh	874,408
			3. Saharanpur	705,478
			4. Bareilly	903,668
			5. Jhansi	505,693
			6. Kanpur	2,765,348
			7. Allahabad	1,112,544
			8. Lucknow	2,817,105
			9. Varanasi	1,198,491
			10. Ghaziabad	1,648,643
			11. Agra	1,585,704
			12. Rampur	325,313
34.	Uttarakhand	1	1. Dehradun	583,971
35.	West Bengal	4	1. New Town Kolkata	36,541
			2. Bidhannagar	633,704
			3. Durgapur	571,000
			4. Haldia	272,000

Source: PIB (Release ID: 126384).

Notes: *Jammu & Kashmir has asked for more time to decide on the potential smart city.

**12 cities have been shortlisted from Uttar Pradesh against 13 cities allocated to the state.

Annexure 2.2 New Projects Sanctioned Under Swadesh Darshan During 2016–2017 (as on 31 December 2016)

S. No.	State/UT	Name of the Circuit	Name of the Project
1.	Goa	Coastal Circuit	Development of Coastal Circuit (Sinquerim–Baga, Anjuna–Vagator, Morjim–Keri, Aguada Fort and Aguada Jail) in Goa
2.	Jammu and Kashmir	Himalayan Circuit	Integrated Development of Tourism Infrastructure Projects in the State of Jammu and Kashmir

(continued)

(continued)

S. No.	State/UT	Name of the Circuit	Name of the Project
3.	Telangana	Tribal Circuit	Integrated Development of Mulugu–Laknavaram–Medavaram–Tadvai–Damaravi–Mallur–Bogatha Waterfalls as Tribal Circuit in Telangana
4.	Meghalaya	North East Circuit	Development of Umiam (Lake View), U Lum Sohpetbneng Mawdiangdiang Orchid Lake Resort, Meghalaya
5.	Madhya Pradesh	Buddhist Circuit	Development of Buddhist Circuit in Sanchi–Satna–Rewa–Mandsaur–Dhar in Madhya Pradesh
6.	Kerala	Spiritual Circuit	Development of Sabarimala–Erumeli–Pampa–Sannidhanam as a Spiritual Circuit in District Pathanamthitta, Kerala
7.	Karnataka	Coastal Circuit	Development of Coastal Circuit in Dakshin Kannada Dist., Uttar Kannada Dist. & Udupi Dist. in Karnataka
8.	Manipur	Spiritual Circuit	Development of Spiritual Circuit-Shri Govindajee Temple–Shri Bijoy Govindajee Temple–Shri Gopinath Temple–Shri Bungshibodon Temple–Shri Kaina Temple, Manipur
9.	Gujarat	Heritage Circuit	Development of Heritage Circuit in Ahmedabad–Rajkot–Porbandar–Bardoli–Dandi in Gujarat
10.	Haryana	Krishna Circuit	Development of Tourism Infrastructures at places related to Mahabharata in Kurukshetra, Haryana
11.	Rajasthan	Krishna Circuit	Integrated Development of Govind Dev Ji Temple (Jaipur), Khatu Shyam Ji (Sikar) and Nathdwara (Rajsamand) in Rajasthan

S. No.	State/UT	Name of the Circuit	Name of the Project
12.	Sikkim	North East India Circuit	Development of Tourist Circuit Linking Singtam–Maka–Temi–Bermoik Tokal–Phongia–Namchi–Jorethang–Okharey–Sombaria–Daramdin–Jorethang–Melli (Exit) in Sikkim
13.	Madhya Pradesh	Heritage Circuit	Development of Heritage Circuit (Gwalior–Orchha–Khajuraho–Chanderi–Bhimbetka–Mandu) Madhya Pradesh
14.	Kerala	Spiritual Circuit	Development of Sree Padmanabha Aranmula-Sabarimala as a Spiritual Circuit in Kerala
15.	Bihar	Spiritual Circuit	Development of Jain Circuit: Vaishali–Arrah–Masad–Patna–Rajgir–Pawapuri–Champapuri as Spiritual Circuit in Bihar
16.	Bihar	Spiritual Circuit	Integrated Development of Kanwariya Route–Sultanganj–Dharmshala–Deoghar as Spiritual Circuit in Bihar
17.	Odisha	Coastal Circuit	Development of Gopalpur, Barkul, Satapada and Tampara as Coastal Circuit in Odisha
18.	Nagaland	Tribal Circuit	Development of Tribal Circuit (Mokokchung–Tuensang–Mon) in Nagaland
19.	Uttarakhand	Heritage circuit	Integrated Development of Heritage Circuit in Kumaon Region–Katarmal–Jogeshwar–Baijnath–Devidhura in Uttarakhand
20.	Jammu and Kashmir	Himalayan Circuit	Integrated Development of Tourist Facilities at Jammu–Rajouri–Shopian–Pulwama under Himalayan Circuit theme in Jammu and Kashmir

(continued)

(continued)

S. No.	State/UT	Name of the Circuit	Name of the Project
21.	Jammu and Kashmir	Himalayan Circuit	Integrated Development of Tourist Facilities under the Construction of Assets in lieu of those Destroyed in Floods in 2014 under PM Development Package for Jammu and Kashmir
22.	Jammu and Kashmir	Himalayan Circuit	Integrated Development of Tourist facilities at Mantalai–Sudhmahadev–Patnitop under Himalayan Circuit Theme in Jammu and Kashmir
23.	Jammu and Kashmir	Himalayan Circuit	Integrated Development of Tourist Facilities at Anantnag–Kishtwar–Pahalgam–Daksum–Ranjit Sagar Dam under Himalayan Circuit Theme in Jammu and Kashmir
24.	Jammu and Kashmir	Himalayan Circuit	Integrated Development of Tourist Facilities at Gulmarg–Baramulla–Kupwara–Leh Circuit under Himalayan Circuit Theme in Jammu and Kashmir
25.	Uttar Pradesh	Buddhist Circuit	Development of Buddhist Circuit–Srawasti, Kushinagar and Kapilvastu in Uttar Pradesh
26.	Uttar Pradesh	Ramayana Circuit	Development of Chitrakoot and Shringverpur as Ramayana Circuit in Uttar Pradesh
27.	Andaman and Nicobar Islands	Coastal Circuit	Development of Coastal Circuit (Long Island–Ross Smith Island–Neil Island–Havelock Island-Baratang Island–Port Blair) in Andaman and Nicobar
28.	Tamil Nadu	Coastal Circuit	Development of Coastal Circuit (Chennai Mamallapuram–Rameswaram–Manpadu–Kanyakumari) in Tamil Nadu

S. No.	State/UT	Name of the Circuit	Name of the Project
29.	Uttar Pradesh	Spiritual Circuit	Development of Spiritual Circuit (Ahar-Aligarh-Kasganj-Sarosi (Unnao)-Pratapgarh-Kaushambi-Mirzapur-Gorakhpur-Domariyaganj-Basti-Barabanki-Azamgarh-Kairana-Baghpat-Shahjahanpur) in Uttar Pradesh
30.	Uttar Pradesh	Spiritual Circuit	Development of Spiritual Circuit II (Bijnor-Meerut-Kanpur Dehat-Banda-Ghazipur-Salempur-Ghosi-Ballia-Ambedkar Nagar-Aligarh-Fatehpur-Deoria-Mahoba-Sonbhadra-Chandauli-Misrikh-Bhadohi) in Uttar Pradesh under Swadesh Darshan Scheme
31.	Uttar Pradesh	Heritage Circuit	Development of Heritage Circuit (Kalinjar Fort (Banda)-Marhar Dham (Sant Kabir Nagar)-Chauri Chaura, Shaheed Sthal (Fatehpur)-Mavahar Sthal (Ghosi)-Shaheed Smarak (Meerut)) in Uttar Pradesh under Swadesh Darshan Scheme

Source: Ministry of Tourism (2017, pp. 109–111).

References

Ahluwalia, I. J. (n.d.). *Planning for urban development in India*. New Delhi: Indian Council for Research on International Economics. Retrieved 1 January 2018, from icrier.org/Urbanisation/pdf/Ahluwalia_Planning_for_Urban_%20 Development.pdf

Beattie, Martin. (2003). Colonial space: Health and modernity in Barabazaar. *Traditional Dwellings and Settlements Review, 14*(11), 7–19.

Bhave, Amod. (2011). *Urban renewal of Old City Pune* (Unpublished thesis). Department of Urban Planning, School of Planning and Architecture, New Delhi.

Bombay First. (2003). *40 years concept plan for MMR*. Mumbai: Bombay First and McKinsey.

Bugga, V. K. (2014, January). *Urban renewal, redevelopment and regeneration: Challenges/options.* Paper presented in the 62nd NTCP Congress at Pune, ITPI, New Delhi.

Chattopadhyay, Barnika. (2014, January). *Urban renewal of CBD and its adjacent areas of Kolkata: Past initiatives and present strategies.* Paper presented in the 62nd NTCP Congress at Pune, ITPI, New Delhi.

Das Gupta, Moushumi. (2014, 5 January). 480 Lutyens' bungalows in Delhi to be razed, rebuilt. *Hindustan Times,* New Delhi.

DDA. (1990). *Master Plan for Delhi, 2001.* New Delhi: Delhi Development Authority.

———. (2007). *Master Plan for Delhi, 2021.* New Delhi: Delhi Development Authority.

———. (2010). *Zonal Development Plan, Zone A 'Walled City'.* New Delhi: Delhi Development Authority.

Department of Urban Development, Housing and Local Self Government. (2009). *Affordable Housing Policy 2009.* Jaipur: Government of Rajasthan.

DMU-JNNURM. (2013). *Progress report, 31st March 2013.* New Delhi: MoUD. Retrieved 17 March 2014, from http://urbanindia.nic.in/DMU/JNNURM/DMU-JNNURM.pdf

Dutta, Bikram Kumar, & Bandyopadhyay, Sanhita. (2014, January). *Urban renewal for Shahjahanabad: A critical appraisal.* Paper presented in the NTCP Congress at Pune, ITPI, New Delhi.

Dutta, Sourovee. (2014, January). *Challenges and options of urban regeneration process exploring the relevance of Patrick Geddes's 'Sociological Approach' at the context of Indian organic city.* Paper presented in the NTCP Congress at Pune, ITPI, New Delhi.

Ekram, Lailun Nahar. (1989). *Slum networking of Indore City.* Technical review summary for Aga Khan Award in Architecture. Retrieved 14 April 2014, from www.akdn.org/architecture/pdf/1826_pdf

Ghoge, Ketaki, & Kamath, Naresh. (2012, January 4). Dharavi redevelopment gets nod. *Hindustan Times,* Mumbai.

Government of Delhi. (2002). *Economic Survey Delhi 2001–2002.* New Delhi: Government of Delhi.

———. (2013). *Economic Survey Delhi 2012–2013.* New Delhi: Government of Delhi.

———. (1962). *Town and country planning in India.* New Delhi: Town and country Planning Organisation, Ministry of Health.

Hindustan Times. (2017). Kalkaji slum dwellers to get DDA flats, 11 December 2017, New Delhi.

Isore Sandip, N. (2014, January). *Urban renewal scheme through cluster redevelopment approach: Case study Bhendi Bazar, Mumbai.* Paper presented in the 62nd NTCP Congress at Pune, ITPI, New Delhi.

Jagmohan. (1994). Shahjahanabad, the seventh city of Delhi: A political and socio-cultural profile. *Spatio-economic Development Record,* 1(2, May–June), 5–11.

Kshirsagar, J. B., & Srinivas, R. (2014, January). *Consequences of JNNURM*. Paper presented in the NTCP Congress at Pune, ITPI, New Delhi.

Kumar, Vikram. (2013, July 16). Redevelopment plans for part of Kidwai Nagar approved thirty projects to change the face of Delhi: Kamal Nath reveals grand design to reboot government colonies. *Mail Online India*.

Kumara, H. S. (2014, January). *Urban imbroglio and planning for urban renewal challenges and options for Indian cities: A case of Mysore city*. Paper presented in the 62nd NTCP Congress at Pune, ITPI, New Delhi.

Mehra, Sunil Kumar. (2014, January). *Regulatory and institutional mechanism for redevelopment in Delhi: The vision of Master Plan 2021 and further possibilities.* Paper presented at the 62nd NTCP Congress at Pune, ITPI, New Delhi.

Mehta, Meera, & Mehta, Dinesh. (2010). A glass half full? Urban development (1990s to 2010). *Economic & Political Weekly, 45*(28), 20–23.

Meller, H. (1997). *Patrick Geddes: Social evolutionist and city planner*. London and New York, NY: Routledge.

Ministry of Housing and Urban Poverty Alleviation (MoHUPA). (2005). *Guidelines for integrated housing and slum development programme (IHSDP)*. New Delhi: Government of India.

———. (2007). *The National Urban Housing and Habitat Policy 2007*. New Delhi: Government of India.

———. (2013). *Rajiv Awas Yojana (RAY), scheme guidelines 2013–2022*. New Delhi: Government of India.

———. (2015). *Annual report 2014–2015*. New Delhi: Government of India.

———. (2016a). *Annual report 2015–2016*. New Delhi: Government of India.

———. (2016b). *Pradhan Mantri Awas Yojana: Housing for all (urban)*. New Delhi: Government of India.

———. (2017). *Annual report 2016–17*. New Delhi: Government of India.

Ministry of Railways. (2016). *Memorandum of understanding with Ministry of Urban Development for redevelopment of railway stations*. New Delhi: Press Information Bureau.

Ministry of Tourism. (2017). *Annual report 2016–17*. New Delhi: Government of India.

Ministry of Urban Development (MoUD). (2014). *Guidelines for Swachh Bharat Mission (Urban)*. New Delhi: Government of India.

———. (2015a). *Smart cities, the mission statement and guidelines*. New Delhi: Government of India.

———. (2015b). *Atal Mission for Rejuvenation and Urban Transformation (AMRUT), mission statement and guidelines*. New Delhi: Government of India.

———. (2015c). *AMRUT action plan for 474 cities cleared*. New Delhi: Press Information Bureau.

———. (2015d). *HRIDAY launched*. New Delhi: Press Information Bureau.

———. (2015e). *Guidelines for Heritage city Development and Augmentation Yojana (HRIDAY)*. New Delhi: Government of India.

Ministry of Urban Development (MoUD). (2016). *Shri Vankaiah Naidu inaugurates state of arts Chennai Metro Phase I*. New Delhi: Press Information Bureau.

———. (2017). *Annual report 2016–17*. New Delhi: Government of India.

Modi, Narendra. (2011). *Convenient action: Gujarat's response to challenges of climate change*. New Delhi: Macmillan Publishers.

Mohan, I. (1992). *World of walled cities: Conservation, environmental pollution, urban renewal and redevelopment projects*. New Delhi: Mittal Publications.

Munshi, Neela, & Dave, Deepa. (n.d.). *Integrated multi-modal public transport hub at central business district*. Ahmedabad: Ahmedabad Urban Development Authority.

Nallathiga, Ramakrishna. (2014, January). *From decline to growth path: The experience of urban renewal in Mumbai*. Paper presented in the 62nd NTCP Congress at Pune, ITPI, New Delhi.

Nayar, Kuldip. (2013). *Emergency retold*. New Delhi: Konarak Publishers.

NIUA. (2009). *Appraisal of city development plan, Hyderabad*. New Delhi: National Institute of Urban Affairs.

Patharkar, A. R. (2014, January). *Metabolism of human settlements and urban regeneration*. Paper presented in the NTCP Congress at Pune, ITPI, New Delhi.

Pessina, G. (2011). *Sustainable for whom? Projects and opinions on the Sabarmati River in Ahmedabad*. Ahmedabad: Vastu Shilpa Foundation for Studies and Research in Environmental Design.

Raina, Shanu. (2012). *Development strategy for urban villages* (Unpublished thesis). Department of Urban Planning, School of Planning and Architecture, New Delhi.

SDR News. (2014). Centre-states/UTs meet on urban governance and housing for all ... adopts the national declaration on urban governance and housing for all. *Spatio-economic Development Record, 21*(3/4), 84.

———. (2016). Development of tourism in India. *Spatio-economic Development Record, 23*(6), 156–158.

Sethi, Rajeev. (2014, 14 March). The Kathputli saga. *Times of India*, New Delhi.

Sharma, Renu. (2014). Impact of MRTS: Case study Delhi. *Spatio-economic Development Record, 20*(6), 149–155.

Taneja, Simrandeep. (1996). *Evaluation of resettlement policies: Case study, Delhi* (Unpublished thesis). Department of Urban Planning, School of Planning and Architecture, New Delhi.

The Economist. (2005, 27 January). Inside the slum. *The Economist*, Mumbai.

The Statesman. (2017, 7 May). Yogi wields broom for cleaner UP. *The Statesman*, New Delhi.

The Times of India. (2014a, 21 March). HC asks DDA to decide on Kathputli 'residents'. *The Times of India*, New Delhi.

———. (2014b, 29 March). Lekhi claims scam in Kathputli. *The Times of India*, New Delhi.

The Times of India. (2015, 8 October). U'khand's Sabarmati-like riverfront project Kicked off. *The Times of India*, New Delhi/Dehradun.

———. (2016, 20 December). Kathputli colony hits development road. *The Times of India*, New Delhi.

The Times of India. (2017a, 5 May). The good, the bad and the rubbish: How cities are ranked. *The Times of India*, New Delhi.

———. (2017b). CLEANEST: Quirky & battle-like drive put city of Holkars on top of heap. *The Times of India*, Ahmedabad.

———. (2017c, 7 March). ₹92 crore revamp of Delhi's Nehru Place. *The Times of India*, New Delhi.

Virmani, Deepak. (1994). *Commercialisation and built form in the inner cities: Case study of Shahjahanabad* (Unpublished thesis). Department of Urban Planning, School of Planning and Architecture, New Delhi.

World Bank. (2013). *Urbanisation beyond municipal boundaries nurturing metropolitan economies and connecting peri-urban areas in India.* Washington, DC: World Bank.

CHAPTER 3

Spatial Planning Strategies for Urban Renewal

Introduction

Urban renewal affects people directly. In the renewal process, especially in case of redevelopment of slums, there are gainers as well as losers. This creates conflict of interests. The greatest challenge in urban renewal is to minimise all conflicts and find a solution that rejuvenates the area, improves the quality of life of people and introduces planned development.

Each area is unique and has specific potential, problems and peculiarities. A city is the mosaic of such unique areas which may be old or new, planned or unplanned, natural green or manmade park. For example, at the city level, each land use zone, such as residential, commercial, industrial or recreational, is unique. Spatial character of the residential area is totally different from that of an industrial or commercial zone. This is because of the nature of activities and the pattern of resultant land uses that exist in such areas. Even within a specific land use zone, there may be unique pockets. For example, a residential neighbourhood may have a pocket where high-income group (HIG) people live; it may also have slum pockets, mixed land use such as streets, a large park or a cluster of heritage buildings. Accordingly, the spatial planning strategy for the renewal of this neighbourhood should also be different for different areas—redevelopment/in situ upgradation of slum pockets and conservation of park as well as heritage areas. One solution may not fit all situations and therefore, renewal of an area may require a combination of several strategies. The Walled City of Delhi (Shahjahanabad) presents a good example of this observation. This area has many renewal zones, which is why the strategy of renewal of Walled City Delhi, as per MPD-2021, is conservation in a heritage zone; redevelopment for severely dilapidated areas; and in situ upgradation for other traditional zones (DDA, 2007).

Theoretically, strategy may be defined as a plan of action to achieve a set goal. There could be two types of strategies: (a) non-spatial and (b) spatial. The non-spatial strategies are those that are not associated with land and land use pattern. These strategies, in the context of urban renewal, generally, deal with urban governance and include operating rules, regulations, powers, functions, procedures, institutional mechanism, organisational setup, efficiency, accountability, transparency, community involvement and such others. The transformation of urban governance and management can be accomplished through the non-spatial strategy of reforms which is discussed in Chapter 4.

Spatial planning strategy is defined as a plan of action that aims at providing solution to specific problems through land use planning and spatial development approaches. Taking into account the urban renewal initiatives in India, discussed in Chapter 2, the following 12 spatial planning strategies have been identified:

1. Clearance
2. Redevelopment/cluster redevelopment
3. Relocation/resettlement/rehabilitation
4. Dispersal/decentralisation
5. Adaptive reuse
6. Re-densification
7. Regularisation

8. In situ upgradation/environmental upgradation
9. Restoration/revitalisation/retrofitting
10. Conservation
11. Restructuring
12. Creation of underground spaces

Following sections attempt at defining and briefly discussing these strategies and their applicability.

Clearance

Clearance can be defined as a strategy of physical removal of an unauthorised occupation and/or dilapidated structures in a blighted area. This is probably the first strategy that was applied to slum areas under a slum clearance act. This is applicable in situations where the area is encroached upon through illegal occupation and the area is

- required for the designated use as shown in a master plan;
- obstructing traffic, causing accidents, delays and congestion;
- coming in the way of a master plan proposed road; or
- affecting the visual and aesthetic quality and the image of city.

Under this strategy, the encroachment is cleared, buildings are demolished and the site is developed for the designated purpose as per the layout plan/master plan.

In 2009–2010, large-scale clearance of slums, located along Yamuna Pushta and other places in Delhi, was made before the commencement of Commonwealth Games for the reasons such as widening roads, security and aesthetic. In December 2013, the Ministry of Railway demolished a slum located on their land in Mansarovar Park, Delhi. In another case, the same year, the DDA's attempt of slum demolition was taken up in Mayur Vihar. However, it was foiled by the intervention of a political party (Banda and Sheikh, 2014).

In the past, no provision was made, even on humanitarian grounds, for assisting the illegal occupants vacated from the site. Now, however, such strategy by itself is socially and politically not acceptable. 'The rehabilitation and resettlement of people living in unauthorised colonies and jhuggis' is one of the promises of almost all the political parties in their election manifesto.

Application of this strategy now, in almost all cases, has to cater to the affected families by combining the clearance strategy with another spatial or non-spatial strategy such as payment of compensation (non-spatial) or relocation on a plot of land (spatial). A large area of land owned by railways, defence, ports and other central government agencies is occupied by slums and such lands cannot be cleared of encroachment by slum dwellers unless their relocation/rehabilitation is ensured.

Redevelopment/Cluster Redevelopment

As mentioned in Chapter 1 and explained in detail in Figure 5.2 (Chapter 5), redevelopment is a process of demolition and reconstruction of buildings. This strategy of renewal is applicable to dilapidated areas with crumbling structures declared unfit for human habitation or occupation for any other purpose, commercial or industrial. The strategy of redevelopment is also applicable to areas which have outlived their economic life or areas which have not been developed to their full potential of permissible FAR/FSI.[1]

A few examples of the application of this strategy, as discussed in Chapter 2, include slum redevelopment of Dharavi and Bhendi Bazaar in Mumbai. Examples of redevelopment of areas that have outlived their economic life due to changes in government policy and master plan provisions include mill area redevelopment in Mumbai and redevelopment of government housing colony at East Kidwai Nagar, New Delhi.

---

[1] FAR/FSI is the ratio of the total built up area to the plot area. FAR is expressed as percentage and FSI is expressed as ratio. Accordingly, 100 FAR is the same as 1 FSI.

Patharkar (2014) argues that the redevelopment of a single building depends upon the financial capability of the owner who, in most of the cases, is poor. As a result, the area remains underutilised and in the state of blight which may be dangerous to the occupants and the community. Also, due to financial constraints, the owner may not be in a position to utilise the full potential of the site. If a cluster of dilapidated buildings is identified and property owners join to redevelop the area, it will have better access to finance, greater flexibility in design, better provision of roads, open spaces and facilities and services. Recognising this, Government of Maharashtra decided to support and promote cluster redevelopment through granting higher FSI/FAR.

Cluster redevelopment can be defined as a strategy where the different owners of buildings join hands and pool their land for redevelopment as per the scheme (Figure 5.2 and Annexure 5.4; Chapter 5). Implementation of the cluster redevelopment strategy has generally been a joint effort of people, developer and the planning authority. It is a win-win situation for all. The original owners get better and safe tenements without financial investment. The developer gets profit on his investment by selling the additional FSI and the planning authority/local body gets public amenities fully developed at no additional cost.

Cluster redevelopment strategy is also applicable to industrial areas. In 1996, the Supreme Court of India had directed the closure of industrial units functioning in non-confirming and residential areas in Delhi. On the ground, several residential areas with a large-scale concentration of industrial units were located; in character and activities, these areas were more industrial than residential. Considering this, the Government of Delhi decided to follow the strategy of cluster redevelopment for such industrial areas. The MPD-2001 was amended with the provision that the areas with industrial concentration may be notified by the Government of Delhi as industrial clusters for redevelopment. As per the guidelines notified by DDA, an industrial cluster for redevelopment is a minimum contiguous area of 4 acres (1.6 ha) having more than 70% plots under industrial use (DDA, 2007, Section 7.6.2.1).

Subsequently, the Delhi State Industrial and Infrastructure Development Corporation (DSIIDC) in association with the concerned

Sub-divisional Magistrates identified 22 clusters for notification. These industrial clusters, notified for redevelopment, included Samaypur Badli, Shahdara, Anand Parbat, Jawahar Nagar, Sultanpur Majra, Hastsal Pocket-A, Naresh Park Extension, Libaspur, Peeragarhi Village, Khyala, Hastsal Pocket-D, Shalimar Village, New Mandoli, Nawada, Rithala, Swarn Park Mundka, Haiderpur, Karawal Nagar, Dabri, Basai Darapur, Prahladpur Bangar, Mundka South and Mundka Phirni (*The Hindu*, 2012).

Cluster redevelopment strategy has been applied successfully in United States of America, China and Singapore. As discussed in Chapters 2 and 5, redevelopment strategy is mostly applied along with strategy of temporary or permanent relocation/resettlement.

Relocation/Resettlement/Rehabilitation

Relocation refers to the temporary or permanent shifting of the families affected by a redevelopment project to a different site or another part of the same site. The strategy of temporary relocation is applied to accommodate the affected families for the time being and, on completion of buildings, bring them back to their allotted new tenements. In the redevelopment of Kathputli Colony, Delhi (Chapter 2), the temporary accommodation has been provided at another site located at Anand Parbat.

The strategy of permanent relocation is applicable to public purpose project sites under unauthorised occupation that is required for implementing the project. As given in Annexure 5.6, the land-owning agency makes a specific request to the authorities and following the procedure, the affected families are relocated permanently on allocated individual plots or tenements. In Delhi, the policy of allocating plots is replaced with the allocation of built-up accommodation of around 25 sq. m with common areas and facilities. In a case,[2] the Delhi High Court, pronouncing the judgment, directed that such relocation will happen in consultation with each of them (affected people) in a

---

[2] *Mukandi Lal & Others v/s Municipal Corporation of Delhi & Others*, Writ Petition (Civil) 9246 of 2009.

'meaningful manner' and that state agencies will ensure that basic civic amenities, consistent with the 'right to life and dignity' of each of the citizens in the jhuggis, are available at the site of relocation. This judgement provides legal support to humane urban renewal (Principle 1, Chapter 1) and ensures social justice in urban renewal programmes.

It should be noted that the relocation strategy is applicable to renewal of all areas—residential, industrial and commercial. The nature of relocation (temporary or permanent) and the process remains similar. As mentioned earlier, in 1996, the Supreme Court of India had directed the closure of industrial units functioning in non-confirming and residential areas in Delhi. In view of the large-scale loss of production and employment, the Government of Delhi had decided to start a scheme for permanent relocation of industrial units affected by this order and required to shut down. An industrial site was developed at Bawana for the relocation of industries affected by the Supreme Court order.

People living in an area evolve social and economic linkages. In spatial planning terms, these refer to people's interrelationship with the school, health centres/clinics, houses of friends and relatives and places of worship and work. In the process of urban renewal by relocation, all these linkages are generally disturbed, and it is difficult and time consuming to re-establish the links, especially related to jobs. In a democratic country, the interest of people is supreme and forms the basis of development policies and therefore, any relocation strategy requires additional efforts to rehabilitate the project-affected people by providing them affordable housing and job opportunities and access to transport facility if the relocated site is far away. Rehabilitation, therefore, refers to the provision of opportunities to persons affected by relocation to re-establishing their social and economic linkages by additionally providing access to job opportunities and public transport. Relocation and rehabilitation normally work as a package.

Dispersal/Decentralisation

Dispersal refers to the strategy of transforming an area by shifting activities such as large industries, wholesale commerce, warehousing, truck terminals and bus stands, which attract or generate a large volume of traffic and adds to congestion, pollution and hardships to people. The inner core areas of most of the old cities have such concentration of land uses. Most of the master plans suggest the policy of dispersal/decentralisation to decongest core area.

Sometimes, this strategy is also used in very high-density congested areas for the dispersal of population by reducing the density at the time of renewal. In practice, as mentioned in Chapter 2, strategy of renewal with reduced intensity of development (reduced FAR or density) has not gained favours from owners of properties as well as developers. Accordingly, they prefer repairs to renewal. For example, the first MPD (MPD-1962), proposed the reduction of density of the Walled City from 1,500 pph to 100–150 pph, but nothing happened. Dutta and Bandyopadhyay (2014) observed that the proposal of the dispersal of population was impractical in nature and no urban renewal projects/schemes were made. The MPD-2001 (the second in line) dropped this approach (of reducing density) and introduced shifting of activities, such as noxious and hazardous industries and trades, to check further industrialisation and commercialisation of the area. Shifting of Crawford Market from Mumbai to Navi Mumbai is an example of dispersal strategy. It has reduced the congestion in the area but the market still continues as a retail outlet for vegetable and fruits. This also provided the nucleus for the development of housing in Navi Mumbai. The closing of Delhi Cloth Mill, shifting of a bus stand from Old Delhi Railway Station and shifting of the wholesale vegetable market to Azad Pur are some example of this strategy in Delhi.

This strategy should normally be clubbed with the strategy of adaptive reuse of the site vacated by dispersal of activities.

Adaptive Reuse

Adaptive reuse can be defined as the strategy of renewal to reuse the sites made available by shifting of large-scale industries or wholesale markets or sites/buildings located in restricted zones around heritage monuments (see conservation). These adaptive uses should be conforming and compatible and should make up the deficiencies in the area as per the need of the community. Accordingly, they can be used as a park, playground, parking, residential flats, guest houses, commercial offices, retail commercial, auto-showrooms (no servicing), small-scale non-polluting flatted factories, marriage halls or a combination these and more as applicable or permissible.

For example, in Delhi, sites are available at Kishanganj by the closure of the Delhi Cloth Mill (10.8 ha) and on GT Road by the closure of Birla Mill (16 ha) for adaptive reuse as flatted factories/residential flats (Mehra, 2014). In Wazirpur Industrial Area, several sites are now redeveloped as auto showrooms or marriage halls. In the Islands of Mumbai, mill sites are available for redevelopment, and some of them have already been redeveloped as residential complexes. In Thane and Mulund, vacated industrial sites were reused for residential development, which provided much needed housing and commercial space to the city. In case of Thane, industrial sites located along Kolshet–Balkum road are being used for residential purposes, which added to the spatial spread of the city along roads connecting other towns such as Bhiwandi and Bhayander (Lele and Shirodkar, 2014).

The strategy of adaptive reuse may be applied to the conservation of certain heritage buildings such as traditional *haveli*s[3] in Rajasthan. Accordingly, the exterior of the buildings can be conserved as heritage structures and the interior of the *haveli* may be converted to a heritage guest house/hotel or any other compatible use. Such adaptive reuses of the heritage structures are desirable in conservation efforts to ensure sustainability.

Re-densification

Re-densification refers to increasing the density in an area having sub-optimal use of land and infrastructure which are uneconomical to maintain and sustain. Accordingly, re-densification is a strategy of the urban renewal of low-density areas by increasing their density or FAR/FSI to make them economically viable and functionally sustainable.

For example, in New Delhi, the historic British-period Bungalow Zone has a very low density of 0.7 DU per hectare (du/ha) and most

---

[3] Palatial traditional houses.

of the buildings are unsafe and are more than 80–90 years old. It is being renewed following the strategy of re-densification. In the first phase, Sunehari Bagh, covering an area of 29.89 ha and having 21 bungalows, was renewed to accommodate 32 bungalows in the same area, maintaining the same heritage character of the buildings and their surroundings (Das Gupta, 2014).

With the augmentation of basic services, road capacity and transport network, the carrying capacity of the area is also increased and in such cases, strategy of re-densification becomes desirable. While rejuvenating areas under AMRUT (MoUD, 2015a), an assessment of carrying capacity should be made in such areas and the extent of re-densification may be recommended.

Regularisation

A colony or development comprising contiguous area is termed as unauthorised if its layout and building plans are not approved by the concerned authority/agency. There are hundreds of such colonies in the big Indian cities and the people living there are deprived of facilities, services and a reasonably good quality of life. The strategy of regularisation refers to providing legal status to an otherwise unauthorised colony through a legal process. The basic objective of this strategy is to ensure the provision of basic infrastructure and improve the living environment after regularisation.

Application of this strategy requires legal support. This strategy, as per MPD-2021, is NOT applicable to unauthorised colonies that are occupied by HIG people; or fall in forest areas, or pose hindrance to provision of infrastructure (roads, railway); or have more than 50% plots un-built; or violate the provisions of Ancient Monuments and Archaeological Sites and Remains Act, 1958 (DDA, 2007).

The strategy is applied in most of the large cities in India. It is a politically popular strategy during elections when unauthorised colonies are rampantly regularised to gain votes. Probably, that is why unauthorised colonies keep on growing in number in the hope of being regularised during the next election. This strategy is applied along with the strategy of in situ upgradation.

In situ Upgradation/Environmental Improvement/Upgradation

In situ upgradation is the strategy of urban renewal without displacing the people to provide on the same site the required physical, social and economic infrastructure to improve the living and working conditions. This strategy is applicable to any slum cluster or blighted area.

This strategy of in situ upgradation is being applied to practically all slum areas under socio-political considerations, as such areas cannot be cleared without relocation and rehabilitation which, in most cases, is difficult due to the cost of land and its non-availability in large cities. Under such circumstances, to provide social justice to people (see Chapter 1), the objective is to ensure basic services and amenities in the area and improve their living conditions.

In case of public project area, where a part of the land is encroached by the people, the objective is to recover the remaining portion of the site for the assigned project and in situ upgradation of the slum pocket. The benefits of this strategy are (a) protection of people from displacement on humanitarian grounds, (b) saving on the cost of relocation and rehabilitation, (c) saving of time and cost escalation from delays due to litigations and (d) implementation of the project.

In situ upgradation of slums is the most favoured strategy being followed in Indian cities. Networking of slums and in situ upgradation at Indore, Ahmedabad and Vadodara are successful examples of the application of this strategy (Chapter 2). In situ upgradation is also applicable to blighted commercial and industrial areas. This strategy also includes the introduction of new technology in the industrial processes or transport and communication systems in the area.

Restoration/Revitalisation/Retrofitting

Restoration, in the context of urban renewal, refers to the reintroduction of economic activities and infrastructure to revitalise an area where the cause of decay is the loss of economic base or ailing economic health. Urban revitalisation is the process of introducing spatial and economic changes. It injects new life into stagnated areas by increasing accessibility, creating more jobs and business opportunities, improving the standard of living, reviving the real estate values and improving the image and identity of the area.

Retrofitting strategy aims at making an existing area resilient to withstand disasters such as earthquake by disaster proofing the buildings. Retrofitting strategy has been promoted by the Smart City Mission where existing built-up areas are to be made more efficient and liveable through smart solutions such as green buildings, renewable energy, smart parking, waste management and traffic control (MoUD, 2015b).

Conservation

Conservation refers to the judicious and sustainable use and management of natural or manmade resources in such a manner that their natural, ecological, architectural, historical and socio-cultural significance, as applicable, is maintained. Conservation strategy for an area being renewed is therefore applicable to heritage buildings, sites and structures. It is also applicable to ecologically sensitive zones. Conservation strategy is desirable and should be applied to non-heritage planned areas having good quality buildings, open spaces, avenues, and unique architectural or urban design qualities.

In MPD-1962 (the first plan), in order to protect the spread of blight, conservation areas were identified in the Walled City Shahjahanabad and included Katra Neel, Ballimaran, Dariba Kalan and New Darya Ganj. MPD-2021 has added other conservation areas such as Lutyens Bungalow Zone, Humayun's Tomb Complex and Chirag Delhi. It even introduced the idea of developing archaeological parks such as Mehrauli, Tughlaqabad, and Sultan Garhi as a way of conservation of heritage (Chapter 2).

Some of the examples of the application of this strategy in India include the renewal of area around Jama Masjid in Walled City Delhi and the restoration of the traditional Meena Bazar; conservation of the World Heritage Humayun's Tomb in Delhi and conservation of other places such as Charminar area in Hyderabad, temples at Madurai, Srirangam and other temple-towns.

It is highlighted here that the heritage monuments, buildings and sites have a historical, architectural, socio-cultural and religious significance that is recognised at international, national, state or local area level. There are guidelines for the conservation of monuments and sites recognised as world heritage. At the national level, ASI has listed the national monuments which are conserved under the provisions of the Ancient Monuments and Archaeological Sites and Remains (Amendment and Validation) Act, 2010. In fact, it is the heritage sites of state and local significance that are not taken care of. The Indian National Trust for Architectural and Cultural Heritage (INTACH) has listed such places in different states in the country but in the absence of their recognition by the state or local bodies, they remain as mere listings. What is needed, in renewal schemes, is to identify such buildings and sites with local community participation and also assess the significance they (people) attach to these places. Depending upon the level of significance conservation strategy may be decided. In some cases, it may include sensitising people about conservation. According to CDP of Jaipur, due to the lack of awareness of heritage conservation, heritage buildings are treated only as commercial spots. They continue to be in a state of deterioration. Little attention is paid to the development of infrastructure facilities near the tourists' spots. As a consequence, the tourism industry is facing fluctuations (NIPFP, 2006, p. 3). Conservation of buildings and sites may not be successful if they are not supported by people.

As mentioned earlier, the strategy of adaptive reuse of certain heritage buildings is desirable in conservation efforts to ensure sustainability of the heritage structure (see Chapter 5).

Restructuring

Restructuring, in the spatial planning context, refers to the re-organisation of land use pattern of the area being renewed with a view to accommodating new demands generated by the policy change, removal of non-compatible land uses and the introduction of new activities and transport system. For example, as discussed earlier, most of the master plans have recommended dispersal as the strategy to renew the core area of cities and proposed shifting of large-scale industries, wholesale commercial areas, bus stands and such other activities; however, they are vague on the reuse of the vacated sites and totally silent on what happens to its surroundings in terms of transformation in economic activities, land use pattern, traffic characteristics, breaking of socio-economic linkages and evolution of new activity pattern, linkages, circulation system and transport network. The result of all these happenings could be spatial and economic restructuring.

One of the most visible changes that has triggered the process of restructuring of cities in India is the introduction of MRTS (see Chapter 2). This restructuring process has started in Delhi where MPD-2021 has introduced transit-oriented development (TOD) along the MRTS corridors.

With spatial growth and spread, Mumbai city has restructured itself with the development of an alternative commercial centre at Bandra Kurla area. This commercial complex will further restructure the areas around Bandra Kurla.

Creation of Underground Spaces

Non-availability of land for the provision of amenities and public spaces is one of the biggest problems in old congested areas. Under such circumstances, the creation of underground spaces for parking, markets and provision of other facilities and services become necessary, desirable and a viable option. The underground spaces could be dead spaces or lively public spaces frequented by people. Underground metro rail stations have opened immense opportunities for such lively public spaces. Such underground stations should be conceived as public spaces and designed accordingly. This will be a big boon and centre of attraction in congested areas such as the Walled City, Delhi.

Underground Palika Bazar clubbed with multi-storey parking facility in Connaught Place, New Delhi, is an example of underground public space created as a result of widening of Panchkuian Road, New Delhi.

Summing Up

In literature and also in actual practice, in the absence of well-defined and acceptable definitions, various terms are being used for the same strategy. Terms such as relocation, resettlement and rehabilitation can be seen as interchangeable to mean the same strategy. This chapter is an attempt to identify and define various spatial strategies that are being used in the urban renewal process. It also highlights that more than one strategy may be needed in an urban renewal scheme. For example, a redevelopment strategy incorporated relocation and resettlement as part of the process. Similarly, an area may have unique pockets with specific problems and potential. In that case, there may be a need for the application of different strategies for different pockets. For example, an area may have a slum pocket, a very low-density planned residential area and a heritage area. Accordingly, the strategy applied may be in situ upgradation of the slum area, redensification of planned residential area and conservation of heritage area.

References

Banda, Subhadra, & Sheikh, Shahana. (2014). Glaring loopholes: Delhi government's guidelines for rehabilitation/resettlement of slum dwellers. *Economic & Political Weekly, 49*(4).

Das Gupta, Moushumi. (2014, 5 January). 480 Lutyens bungalows in Delhi to be razed, rebuilt. *Hindustan Times*, New Delhi.

DDA. (2007). *Master Plan for Delhi, 2021*. New Delhi: Government of Delhi.

Dutta, Bikram Kumar, & Bandyopadhyay, Sanhita. (2014, January). Urban renewal for Shahjahanabad: A critical appraisal. Paper presented in the 62nd NTCP Congress at Pune, ITPI, New Delhi.

MoUD. (2015a). *Atal Mission for Rejuvenation and Urban Transformation (AMRUT): Mission statement and guidelines*. New Delhi: Government of India.

———. (2015b). *Smart cities the mission statement and guidelines*. New Delhi: Government of India.

Lele, M. D., & Shirodkar, Smita. (2014, January). *Urban renewal: An overview*. Paper presented in the 62nd NTCP Congress at Pune, ITPI, New Delhi.

Mehra, Sunil Kumar. (2014, January). *Regulatory and institutional mechanism for redevelopment in Delhi: The vision of Master Plan-2021 and further possibilities*. Paper presented in the 62nd NTCP Congress at Pune, ITPI, New Delhi.

NIPFP. (2006). *Jaipur city development plan: An appraisal report*. New Delhi: The National Institute of Public Finance.

Patharkar, A. R. (2014, January). *Metabolism of human settlements and urban regeneration*. Paper presented in the 62nd NTCP Congress at Pune, ITPI, New Delhi.

The Hindu. (2012, 12 June). Delhi industrial clusters set for a face lift. *The Hindu*, New Delhi.

CHAPTER 4

Reforms as Strategy for Rejuvenating Urban Governance and Promoting Urban Renewal

Introduction

As defined in Chapter 1, reforms refer to the strategy of making a system better by introducing changes necessary to improve its performance, accountability and effectiveness. Since city is a system, urban reforms are strategies to rejuvenate the performance in managing and governing a city in efficient, transparent and accountable manner. This chapter discusses the various reforms, introduced by different programmes/missions, that provide legal support, improve institutional mechanism and promote public participation and private sector involvement to achieve the goal of urban transformation in India.

Rationale for Reforms

Before 1992, when the 74th Amendment to the Constitution became an Act of Parliament, the urban management and governance scenario in India was in a bad shape. The tax collection was poor; there was an over dependence on the government grants; service provision was not sustainable as cost recovery was poor; maintenance of accounts was irregular or faulty; there was a lack of transparency in official dealings; buildings in core areas and old part of cities were ill maintained due to Rent Control Act, which fixed very low rents and supported to concerns of tenants more than rational and balanced provisions favouring both the tenants and the owners.

ULBs were redundant as the state governments were reluctant in holding municipal elections. There was no law that ensured regular election and establishment of local governance institution. Urban services were provided by utility boards. The Constitution (74th Amendment) Act, 1992 (74th CAA) ensured that municipalities are constituted through election to serve as the third tier of government. It also ensured that ULB elections are held every five years. The Act directed states to constitute such bodies and assign them financial and administrative powers, authority and also the responsibility to prepare plans of economic development and social justice, and implement schemes in relation to 18 functions listed in the 12th Schedule (Annexure 4.1). This Schedule includes, among other matters, functions such as urban planning including town planning, slum improvement/upgradation and provision of urban services. The 74th CAA was a landmark act in the urban governance and management. It did establish the ULBs. Elections are held regularly every five years. However, the performance of ULBs could not improve as expected.

Noting this state of affairs, the Government of India followed urban renewal strategy that was linked with reforms and from time to time introduced programmes such as JNNURM 2006–2013, RAY 2013–2022, AMRUT 2015–2020 and PMAY 2013–2022. Chapter 2 (Urban Renewal Initiatives in India) provides details of these programmes, including aims, objectives and coverage, and financial allocation is discussed in Chapter 6 (Resource Mobilisation for Urban Renewal). This chapter specifically focuses on the reforms that are necessary to face the challenges of urban renewal and implementation of different programmes.

Objectives

The objectives of these reforms, under various schemes/missions, mostly include the following:

1. Strengthening various institutions responsible for planning and implementation
2. Improving functional efficiency, accountability and transparency
3. Creating an environment that is conducive to doing business through enacting enabling legislations, development controls and rules
4. Simplification of procedures to ensure timely implementation of programmes and promote participation of stakeholders, investors and private sector in the process of urban transformation

The following sections present a short critical account of reforms and their implementation status.

Reforms under JNNURM

Scope and Coverage

JNNURM (as discussed in Chapter 2) noted the state of affairs of ULBs and introduced 23 reforms in their institutional, financial and governance structures to enable them to perform in an efficient, accountable and transparent manner (Table 4.1).

Since, for implementing some of the reforms, an action was required at the state government level, the 23 reforms were divided into two groups: (a) state-level reforms and (b) ULB-level reforms. Again, to ensure compliance with priority reforms within the mission period of 7 years, 13 reforms were made compulsory and the remaining 10 were optional. As shown in Table 4.1, there were six state-level mandatory reforms and seven ULB-level reforms. It was a carrot and stick approach and therefore, reforms were linked with the release of funds for different urban renewal projects.

For effective implementation of these reforms, the state government and ULBs/parastatals entered into an MoA with the central government, indicating their commitment to implement the respective mandatory and optional reforms and specifying milestones to be achieved during the mission period. The signing of this tripartite MoA was a necessary condition to access central assistance and release of funds.

This section presents the performance of the state governments and ULBs in implementing the JNNURM reforms.

Table 4.1 Reforms under JNNURM

Mandatory Reforms at State Level	Optional Reforms
1. Decentralisation: 74th Constitutional Amendment 2. Urban Land (Ceiling and Regulation) Act (ULCRA) Repeal 3. Reform Rent Control Law 4. Enactment of Public Disclosure Law 5. Enactment of Community Participation Law 6. Assign city planning and other functions to ULB	1. Bye-laws revision: Streamline process for construction 2. Simplify land use conversion 3. Property Title Certification system in ULBs 4. Earmarking for EWS/LIG 20–25% land in housing projects 5. Computerised registration of land and property 6. Revision of bye-laws: for compulsory rainwater harvesting 7. Reuse of recycled water 8. Administrative reforms 9. Structural reforms 10. Encouraging public-private partnership (PPP)
Mandatory Reforms at ULB Level	
1. Double entry accrual based accounting system 2. E-Governance: IT(Information Technology)/GIS (Geographical Information System) applications 3. Property tax reform 4. Levy of user charges: Full recovery of O&M (operation and maintenance) 5. Internal budget earmarking: Basic services for poor 6. Provision of services to poor 7. Specially, tenancy security	

Source: Based on MoHUPA (2005), Annexure B.

Implementation of Mandatory State-level Reforms

As per DMU-JNNURM Report (2013a), the status of state-level reforms, as on 31 March 2013, is summarised in Table 4.2. The reform agenda, as evaluated by DMU-JNNURM, includes the following:

1. Implementation of the Constitution (74th Amendment) Act, 1992 (74th CAA)
2. Reforms in Rent Control Law
3. Reduction in stamp duty
4. Enactment of Community Participation Law (CPL)
5. Enactment of Public Disclosure Law
6. Property titles

Implementation of the 74th CAA

Reforms related to the 74th CAA include the transfer of the Twelfth Schedule (Annexure 4.1) functions and constitution of Metropolitan Planning Committees (MPCs).

Transfer of Twelfth Schedule Functions: As shown in Annexure 4.1, there are 18 functions that are to be transferred to the ULBs by the state governments. According to DMU-JNNRUM report, 12 states (33%) could *not* transfer all the functions to the ULBs as envisaged in the Twelfth Schedule of 74th CAA. Most of the other states (67%) have either assigned all functions to the ULBs or evolved a mechanism to associate ULBs with the concerned parastatal agencies that are currently performing the specific function (say urban planning, firefighting, etc.). The argument given for pursuing this approach was 'lack of capacity of ULBs', including the lack of skilled manpower, to perform the function. Some other arguments, for not devolving urban planning function to ULBs, were jurisdiction of ULBs which is limited to the municipal boundary, while urban development plan covers areas beyond this line. In addition, since large cities comprise several municipalities, as agglomeration, this function cannot be assigned to ULBs. These arguments appear to be weak and indicate a lack of political and administrative will. Technical capabilities can always be improved effectively after assigning the function which will actually generate the demand for technical staff in ULBs and give a push to the process of capacity building.

The reason for transferring urban planning function from state to ULBs has been the fact that the master plan of city deals with city-specific social, economic and spatial development issues and provides a future course of strategies and actions. It is therefore best tackled by the respective ULBs. This will provide the ownership of the development plan and a commitment of the local body to implement the plan for orderly development of the city. It will create the accountability of ULB to people and electorate.

According to the MoUD, 15 states/UTs have transferred the urban planning and the delivery of urban infrastructure to ULBs in their respective states; these states include Andhra Pradesh, Assam, Chhattisgarh, Haryana, Himachal Pradesh, Karnataka, Madhya Pradesh, Maharashtra, Odisha, Rajasthan, Gujarat, Kerala, Tamil Nadu, Tripura and West Bengal (CAG, 2012, Section 4.2.1.3).

Constitution of MPCs: The 74th CAA (Article 243 ZE) provides for the constitution of MPCs for the preparation of a development plan after consolidating plans of all ULBs and panchayats located in the metropolitan areas. Since MPC is constituted for a city/urban agglomeration of 10 lakh or more population, this provision is not applicable to 14 states which do not have such large cities. Delhi is exempted from the constitution of MPC. As on 31 March 2013, only four states/UTs—Chandigarh, Jharkhand, Madhya Pradesh and Uttar Pradesh—had not constituted MPC; five states—Andhra Pradesh, Gujarat, Tamil Nadu, Rajasthan and Karnataka—had constituted the MPCs, but they are not yet operational (Table 4.2).

Reform in Rent Control Law

As discussed in Chapter 1, one of the causes of urban blight, in old part of cities, is low rent paid by the tenants. Reform in Rent Control Laws, therefore, aims at reducing conflicts between the house owner and tenants; making the repair and maintenance of building viable;

Table 4.2 Status of State/UT-level Reform Under JNNURM (31 March 2013)

Nature of Reforms	Number of States/UTs (% of total 36 states/UTs)	Name of States/UTs
Implementation of the 74th CAA		
No transfer of Schedule 12 functions in Act	12 (33)	Arunachal Pradesh, Assam, Chandigarh, Goa, Jammu and Kashmir, Manipur, Meghalaya, Mizoram, Nagaland, Rajasthan, Sikkim, and Uttarakhand
No constitution of MPCs	4 (11)	Chandigarh, Jharkhand, Madhya Pradesh, and Uttar Pradesh
MPCs constituted but not yet operational	5 (14)	Andhra Pradesh, Gujarat, Tamil Nadu, Rajasthan and Karnataka
Not amended the Rent Control Act	13 (36)	Andhra Pradesh, Arunachal Pradesh, Assam, Bihar, Goa, Gujarat, Haryana, Jammu and Kashmir, Kerala, Maharashtra, Meghalaya, Puducherry, and Punjab
Not yet reduced stamp duty (including the surcharge) to 5%	5 (14)	Bihar, Haryana, Jammu and Kashmir, Kerala, and West Bengal
Not yet passed Community Participation Law	8 (22)	Arunachal Pradesh, Bihar, Goa, Meghalaya, Puducherry, Punjab, Odisha, and Uttarakhand
Not yet passed Public Disclosure Acts	3 (8)	Chandigarh, Goa, and Mizoram
Property titles		
Number of states that HAVE NOT BEEN able to guarantee property titles or insure titles	36 (100)	ALL

Source: Based upon DMU–JNNURM (2013a) Format 5 and Format 7.

increasing rental housing stock; promoting better relationship between house owners and tenants; and reducing litigations and improving the quality of life in blighted areas. This reform will also result in the increase in property tax revenue of ULBs. As on 31 March 2013, most (64%) of the states and UTs had incorporated reforms in their respective Rent Control Act to boost renewal of old areas. The 13 states that did not amend the Rent Control Act are Andhra Pradesh, Arunachal Pradesh, Assam, Bihar, Goa, Gujarat, Haryana, Jammu and Kashmir, Kerala, Maharashtra, Meghalaya, Puducherry and Punjab (Table 4.2).

Reduction in Stamp Duty

One of the barriers to the efficient and transparent functioning of the real estate market has been the high rate of stamp duty (more than 10%) on the conveyance of transaction. The high rate of stamp duty discourages buyers to register the actual or market value of the property. This is a loss of revenue to the government, a cause of corruption in the real estate market and a reason for black money transactions. Lowering the stamp duty encourages buyers to pay duty on the actual price, improve revenue collection of the government, reduce corruption and black money generation and boost the real estate market. JNNURM, therefore, introduced this reform to reduce stamp duty from 10% to 5% or below, including surcharges. This reform has been quite successfully implemented and only five states—Bihar, Haryana, Jammu and Kashmir, Kerala, and West Bengal—did not implement it (Table 4.2).

To encourage the registration of property in the name of women, some states have further reduced the stamp duty for women. For example, in Uttarakhand, the duty has been reduced to 5% for men and 3.75% for women; in Delhi, the duty was reduced to 6% (instead of 5% as required) for men and 4% for women. When questioned by the Comptroller and Auditor General (CAG) on not following the spirit of the reform to reduce duty to 5%, Delhi State argued that it has achieved the Mission guidelines as the average of 6 and 4 is 5%, which was rejected by the auditors (CAG, 2012, p. 31).

Community Participation Law

The objective of CPL is (a) to strengthen municipalities by institutionalising citizens' participation by creating a three-tier structure at city level—municipal corporation, wards committee and area sabha (comprising all registered voters in the area as members); (b) to define functions, duties and power at each tier; (c) to provide devolution of funds, functions and functionaries at each level and (d) to involve citizens in municipal functions such as setting priorities, budgeting, monitoring and serving as a pressure group for the compliance of regulations. As shown in Table 4.2, most (78%) of the states have passed CPL, but eight states have not taken any action in this respect. These states are Arunachal Pradesh, Bihar, Goa, Meghalaya, Puducherry, Punjab, Odisha and Uttarakhand. Delhi argued that their Bhagidari System should suffice as CPL. CAG questioned: How can this system be substituted for an agenda of reform of enactment of CPL (CAG, 2012, p. 32)? According to the Best Practices (Government of India, n.d.), Andhra Pradesh has enacted the CPL and amended Municipal Law in 2008, framed the Rules in 2010 and also selected the members of all Area Sabhas as per the provision of the Rules during the same year.

Public Disclosure Law

The objective of Public Disclosure Law is to ensure transparency and accountability in the functioning of ULBs through quarterly publication of performance information to all stakeholders. This Law supplements the RTI Act, 2005, by making available regular information on ULB activities, suo-motu. Most (92%) of the states have made provision of public disclosure of information, except Chandigarh (UT), Goa and Mizoram (Table 4.2).

According to the Best Practices in JNNURM Reforms (Government of India, n.d.), effort of three states—Karnataka, Haryana and Rajasthan—are praiseworthy. Karnataka has enacted The Karnataka Local Fund Authorities Fiscal Responsibility Act, 2003, under which every ULB will have to disclose annual budget, annual accounts and the annual report. Haryana has enacted the Haryana Municipal Public

Disclosure Act, 2008, and Municipal Corporation of Faridabad has already started disclosing a variety of information on a portal. This has brought transparency in governance and awareness regarding projects and functions of the municipalities in the state. Rajasthan has amended the Rajasthan Municipality Act, 2009, to incorporate public disclosure. According to CAG (2012), the nature and mode of the implementation of this Act varied from state to state.

Guarantee of Property Title to Urban Poor

As seen from Table 4.2, none of the states was able to implement this reform of JNNURM.

Implementation of Mandatory ULB-level Reforms

Table 4.3 indicates the commitment made by the ULBs, in the MoA, to implement the mandatory reforms under JNNURM. These reforms include the following:

1. Double entry accounting system (DEAS)
2. E-governance
3. Property tax
4. User charges
5. Conversion of agricultural lands for urban use
6. Property titles

Double Entry Accrual-based Accounting System

The objective of double entry accrual based accounting system is to introduce a modern system of financial management that makes the performance of ULBs transparent and self-reliant. A look at Table 4.3 indicates that a majority (81.1%) of ULBs have agreed to introduce double entry accrual based accounting. According to CAG (2012), among seven states visited by the auditors, the only ULB that has actually finalised the accounts based on the reform (double entry accrual based accounting system) is Greater Hyderabad Municipal Corporation. The other ULBs had started the process or in some cases, completed the process but had not actually shifted to the new accounting system.

E-governance

E-governance reform aims at improving the governance and services delivery systems of ULBs through the application of ICT so that their performance is user-friendly, efficient and effective. The focus was to identify services for e-governance and set benchmarks to be achieved so that the reach of the delivery of services to the people is improved.

As indicated in Table 4.3, some 37 (56.9%) ULBs have implemented the e-governance reform. Best Practices in JNNURM Reforms, in this regards, are available from Pimpri-Chinchwad, Hyderabad, Surat, Kolkata, Mysore, Cochin, Bengaluru, Delhi, Jaipur, Ajmer and Ranchi. In Karnataka, e-governance has been introduced in all the 213 ULBs (Government of India, n.d.).

Property Tax

Property tax is the single most important source of tax revenue of an ULB. In spite of this, most of the ULBs do not have proper record of properties and therefore, the tax collection is poor. The JNNURM reforms, in this respect, include proper mapping of all properties using GIS, making the system capable of self-assessment of property tax by the owners of properties and achieve coverage efficiency of 85% and tax collection efficiency of 90%. Some 61.5% ULBs have committed to cover more than 85% of the number of properties in their respective cities for the collection of property tax. Good practice, in this respect, is recorded in case of ULBs such as Vijayawada, Patna, Delhi, Kanpur, Agra, Meerut and Puri. This has increased the property tax collection efficiency by 10% in case of Puri and 20% in case of Delhi (Government of India, n.d.).

User Charges

The objectives of levying user charges are to recover 100% cost of operation and maintenance and to make the service provision

Table 4.3 ULB-level Reforms Committed up to Seven Years Under JNNURM (31 March 2013)

Nature of Reforms	No. of Cities (% out of 65)
DEAS	
Migrated to double entry accrual based accounting	53 (81.5)
E-governance	
Have been able to implement e-governance	37 (56.9)
Property tax	
More than 85% coverage of properties for taxation	40 (61.5)
Less than 85% coverage of properties for taxation (as per commitment)	25 (38.5)
Tax collection to tax demanded ratio more than 90%	31 (47.7)
Tax collection to tax demanded ratio less than 90% (as per commitment)	34 (52.3)
User charges	
100% collection of O&M cost incurred in providing services such as water supply	23 (35.4)
Less than 100% collection of O&M cost incurred in providing services such as water supply (as per commitment)	42 (64.6)
Conversion of agricultural lands for urban use	
Number of cities that have simplified the procedure for conversion of agricultural land for urban use	52 (80)
Property titles	
Number of states that have been able to guarantee property titles or insure titles	Nil (0)

Source: DMU-JNNURM (2013b) Format 6/7.

sustainable. As can be seen in Table 4.3, some 35.4% ULBs committed to levy 100% user charges and remaining (64.6%) agreed to levy less than 100%; but, according to CAG (2012, p. 24), out of 39 mission cities selected for audit, only 7 (18%) cities introduced mechanism for the collection of water charges. These cities include Visakhapatnam, Ahmedabad, Pune, Imphal, Raipur, Lucknow and Haridwar.

In case of user charges for solid waste management, in the sample of same 39 mission cities, only 5 (13%) cities could achieve the objective. These cities are Ahmedabad, Indore, Nagpur, Pune and Lucknow (CAG, 2012).

Conversion of Agricultural Lands for Urban Use

This reform focuses on the simplification of the legal and procedural framework for the conversion of agricultural lands for non-agricultural purposes. As on 31 March 2013, a majority of ULBs (80%) agreed to implement this reform (Table 4.3).

Property Titles

As shown in Table 4.3, none of the ULBs or parastatals had implemented this reform as the state government also failed to do so (Table 4.2).

Internal Earmarking of Funds

Internal earmarking of funds in the municipal budget for provision of BSUP was committed by various ULBs, as indicated in Table 4.4. A total of 6 ULBs committed up to 10% funds, 17 agreed to commit funds between 10% and 20% and a commitment of 20–25% funds was made by 13 ULBs. It is noted that a higher percentage of more than 25 was committed by 22 ULBs. However, the actual pattern of implementation of this reforms indicates that only 4 ULBs (Itanagar, Aizawl, Imphal and Kohima) out of 65 (10%) had actually fulfilled their commitment by 31 December 2013.

Implementation of Optional Reforms

The optional reforms under JNNURM include the following:

1. Bye-laws revision, covering provision for
    i. streamlining the approval process for construction,
    ii. compulsory rainwater harvesting (RWH) and
    iii. reuse of recycled water.

Table 4.4 Commitment to Internal Earmarking of Funds in the Budget for Basic Services for Urban Poor (31 December 2013)

Percentage Committed	ULBs Committing*		ULBs Which Have Actually Implemented the Commitment**	
	No.	Name	No.	Name
Up to 10	6	Kanpur, Shimla, Chandigarh, Itanagar, Panaji, Shillong	1	Itanagar
10–20	17	Lucknow, Ludhiana, Delhi, Jabalpur, Pune, Agartala, Meerut, Raipur, Bodhgaya, Ahmedabad, Rajkot, Faridabad, Jammu, Srinagar, Aizawl, Amritsar, Nainital	1	Aizawl
20–25	13	Surat, Nagpur, Guwahati, Kohima, Ajmer, Pushkar, Chennai, Coimbatore, Madurai, Allahabad, Agra, Varanasi, Dehradun, Haridwar	2	Imphal, Kohima
More than 25	22	Bhubaneshwar, Mathura, Indore, Bangalore, Mysore, Puducherry, Navi Mumbai, Bhopal, Ujjain, Kolkata, Nanded, Gangtok, Vadodara, Nashik, Hyderabad, Vijayawada, Tirupati, Visakhapatnam, Thiruvananthapuram, Imphal, Patna, Kochi	–	–
Not specified	7	Porbandar, Ranchi, Jamshedpur, Dhanbad, Jaipur, Asansol, Puri		
Total	65	–	4	–

Sources: * DMU-JNNURM (2013b).
** Government of India (n.d.).

2. Property Title Certification System in ULBs
3. Earmarking for EWS/LIG: 20–25% land in housing projects
4. Computerised registration of land and property
5. Administrative reforms

6. Structural reforms
7. Encouraging PPP

Bye-laws Revision

Streamlining the approval process for building: Both development and renewal efforts require the approval of plans and projects before implementation. This, under the current bye-laws, has to follow a complex process that takes a long time. Thus, the objective of this reform has been to streamline the approval process, make it simple, transparent, quick and development-oriented. In their MoA, 63 ULBs had committed to implement this reform. According to CAG (2012), however, 21 ULBs could not implement the reform. There are only three good examples of this reform from states such as Uttarakhand, Assam and Gujarat (Government of India, n.d.). In Uttarakhand, a single window clearance system has been established at Dehradun and Nainital. Building permission is granted in one day for residential structures and it takes three days for commercial buildings. A Citizen's Charter has been prepared that gives the approval process and the time taken for approval in different cases. In Assam, ULB of Guwahati had modified the bye-laws in 2005–2006 to reduce the building approval time from 75 days to 30 days. In Gujarat, Surat Municipal Corporation (SMC) modified the laws in 2006–2007 to introduce e-submission and e-processing for transparency and to reduce the approval time form 60 days to 15 days.

Compulsory RWH: This reform is to cope with the problem of depleting groundwater table in the country and also to promote the conservation of water by people. According to the report of the MoUD, as presented to the CAG (2012), 67 ULBs had committed to this reform and 61 ULBs had reported compliance to their commitment. However, from the Best Practices in JNNURM Reforms (Government of India, n.d.), there are only two examples—Chennai and the Faridabad—that have actually implemented the reform. In Tamil Nadu, The Ground Water Regulation Act, 1987, was amended in October 2002 to incorporate compulsory RWH for new buildings. To install RWH structures for existing buildings, a timeframe of one year from the date of notification of the Act was given to the owners. The Tamil Nadu Municipalities Building Regulation Rules, 1972, and Multi-Storeyed and Public Building Rules, 1973, were modified in October 2002 to make provisions for the conservation of rainwater. An ordinance was promulgated in July 2003 to amend the laws relating to municipal corporations and municipalities in the state for the provision of RWH structures in all the building. Chennai is showing good results in RWH. Similarly, in Faridabad, the bye-laws were revised in 2006 to include RWH in all new buildings.

Reuse of recycled water: Reuse of recycled water refers to using domestic wastewater from bathroom and kitchen a second time for an appropriate use after primary/secondary treatment as required. This reform aims at ensuring dependable, environmentally sustainable and cost-effective water supply system for residential areas. The reuse of recycled water can be at the level of an individual house, group-housing area or neighbourhood. According to MoUD report to CAG, 94% (61 out of 65) ULBs committed to this reform in their MoA, but 31% (19 out of 61) ULBs could not implement their commitment by 2010–2011. The recycled water could also be used for cooling purposes in industrial processes.

Property Title Certification System in ULBs

The basic objective of creating property title certification system in ULBs is to create a public record of title which would truly describe the property as well as the title and has a system for reflecting any transaction in real time (CAG, 2012). In urban renewal projects, it is of utmost importance to know the boundary of the property and its ownership. In the absence of this information, the plans cannot be prepared and approved. Lack of such information or incorrect information would invite conflicts and litigations and cause delays in the implementation of projects. Unfortunately, no ULB could implement this reform. It was because property certification is the responsibility of revenue department and requires action by the state governments.

Earmarking 20–25% Land in Housing Projects for EWS/LIG

One of the reasons for the growth of slums in cities is lack of supply of developed land for EWS and LIG. To ensure regular supply of developed land for housing urban poor, such a reform was necessary. According to MoHUPA, 62 ULBs that had committed for this reform have implemented it. According to Thornton (2011), however, the reform process was in progress in all cases. According to the Best Practices in JNNURM Reforms (Government of India, n.d.), only the Urban Development Department, Jharkhand, had issued an order earmarking 25% land for EWS in housing projects. This indicates the actual state of affairs and the value of the commitments to the reforms by the ULBs.

Computerised Registration of Land and Property

The present system of registration of land and property is manual which takes time and it results in corruption as well. The objective of this reform was to promote an efficient real estate market where the transactions are smooth, barrier-free and transparent (CAG, 2012, Chapter 10). According to MoUD, 63 ULBs were committed to the reform and 49 implemented their commitment. Two good examples are available from Andhra Pradesh and Karnataka. Andhra Pradesh achieved this reform in 2006–2007 through the implementation of Computer-aided Administration of Registration Department (CARD) project. This drastically reduced time for a variety of services as indicated in Table 4.5.

The impact of this project is encouraging and it has increased the productivity of employees and has led to increase in the number of registrations, and thus increase in revenue to the government.

Karnataka, also in 2006–2007, developed and introduced a software known as 'Kaveri' for services such as registration of properties, valuation of properties, scanning of architectural documents, report vendor management system and data transmission. This resulted in speedy functioning, better storage and retrieval of data and growth in revenue collection of the ULB.

Table 4.5 Reduced Time Taken for a Variety of Services due to Implementation of CARD in Andhra Pradesh and Karnataka

Service	Time Taken by Manual Operation	Time Taken by CARD (minutes)
Encumbrance certificate	1–5 days	10
Verification of property	1 hour	10
Sale of stamp paper	30 minutes	10
Document writing	1 day	30
Registration	1–7 days	60
Certified copy of documents	1–3 days	10

Source: CAG (2012).

Administrative Reforms

The objective of administrative reforms was to enhance the administrative efficiency of ULBs through capacity building and improving human resource development practices. According to MoUD, 48 ULBs had committed to this reform but only 23 (48%) could implement the reform. CAG (2012) audited 39 ULBs and found that only 13 (33%) had implemented the administrative reforms. Thornton (2011) noted that in implementing this reform, the ULBs had either reduced the staff or not filled the vacant posts. This was not the intent of this reform.

Structural Reforms

According to Thornton (2011, p. 113), structural reforms in the context JNNURM require defining the roles of many line departments and innumerable parastatal agencies which are still occupying the urban space that rightfully and constitutionally (74th CAA) belong to ULBs. It also requires setting up of new institutional mechanism to perform new roles and responsibilities as per the Twelfth Schedule of 74th CAA, particularly urban planning, regulation of land-use and slum improvement and upgradation. It appears that a majority of states could not understand the spirit of this reform. The Best Practices in JNNURM Reforms compiled by the MoUD record the efforts of Bihar, Odisha and Maharashtra (Government of India, n.d.). In Bihar, 114 posts of city managers have been created by the Urban Development and Housing Department to perform tasks pertaining to the planning and implementation of works related to central government programmes and projects as well as administration and accounts.

In Odisha, 222 posts of supporting staff have been created in ULBs. For discharging town planning function assigned to 41 ULBs in the state, Housing and Urban Development Department has created 64 posts of sub-professional staff, 15 posts of senior draftsman and 112 posts administrative staff.

Maharashtra spelt out the aim of these structural reforms as to provide an enabling and supporting institutional context for governance improvements to strike roots and sustain them (Government of India, n.d.). The objectives for accomplishing this aim are as follows:

1. Reforms in the institutional structures of urban management at the state level
2. Creation of a cadre of municipal staff for different disciplines
3. Decentralisation of municipal administration, and synchronisation of internal jurisdictions
4. Organisation structure review and optimisation of staffing patterns

Implementation of these reforms requires concurrent actions at both the state and ULB levels. Accordingly, the state has formulated Maharashtra Municipal Councils, Nagar Panchayat, and Industrial Township (Absorption, Recruitment and Service Conditions) Rules, 2006 and created the following six cadres of municipal services:

1. Municipal Engineering Service (Civil/Electrical/Computer)
2. Municipal Water Supply, Sewerage and Sanitation Engineering Service
3. Municipal Audit and Accounts Service
4. Municipal Taxation and Administrative Service

5. Municipal Fire Service
6. Municipal Town Planning and Development Service

The benefits of cadre formation will be that the appointment of city managers will be through centralised and unified selection processes which will ensure basic minimum qualifications and good quality of personnel and eliminate bias in hiring. The experiences and competencies will be leveraged across cities through the lateral movement of the city managers.

Encouraging Public–Private Partnership

Public–private partnership (PPP) refers to participation through a contract or concession agreement between the government or a statutory entity on the one hand and a private company on the other for delivering an infrastructure service on the payment of user charges. The infrastructure services can be water supply, sewerage, drainage, solid waste management, electricity supply and construction of roads. A total of 63 ULBs committed to this reform and 55 (87%) ULBs implemented it. It was sometimes confused with the outsourcing of projects to the private sector. According to CAG (2012), this reform requires the state government to formulate PPP policy, legal and regulatory framework, a methodology for the selection of private sector partner and other modalities which none of the states could do. Application of this model has been reported by Puducherry, Guwahati, Chennai, Jaipur, Mysore and Pimpri-Chinchwad for solid waste management. Ahmedabad applied this in water supply, sewerage and transport projects.

Reforms under Rajiv Awas Yojana

Objective

As mentioned in Chapter 2, RAY 2013–2022 was also a reform-oriented programme. The objective of reforms under RAY was to introduce the enabling provisions to address some of the causes leading to the creation of slums.

Scope

According to RAY Scheme Guidelines (Government of India, 2013, pp. 15–16), the reforms focused on the urban governance by way of improving capacities, bringing in fiscal prudence, creation of land bank, introduction of simplified processes and procedures for the following:

- Creating affordable housing stock
- Bringing in inclusive planning
- Providing security of tenure to slum dwellers

Driving on the experience of JNNURM in providing the BSUP, RAY introduced two categories of reforms—the mandatory reforms and the optional reforms.

Mandatory Reforms

The mandatory reforms provided legal empowerment to the urban poor and ensured the supply of land and fiscal resources for the provision of basic services to improve quality of life and mainstreaming urban poor so that incidence of slum formation was minimised. These reforms included the following:

1. Commitment and willingness to assign mortgageable and renewable, long-term (15 years) inheritable lease rights to slum dwellers who have been a resident of the slum for more than 5 years.
2. Reservation of 15% of residential FAR/FSI or 35% of DUs for EWS/LIG categories, whichever is higher, with a system of cross-subsidisation in all future housing projects in accordance with guidelines to be prescribed by MoHUPA.
3. A non-lapsable earmarking of 25% of the budget of the municipality to provide basic services to the urban poor.
4. Creating and establishing a municipal cadre for social/community development and urban poverty alleviation during the plan period.

The Government of India was serious about giving property rights to urban poor, and prepared a draft Model Property Right to Slum Dwellers Act, 2011, and sent to all states and UTs for their comments and suggestions. This model act had four important provisions: (a) every landless person living in slums in any urban area shall be entitled to a dwelling space at an affordable cost; (b) to ensure women empowerment, the legal entitlement shall be given in the name of the female head of the household or in the joint name of the male head of the household and his wife; (c) to check the misuse of the dwelling space, so provided, the draft provides that the dwelling space shall not be sold or mortgaged for the purpose of raising housing loan and (d) the Act provides for constitution of the City/Urban Area Slum Redevelopment Committee for carrying out functions specified and constitution of Slum Redevelopment Authority for monitoring the implementation of the Act.

Optional Reforms

The optional reforms were focused at providing enabling climate to promote affordable housing stock and covered the following:

1. Formulation of state policy for affordable housing
2. Amendments of the master plans to provide for inclusive growth through inclusionary zoning and other measures for inclusive development
3. Simplification of the processes and procedures of sanctioning buildings
4. Simplification of building bye-laws concerning development and housing projects to provide single window-based quick approvals in order to reduce transaction costs
5. Amendments in the Rent Control Act balancing the interest of landlords and tenants

The states and UTs were required to indicate their commitment to and timeline for the implementation of these reforms.

Reform Incentive Fund

With a view to encouraging states and UTs to take up optional reforms, a Reform Incentive Fund (RIF) was constituted. RIF was constituted out of funds remaining unutilised by states/UTs against their allocation for initial three years from the date of approval of the scheme. The states/UTs that successfully carried out the optional reforms were eligible to pose projects for funding under this fund after three years of implementation of the scheme (Government of India, 2013, pp. 14–15).

Reforms Under AMRUT

Background

As discussed earlier in this chapter, the reform process of JNNURM followed by RAY ended, basically as a mere statement of commitment to follow reforms given by the state government or ULBs. It did not give positive and tangible results. As noted by CAG (2012) and Thornton (2011), the state government/ULBs could not actually achieve the committed reforms as envisaged under JNNURM. In some cases, such as administrative reforms, the ULBs could not understand the basic intent of the reforms. The linking of reforms with the release of funds could also not be successful and caused delays and disinterest among ULBs towards the Mission.

Objective

The objectives of the reforms under AMRUT, introduced in 2015, are to improve service delivery, mobilise resources and to make municipal functioning more transparent and functionaries more accountable (MoUD, 2015a, p. 6). It is a CSS and the total outlay is of ₹50,000 crore for five years (2015–2020).

Coverage

As mentioned in Chapter 2, AMRUT covers 500 cities and includes a set of 11 reforms. Learning from the mistakes of JNNURM, AMRUT reforms have specified 'milestones' and 'timelines' as given in Annexure 4.2. The eleven reforms are as follows:

1. E-governance
2. Constitution and professionalisation of municipal cadre (new)
3. Augmenting double entry accounting
4. Urban planning and city-level plans (new)
5. Devolution of funds and functions
6. Review of building bye-laws
7. Set up of financial intermediary at the state level (new)
8. (a) Municipal tax and fees improvement and (b) improvement in levy and collection of user charges
9. Credit rating (new)
10. Energy and water audit (new)
11. SBM (new)

This list includes five reforms that are in continuation with those introduced by JNNURM and covers e-governance, augmentation of DEAS in ULBs, devolution of functions as per the Twelfth Schedule (Annexure 4.1), review of building bye-laws and improvement in municipal taxes and fees coverage and improvement in levy and collection of user charges.

The new reforms include the constitution and professionalisation of municipal cadre; urban planning and preparation of city-level plans; setting up of financial intermediary at the state level and the introduction of systems for credit rating; energy and water audit and management of waste. These reforms under AMRUT, however, are more result-oriented as each reform has a set of milestones and respective implementation timeline to meet. For example, as given at serial number 4 in Annexure 4.2, the reforms for urban planning and preparation of city level plans, under AMRUT, include the following seven milestones and timeline to meet.

AMRUT Reforms for Urban Planning and City-level Plans: Milestones and Timeline to Meet

Milestones	Timeline (Months)
1. Preparation of the master plan using geographical information system (GIS)	48
2. Preparation of SLIPs and SAAP	6
3. Establish urban development authorities	36
4. Make action plan to progressively increase green cover in cities to 15% in 5 years	6
5. Develop at least one children park in the city every year	Every 12
6. Establish a system for maintaining parks, playground and recreational areas relying on PPPP model	12
7. Make a state-level policy to implement the parameters given in National Mission for Sustainable Habitat	24

Source: Government of India (2015).

Since the financing pattern of AMRUT (see Chapter 6) includes the Central Government grant which is limited to one-third to 50% of the project cost, the state governments/ULBs are required to raise rest of the funds through pool-financing, access to external funds or floating municipal bonds or private investment. Accordingly, there are new reform such as setting up of financial intermediary at state level and making it operational and introduction of system of credit rating of the ULBs.

AMRUT reforms may be called as the new *avatar* of JNNURM reforms with a difference. The difference is that JNNURM was a reform-linked mission where release of funds was tied up with compliance of reforms, while AMRUT reforms are incentive-driven where 10% of the annual budget will be released, as incentive, for achieving milestones and implementation within the timeline set for reforms by the state governments/ULBs. This makes 90% fund freely available to complete the projects and meet administrative and office expenses without delays (Chapter 6). This approach appears to be more practical and efficient.

On the basis of their achievements, in September 2015, 19 states and 1 UT were rewarded with the performance incentive for promoting urban reforms under AMRUT for the year 2015–2016. The focus of reforms during the year 2015–2016 was e-governance, double entry accounting, improvement in the collection of municipal tax and user charges, energy and water audit and single window clearance. Tamil Nadu and Chandigarh topped the list of performing states/UTs. The focus for 2016–2017 is online building plan permission in all the 53 cities with million-plus population, use of energy efficient pumps, reuse of treated water and planning for urban flood mitigation (MoUD, 2015b).

For financing urban renewal projects through loans (Chapter 6), creditworthiness of ULB is a precondition. Accordingly, credit rating of ULBs has been added as a new reform under AMRUT. This will enable them to issue municipal bonds to raise resources from the financial market. The process has already started in most of the 500 mission cities.

Implementation of AMRUT Reforms

According to the office memorandum (MoUD, 2017a), the status of the implementation of two AMRUT reforms—credit rating and energy efficiency in water pumps and street lights—in case of eight states is as shown in Table 4.6.

In March 2017, 'investment grade' (up to BBB⁻) credit rating was awarded to 94 ULBs, spread over 14 states in the country. The top ranking ULBs were NDMC, Navi Mumbai and Pune with AA+ rating (Annexure 4.3). This rating has injected enormous confidence in ULBs. According to Vandana Ramnani (2017), cities with A+ and above rating are planning to raise from the market about ₹50,000 crore. These include NDMC, SMC and Greater Visakhapatnam Municipal Corporation (GVMC).

Credit ratings are assigned to ULBs on the basis of an assessment of the assets and liabilities, revenue streams, resources available for capital investments, double entry accounting practice and other governance practices, which is prepared by an independent agency.

Table 4.6 Implementation of AMRUT Reforms by Eight States (April 2017)

State	No. of Mission Cities Total	Credit Rating In Progress	Credit Rating Awarded	Energy Efficiency Water Pumps	Energy Efficiency Street Lights
Telangana	12	8	4	1	12
Tamil Nadu	28	28	0	0	0
Uttar Pradesh	61	61	0	61	0
Manipur	1	0	0	0	0
Chhattisgarh	9	7	2	9	4
Maharashtra	44	24	10	0	0
Delhi	4	0	1	0	3
Assam	4	1	0	0	1

Source: Based upon MoUD (2017a).

During 2016–2017, 20 states/UTs had achieved milestones and implementation timeline set for reforms and were awarded the reform incentive totalling ₹400 crore (Table 4.7).

Swachh Bharat Mission: Social Reform

SBM is an initiative for social reform in Indian society. It aims at creating an enabling environment for a *jan andolan* (people's movement) to achieve 100% ODF society. SBM also promotes 100% collection and scientific processing of municipal solid waste by the ULBs. The mission has impacted the society and brought in changes in habits. In some cases, revolt by females is seen when they refused to marry to a person who does not have a toilet in the house. The evidence of this social transformation may be indirectly derived from the fact that a recent movie, *Toilet: A Love Story*, made on such a theme was liked by the people and was successful at the box office.

Until December 2016, a total of ₹1,628 had been released to the states. Up to the year 2016–2017, two states, Gujarat and

Table 4.7 Implementation of AMRUT Reforms and Award of Reform Incentive to States and UTs (30 September 2016)

S.No.	States/UTs	Amount Awarded as Reform Incentive (₹ Crore)
1.	Andhra Pradesh	13.62
2.	Bihar	15.04
3.	Chandigarh	0.69
4.	Chhattisgarh	13.00
5.	Goa	1.34
6.	Gujarat	26.72
7.	Himachal Pradesh	3.54
8.	Jharkhand	7.28
9.	Karnataka	29.92
10.	Kerala	15.00
11.	Madhya Pradesh	33.45
12.	Maharashtra	**45.47**
13.	Mizoram	**1.63**
14.	Odisha	**10.27**
15.	Rajasthan	20.80
16.	Tamil Nadu	61.34
17.	Telangana	10.73
18.	Tripura	1.70
19.	Uttar Pradesh	63.47
20.	West Bengal	24.89
	Total	399.99
		Say 400.00

Source: MoUD (2017a).

Andhra Pradesh, and one UT, Chandigarh, have become ODF. It is reported that a total of 545 cities/towns have declared themselves ODF and in case of 468 cities/town, this claim has been certified through third-party certification. It is expected that 739 ULBs will become ODF by March 2017 (MoUD, 2017b, p. 25). Taking into account that India has about 8,000 urban centres, the achievement of the SBM is just about 10%. However, it is a good beginning in social transformation and will continue to have public and government support in future also.

Reforms under PMAY

PMAY (U) does not include reforms. However, it includes six conditions that are mandatory and the states/UTs are required to agree to fulfil these for participating in the mission and to avail of financial assistance from central government.

Objective

Since availability of land is one of the most important components in providing housing to all, including weaker sections, the objective of these mandatory conditions is to create a conducive environment to facilitate the growth of housing sector, including affordable housing.

Mandatory Conditions

The mandatory conditions, imposed by PMAY, to be implemented by the states/UTs, include the following (Government of India, 2015b, p. 15):

1. To make suitable changes in the procedure and rules for changing land use from agriculture to non-agriculture in such a manner that it obviates the need for a separate permission if land already falls in the residential zone earmarked in the master plan of city or area
2. To prepare/amend the master plans earmarking land for affordable housing
3. To put in place a system to ensure single window and time-bound clearance for layout approval and building permissions at ULB level
4. To adopt the approach of deemed building permission and layout approval on the basis of pre-approved layouts and building plans for EWS/LIG housing or exempt approval for houses below certain built-up area or plot area
5. To either legislate or amend existing rental laws on the lines of model Tenancy Act being prepared by MoUD

6. To provide additional FAR/FSI/TDR and relax density norms for slum redevelopment and low cost housing, if so required

Technology Sub-Mission

PMAY also promotes a reform in the form of adoption of modern, innovative and green technologies and building material for faster and quality construction of houses. To implement this, a technology sub-mission under the Mission would be set up which will perform the following functions:

1. Facilitate preparation and adoption of layout designs and building plans suitable for various geo-climatic zones
2. Assist states/cities in deploying disaster-resistant and environment-friendly technologies
3. Coordinate with various regulatory and administrative bodies for mainstreaming and up-scaling the deployment of modern construction technologies and material in place of conventional construction and also coordinate with other agencies working in green and energy efficient technologies, climate changes, etc.
4. Work on following aspects:
    i. Design and planning concepts
    ii. Innovative technologies and materials
    iii. Green buildings using natural resources, ensuring adequate sunlight and air
    iv. Earthquake and other disaster resistant technologies and designs
5. Identify the state- or region-specific needs of technologies and designs for support under this sub-mission
6. Encourage partnerships with willing Indian Institutes of Technology (IITs), National Institutes of Technology (NITs) and planning and architecture institutes for developing technical solutions, capacity building and handholding of states and cities

Reforms under Smart Cities Mission

Smart Cities Mission, in my opinion, has indirectly introduced two reforms in project management; these are as follows:

1. Competitive Cooperative Federalism and City Challenge
2. Special Purpose Vehicle (SPV)

Competitive Cooperative Federalism and City Challenge

The current NDA Government is following a principle of 'cooperative federalism' which recognises that strong states make strong nation and has empowered them to prepare and implement plans of their development. Smart Cities Mission has introduced a reform in the form of healthy competition in the selection process for central assistance. Smart Cities Mission calls it Competitive Cooperative Federalism. There were two stages involved in the selection process:

- Stage 1. Shortlisting of cities by states
- Stage 2. The City Challenge

In the Stage 1, the total number of 100 smart cities was distributed among the states and UTs based upon an equitable criteria, giving equal weightage to urban population and the number of statutory towns in the state/UT. It was followed by an intra-state competition where all cities in the state competed on the basis of scoring criteria (see MoUD, 2015c, pp. 25–32) and in accordance with the total number of smart cities allocated to their state/UT. State government selected the names of the potential smart cities. Based on recommendations of the states/UTs, the list of potential 100 smart cities was announced by MoUD.

In Stage 2, it was an all India competition among the 100 smart cities identified by states/UTs in Stage 1. It was termed as the 'City Challenge'. Each city prepared the smart city proposal (SCP), following a participative process and a set of criteria (see MoUD, 2015c, pp. 33–36) and submitted it to the Evaluation Committee of MoUD. In the first round, 20 cities were selected as smart cities. Those who could not be selected in the first round improved their SCP and submitted for the next round of selection. So far, 60 cities have been selected.

This may be called as the beginning of a new culture of healthy competition among states as well as the ULBs. It ensures equity in Stage 1 which is essential in a democratic set-up. It promotes pan-India inter-city competition in Stage 2 which ensures a good quality output.

Special Purpose Vehicle

The Smart Cities Mission is being implemented through SPVs (see Chapter 6 and Annexure 6.2). Almost all the 60 smart cities selected so far have set up their respective SPVs, as limited company, under the Companies Act, 2013. This is an institutional reform which replaces ULBs for the implementation of smart cities. It undermines the role of ULBs and sidelines them in the process of city building. These SPVs are being opposed by many states and their ULBs that feel competent enough to implement the Smart Cities Mission.

Summing Up

Reforms improve urban governance and ease the administrative, legal and technical bottlenecks to facilitate the process of urban renewal. JNNURM may be credited as the first reform-oriented programme in the urban sector. Looking critically, JNNURM could not do anything other than creating awareness regarding the need for introducing efficiency, accountability and transparency in functioning of ULBs.

According to the CAG (2012), the state government and the ULBs could not fully implement the envisaged reforms as per their commitment. Thus, the objective of improving institutional, financial and governance structure of ULBs to make them efficient, accountable and transparent could not be achieved as envisaged under the JNNURM. There may be several reasons. To implement 23 reforms in a period of 7 years was a bit too ambitious. Some of the reforms, such as those that required amendments in laws and devolution of duties and functions to ULBs, required political will, leadership and administrative support which seemed to be lacking, especially in case of devolution of functions to ULBs as per the 74th CAA. In some cases, such as structural reforms, there was a lack of clarity. There was insufficient political will to support reform agenda, especially PPP and proper pricing of services (Vaidya, 2009). Introduction of user charges required change in the mind-set of the people and politicians which requires a long time.

Some of the states had performed better than others. If one goes by the number of reforms implemented and included in the JNNURM Best Practices, Odisha tops the list. It is followed by Uttarakhand, Andhra Pradesh, Uttar Pradesh and Karnataka (Government of India, n.d.).

The JNNURM ended on 31 March 2012. However, 'the reforms were far from complete by the end of the Mission period' (CAG, 2012). On the recommendation of CAG, an extension of two years up to 31 March 2014 was granted to ULBs by MoUD to complete the reform process already started. Through the Office Memorandum of the MoUD dated 12 May 2015, a further extension was granted up to 31 March 2017 for the completion of all projects sanctioned up to March 2012.

In 2013, the reform agenda of JNNURM was carried forward by RAY (2013–2022) which reduced the number of reforms to nine (four mandatory and five optional) and created a RIF to give fiscal incentives to encourage state governments to take up the optional reforms.

With change in government in the 2014 general elections, the Prime Minister Narendra Modi gave a new mantra—'Reform, Perform, Transform'—and the agenda of urban transformation continues under the new regime. Housing has now become a part of PMAY and the other projects related to urban transformation are being tackled under AMRUT (see Chapter 2).

PMAY-HFA (U) by 2022 does not include any urban reforms directly. However, it imposes six mandatory conditions to be fulfilled by the state governments for the release of funds. Since these conditions create a conducive climate for the growth of housing sector, they are treated as reforms and discussed in this chapter.

AMRUT, launched in 2015, is a reform-oriented programme of urban renewal covering 500 cities. Unlike JNNURM, it has much reduced number of reforms (i.e., 11). These include five JNNRUM reforms and six new reforms. The new reforms include efficient urban planning, energy and water efficiency, cleanliness, establishment of financial institutions, credit rating of ULBs and constitution of municipal cadre. Implementation of AMRUT reforms is not linked with the release of funds as was the case of JNNURM. This is one of the major differences between the two missions. AMRUT reforms are incentive-driven and time/target-oriented. Attaining the milestone and meeting the timeline entitles ULBs to incentive reward. It is a new approach and appears to set a new work culture and healthy competition among ULBs. Urban reforms have now extended to 500 cities under AMRUT which will strengthen the process and coverage of urban renewal in India.

Smart Cities Mission has introduced a competitive approach to development where each state and city competes in a healthy manner and prospers together, contributing to national development. The SPVs introduced the institutional mechanism for implementing the Smart Cities Mission, if replicated for all other projects in future, will kill the ULBs and will require review.

Annexure 4.1 Twelfth Schedule (Article 243W) to the Constitution (74th Amendment) Act, 1992

1. Urban planning including town planning
2. Regulation of land-use and construction of buildings
3. Planning for economic and social development
4. Roads and bridges
5. Water supply for domestic, industrial and commercial purposes
6. Public health, sanitation, conservancy and solid waste management
7. Fire services
8. Urban forestry, protection of the environment and promotion of ecological aspects
9. Safeguarding the interests of weaker sections of society, including the handicapped and the mentally retarded
10. Slum improvement and upgradation

(continued)

(continued)

11. Urban poverty alleviation
12. Provision of urban amenities and facilities such as parks, gardens, playgrounds
13. Promotion of cultural, educational and aesthetic aspects
14. Burials and burial grounds; cremations, cremation ghats/grounds and electric crematoria
15. Cattle pounds, prevention of cruelty to animals
16. Vital statistics including registration of births and deaths
17. Public amenities including street lighting, parking lots, bus stops and public conveniences
18. Regulation of slaughter houses and tanneries

Source: Government of India (1992). Constitution (Seventy-fourth) Amendment Act 1992. Available at http://indiacode.nic.in/coiweb/amend/amend74.htm accessed on 09-02-2018

Annexure 4.2 Reforms, Milestones and Timeline Under AMRUT for Mission Cities

S. No.	Type	Milestones	Implementation Timeline (Months)
1.	E-Governance	**Digital ULBs** 1. Creation of ULB website	6
		2. Publication of e-newsletter: Digital India Initiatives	6
		3. Support Digital India (ducting to be done on PPP mode or by the ULB itself)	6
		Coverage with E-MAAS (from the date of hosting the software) • Registration of birth, death and marriage • Water and sewerage charges • Grievance redressal • Property tax	24

S. No.	Type	Milestones	Implementation Timeline (Months)
		• Advertisement tax • Issuance of licenses • Building permissions • Mutations • Pay roll • Pension	
		• e-procurement • Personnel staff management • Project management	36
2.	Constitution and professionalisation of municipal cadre	1. Establishment of municipal cadre	24
		2. Cadre-linked training	24
		3. Policy for engagement of interns in ULBs and implementation	12
		4. The state will prepare a policy for right-sizing the number of municipal functionaries depending on, say, population of the ULB, generation of internal resources and expenditure on salaries	36
3.	Augmenting double entry accounting	1. Complete migration to DEAS and obtaining an audit certificate to the effect from FY2012–2013 onward.	12
		2. Appointment of internal auditor	24
		3. Publication of annual financial statement on website	Every 12
4.	Urban planning and city level Plans	1. Preparation of the master plan using GIS	48
		2. Preparation of SLIP SAAP	6

(continued)

(continued)

S. No.	Type	Milestones	Implementation Timeline (Months)
		3. Establish urban development authorities	36
		4. Make action plan to progressively increase Green Cover in cities to 15% in 5 years	6
		5. Develop at least one Children Park every year in AMRUT cities	Every 12
		6. Establish a system for maintaining of parks, playground and recreational areas relying on PPPP model	12
		7. Make a state-level policy to implement the parameters given in National Mission for Sustainable Habitat	24
5.	Devolution of funds and functions	1. Ensure transfer of 14th FC devolution to ULBs	6
		2. Appointment of State Finance Commission (SFC) and making decisions	12
		3. Implementation of SFC recommendations within timeline	18
		4. Transfer of all 18 functions to ULBs	12
6.	Review of building by-laws	1. Revision of building bye-laws periodically	12
		2. State to formulate a policy and action plan for having a solar rooftop in all buildings having an area greater than 500 sq. m and all public buildings	12–24

S. No.	Type	Milestones	Implementation Timeline (Months)
		3. State to formulate a policy and action plan for having rainwater harvesting structures in all commercial, public buildings and new buildings on plots of 300 sq. m and above	12–24
		4. Create single window clearance for all approvals to give building permissions	12
7.	Set-up financial intermediary at state level	1. Establish and operationalise financial intermediary—pool finance, access external funds, float municipal bonds	12–18
8.(a)	Municipal tax and fees Improvement	1. At least 90% coverage	12
		2. At least 90% collection	
		3. Make a policy to periodically revise property tax and to levy charges and other fees	
		4. Post Demand Collection Book (DCB) of tax details on the website	
		5. Achieve full potential of advertisement revenue by making a policy for destination specific potential having dynamic pricing module	
8.(b)	Improvement in levy and collection of user charges	1. Adopt a policy on user charges for individual and institutional assessments in which a differential	12

(continued)

(continued)

S. No.	Type	Milestones	Implementation Timeline (Months)
		rate is charged for water use and adequate safeguards are included to take care of the interests of the vulnerable	
		2. Make action plan to reduce water losses to less than 20% and publish on the website	
		3. Separate accounts for user charges	
		4. At least 90% billing	
		5. At least 90% collection	
9.	**Credit rating**	1. Complete the credit ratings of the ULBs	18
10.	**Energy and water audit**	1. Energy (street lights) and water audit (including non-revenue water or losses audit)	12
		2. Making STPs and WTPs more energy efficient	12
		3. Optimize energy consumption in street lights by using energy efficient lights and increasing reliance on renewable energy	
		4. Give incentives for green buildings (e.g., rebate in property tax or charges connected to building permission/development charges)	24
11.	**Swachh Bharat Mission**	1. Elimination of open defecation	36
		2. Waste collection (100%)	

S. No.	Type	Milestones	Implementation Timeline (Months)
		3. Transportation of waste (100%)	
		4. Scientific disposal (100%)	

Source: MoUD (2015a, Annexure 1, pp. 29–30).

Annexure 4.3 Investment Grade Credit Ratings of Urban Local Bodies in India, 2017

Credit Rating		Cities/Towns
Investment grade	AA⁺ (3)	New Delhi Municipal Council (NDMC), Navi Mumbai and Pune
	AA (3)	Ahmedabad, Visakhapatnam and Greater Hyderabad Municipal Corporation
	AA⁻ (4)	Surat, Nashik, Thane and Pimpri-Chinchwad
	A⁺ (5)	Indore, Kishanganj (Rajasthan), Kolkata, Vadodara (Gujarat) and Warangal (Telangana)
	A (1)	Jhunjhunu (Rajasthan)
	A⁻ (8)	Alwar, Bhiwadi, Beawar, Jaipur (Rajasthan), Bhopal, Jabalpur (Madhya Pradesh), Mira-Bhayandar (Maharashtra) and New Town, Rajarhat (West Bengal)
	BBB⁺ (5)	Ajmer, Kota and Udaipur (Rajasthan), Ludhiana (Punjab) and Jamnagar (Gujarat)
	BBB (14)	Kakinada, Anantapur, Kurnool and Tirupati (Andhra Pradesh), Davanagere and Hubbali-Dharwar(Karnataka), Kochi and Trivandrum (Kerala), Panaji (Goa), Kolhapur and Nagpur(Maharashtra), Jodhpur, Nagaur and Tonk (Rajasthan)
	BBB⁻ (12)	Amaravati (Maharashtra), Belgavi (Karnataka), Bharuch and Bhavnagar (Gujarat), Bharatpur, Bhilwara, Bikaner and Hanumangarh (Rajasthan), Chittor and Cuddapah (Andhra Pradesh), Cuttack (Odisha), Ranchi (Jharkhand)

(continued)

(continued)

Credit Rating		Cities/Towns
BB+ (14)		Proddatur, Nandyal and Nellore (Andhra Pradesh), Kollam and Kozhikode (Kerala), Kalol, Nadiad and Navsarai (Gujarat), Nanded and Solapur (Maharashtra), Gangapur City, Dhaulpur, Pali and Sawai Madhopur (Rajasthan)
	BB (14)	Adoni and Tadipatri (Andhra Pradesh), Dwarka (Gujarat), Aizawl (Mizoram), Thrissur (Kerala), Berhampur, Rourkela and Sambalpur (Odisha), Bundi, Churu, Chittorgarh, Hindaun, Jodhpur and Sujangarh (Rajasthan)
	BB⁻ (7)	Adityapur, Chas, Deoghar and Giridih (Jharkhand), Mori (Gujarat), Baran and Jhalawar (Rajasthan)
B+ (3)		Baripada and Puri (Odisha) and Hazaribagh (Jharkhand)
B (1)		Bhadrak (Odisha)

Source: MoHUPA (2017).

Note: As per the reforms timelines suggested by the MoUD, 39 cities that have credit ratings below the investment grade (BBB-) have to undertake necessary interventions for improving the ratings in one year.

References

CAG. (2012). *Performance audit of Jawaharlal Nehru National Urban Renewal Mission*. New Delhi: Comptroller and Auditor General.

DMU-JNNURM. (2013a). *Progress report, 31 March 2013*. New Delhi: Ministry of Urban Development. Retrieved 17 March 2014, from http://urbanindia.nic.in/DMU/JNNURM/DMU-JNNURM.pdf

———. (2013b). *Progress Report, 31 December 2013*. New Delhi: Ministry of Urban Development. Retrieved 17 March 2014, from http://urbanindia.nic.in/DMU/JNNURM/DMU-JNNURM.pdf

Government of India. (n.d.). *JNNURM best practices in urban reforms*. Retrieved 4 June 2015, from jnnurm.nic.in/reforms.html

Government of India. (2013). *Rajiv Awas Yojana (RAY), Scheme Guidelines 2013-2022*, Ministry of Housing and Urban Poverty Alleviation, New Delhi.

MoHUPA. (2005). *Jawaharlal Nehru National Urban Renewal Mission: Guidelines for Basic Services to Urban Poor (BSUP) and Integrated Housing*

& *Slum Development Programme (IHSDP)*. New Delhi: Government of India.
MoHUPA. (2015). *Pradhan Mantri Awas Yojana, Housing for All (Urban): Scheme Guidelines*. New Delhi: Government of India.
MoHUPA. (2017, March). *Credit rating of urban local bodies gain momentum*. Press Release, Press Information Bureau, Government of India, New Delhi. Retrieved 22 December 2017, from http://pib.nic.in/newsite/PrintRelease.aspx?relid=159951
MoUD. (2015a). *Atal Mission for Rejuvenation and Urban Transformation (AMRUT): Mission Statement and Guidelines*. New Delhi: Government of India.
———. (2015b, December). *20 states/UTs rewarded for promoting urban reforms under Atal Mission during 2015–16*. Ministry of Urban Development Press Release, Press Information Bureau, Government of India, New Delhi.
———. (2015c). *Smart city, mission transform nation: Mission statement and guidelines*. New Delhi: Government of India.
———. (2017a). *Office memorandum, no. K-16015/04/2017/AMRUT-II*. New Delhi: Government of India.
———. (2017b). *Annual report 2016–2017*. New Delhi: Government of India.
Ramnani, Vandana. (2017). Over ₹50K cr of muni bonds may be on offer soon as 26 cities get ready to hit mkt. *Money Control*. Retrieved 8 August 2017, from http://www.moneycontrol.com/news/business/real-estate/over-rs-50k-cr-of-muni-bonds-may-be-on-offer-soon-as-26-cities-get-ready-to-hit-mkt-2317907.html
Thornton, Grant. (2011). *Appraisal of Jawaharlal Nehru National Urban Renewal Mission Final Report*, vol. I. New Delhi: Grant Thornton India.
Vaidya, Chetan. (2009). *Urban issues, reforms and way forward in India* (Working Paper No. 4/2009-DEA). New Delhi: Department of Economic Affairs, Ministry of Finance.

CHAPTER 5

Tools and Techniques of Urban Renewal

Introduction

The first principle of the urban renewal (Chapter 1) is that it should be humane and ensure social justice. It should be a participative process which is socially acceptable, legally tenable, physically feasible and economically sustainable. To accomplish these expectations, effective and innovative tools and techniques are required, which include the following:

1. Legal tools
2. Spatial planning tools and techniques
3. Techniques for attracting community participation
4. Implementation and monitoring tools and techniques
5. Outcome assessment tools
6. Resource mobilisation tools

The focus of this chapter is limited to the legal, spatial planning, community participation, implementation and monitoring and outcome assessment of tools and techniques. The tools and techniques of resource mobilisation are discussed in Chapter 6.

Legal Tools

Urban renewal involves changes in property ownership rights and land uses. Legal support to such needs is of utmost importance and an understanding of the provisions of various available legal tools is necessary.

In India, implementation of several renewal programmes has failed due to inadequate and weak legislative framework and deficient guidelines (Chotani and Mallick, 2014; Mehra, 2014). Analysing the town planning acts of some of the states such as Gujarat, Maharashtra, Mizoram, Arunachal Pradesh, Odisha, Goa, Tamil Nadu, Andhra Pradesh and Madhya Pradesh (Table 5.1), Chotani and Mallick (2014) observe that these acts mainly address the problems of city expansion and the regulation of urban renewal is available, in some cases, either as a part of definitions or master plan, zonal plan or town planning schemes. Some of these plans also provide legal support for the urban renewal strategies such as redevelopment, relocation of population or industry and clearance of slums.

As indicated in Table 5.1, direct mention of redevelopment is available in Maharashtra Slum Areas (Improvement, Clearance and Redevelopment) Act, 1971; Delhi Development Authority Act, 1957; Jaipur Development Authority Act, 1982; and Himachal Pradesh Town and Country Planning Act, 1977. Provision for the redevelopment of an area is given indirectly as 'relaying out of land' in Gujarat Town Planning Act, 1976; Andhra Pradesh Town Planning Act, 1920; and Madhya Pradesh Town and Country Planning Act, 1973. The indirect mention of redevelopment of an area as 're-erection/ reconstruction of buildings' is available in Odisha Town Planning and Improvement Trust Act, 1956; Punjab Regional and Town Planning Act, 1995; and Rajasthan Urban Improvement Act, 1959.

Maharashtra Regional and Town Planning Act, 1968; Mizoram Urban and Regional Development Act, 1990; Arunachal Pradesh Urban and Country Planning Act, 2007; and Goa Town and Country Planning Act, 1974, provide legal support for the 'relocation of population or industry' as a strategy of urban renewal. Statutory

Table 5.1 *Statutory Provisions for Urban Renewal in Some of the Town Planning and Development Acts in India*

S. No.	Acts	Nature of Urban Renewal Provisions/Strategy	Plan/Document Where Provision/Mention Is Made
1.	The Delhi Development Act, 1957	Indication of areas required for development or redevelopment	As part of Master Plan/Zonal Plan contents
2.	The Gujarat Town Planning and Urban Development Act, 1976	Laying out or relaying out of land either vacant or already built-up	As part of Town Planning Scheme
3.	The Maharashtra Regional and Town Planning Act, 1966	• Redevelopment of water front area • Relocation of population or industry from over populated and industrially congested areas • Laying out or relaying out of land either vacant or already built upon	As part of Regional Plan
	Maharashtra Slum Areas (Improvement, Clearance and Redevelopment) Act, 1971	• Slum rehabilitation area, SRA • Slum clearance and redevelopment	Part of definition mechanism for preparation and implementation of slum rehabilitation scheme given in the Act
4.	The Mizoram Urban and Regional Development Act, 1990	• Relocation of population • Laying out or relaying out of land either vacant or already built-up • Resettlement of villages and growth centres inhabitants, etc.	• As part of definitions given in the Act • As part of the contents of development scheme
5.	The Arunachal Pradesh Urban and Country Planning Act, 2007	Relocation of population	As part of definition given in the Act

Tools and Techniques of Urban Renewal 159

S. No.	Acts	Nature of Urban Renewal Provisions/Strategy	Plan/Document Where Provision/ Mention Is Made
6.	Odisha Town Planning and Improvement Trust Act, 1956	• Clearance of urban obsolescence • Rebuilding and Rehousing Scheme	• As part of the objectives of preparation of the Master Plan • As part of Improvement Scheme
7.	Goa Town and Country Planning Act, 1974	Relocation of population	Part of definitions
8.	The Uttar Pradesh (Regulation of Building Operation) Act, 1958	To re-erect building/ construction for second or subsequent time	Part of definition
9.	The Tamil Nadu Town and Country Planning Act, 1971	• Area of bad lay out or obsolete development • Reconstruction of buildings/relocation of population	• Part of definitions • Contents of the Master Plan
10.	The Andhra Pradesh Town Planning Act, 1920	Laying out or relaying out of land, either vacant or already built upon	Contents of Town Planning Scheme
	The Andhra Pradesh Urban Areas (Development) Act, 1975	Area required or declared for development or redevelopment	Contents of Zonal Development Plan
11.	Madhya Pradesh Town and Country Planning Act, 1973	Layout or relaying out of land, either vacant or already built upon	Contents of Zonal Plan
12.	The Punjab Scheduled Road and Controlled Areas Restriction of Unregulated Development Act, 1963 (extended to State of Haryana)	• Erection or re-erection of any building	• Contents of the Master Plan

(continued)

(continued)

S. No.	Acts	Nature of Urban Renewal Provisions/Strategy	Plan/Document Where Provision/ Mention Is Made
	Punjab Regional and Town Planning Act, 1995	• Erection or re-erection of any building • Redevelopment or renewal of specific areas	• Part of definitions • As part of contents of the Master Plan
13.	The Rajasthan Urban Improvement Act, 1959	Construction and reconstruction of buildings	Part of the contents of improvement schemes
	The Jaipur Development Authority Act, 1982	• Relocation of the population or industry from overpopulated and industrially congested areas • Redevelopment and improvement of existing built up areas	• As part of the contents of the Master Plan
14.	The Himachal Pradesh Town and Country Planning Act, 1977	Indication of badly lay out areas for redevelopment	Contents of Sectoral Plan

Source: Chotani and Mallick (2014).

provision for 'slum clearance' is available in Odisha Town Planning and Improvement Act, 1956, and Maharashtra Slum Areas (Improvement, Clearance and Redevelopment) Act, 1971.

In the process of urban renewal, it is required that statutory support

1. clearly defines due process to be followed at various stages of urban renewal;
2. empowers institutions and provides authority to plan and implement urban renewal programmes in an area;
3. regulates land matters such as pooling of land by different owners, redevelopment of the area, selling properties and transfer of ownership;
4. empowers the application of various urban renewal strategies and
5. authorises innovative approaches to fiscal resource mobilisation.

Looking objectively, it may be argued that the basic legal provision for the preparation of urban renewal plan is available through the master plans and other detailed plans emanating out of the master plan. DCRs, guidelines, schemes, incorporated in the master plans, in some states, also provide legal support to various requirements related to the urban renewal. Regulation No. 33(9), with its amendments, is considered as a comprehensive urban renewal regulation in Mumbai (Nangnure, 2014).

There's another set of questions: Which institution has the authority to plan and implement urban renewal projects? Should it be the state government, municipal corporation, development authority or any other agency? Probably, this lack of clarity is the main cause of such poor response to urban renewal in India. To illustrate the significance of institutional mechanism with full legal support, for defining powers and functions and other matters, it is worth noting that in Karnataka, with a view to protecting the world heritage site Hampi, an amendment to the Karnataka Town and Country Planning Act, 1961, was made to declare a heritage area as local planning area. After this amendment, Hampi was declared as local planning area and the Hampi World Heritage Area Management Authority Act, 2002 was introduced which paved the way for the constitution of an authority to conserve and manage Hampi. Similarly, to promote conservation of built and natural heritage in Old Delhi, the Shahjahanabad Redevelopment Corporation has been constituted as a non-profit company, limited by shares, under the Section 25 of the Companies Act, 1956.

As mentioned in Chapter 2, the Twelfth Schedule of 74th CAA includes slum improvement and upgradation at entry no. 10 (see Annexure 4.1). Urban renewal, therefore, is a constitutional obligation and the municipalities are the institutions empowered to prepare and implement the plans. But this has not happened. To implement the Smart Cities Mission (Chapter 6), SPVs are being constituted which is, again, not a permanent and reasonable solution.

For matters pertaining to land, it is highlighted that the Constitution of India provides for the right to property under Article 19 (I) (e) as a fundamental right. Article 19 guarantees to all citizens the right to 'acquire, hold and dispose of property' and Article 31 provides that 'no person shall be deprived of his property save by authority of law'. It also provided that compensation would be paid to a person whose property has been 'taken possession of or acquired for public purposes'. In addition, both the state government and the union government are empowered to enact laws for the 'acquisition or requisition of property' (Schedule VII, Entry 42, List III). Mehra (2014) argues that the process of redevelopment has to be exercised under these legal considerations. The fundamental legal tools of a redevelopment agency include the authority to acquire, develop and sell real property. This agency also needs the authority and obligation to relocate persons who have interests in the property acquired by the agency. Master plans also provide legal support on land issues such as pooling land by different owner for renewal purposes.

To undertake and carry out repair work in old buildings, construction of transit camps to provide temporary accommodation in cases of redevelopment projects and to acquire the old dilapidated buildings which are beyond repair, the legal provision is provided by Section 76 of the Maharashtra Housing and Area Development Act, 1976. Section 92 of this Act provides for the acquisition of buildings, at reasonable expense, which are beyond repairs or unfit for habitation and is dangerous or injurious to health and safety of the inhabitants.

As discussed in Chapter 6, there are eight sources of mobilisation of fiscal resource for urban renewal programmes. All these methods need legal support. The Municipal Acts empower the ULBs to levy various taxes. As regards to non-tax-based revenue sources, the power is derived from Town Planning Acts and Rules. For example, MPD-2021 under Para 3.3, has made provision for 'Accommodation Reservation (AR)' and granting 'TDRs' in case of social infrastructure projects. The same Para also provides for granting enhanced FAR for specified redevelopment areas.

In India, hardly any comprehensive plan of urban renewal is available. However, as mentioned in Chapter 2, there are a few isolated initiatives taken by local authorities of some cities such as Mumbai, Delhi and Hyderabad. Considering the recent thrust on urban renewal, there is, therefore, a need to prepare urban renewal plan within the framework of the Master Plan as its sub-plan so as to provide the necessary legal support.

Spatial Planning Tools and Techniques

The difference of recording, analysing, presenting and making decisions on the future course of action for urban transformation includes policies, programmes, processes, guidelines, norms and standards, spatial plans/land use plans/schemes and detailed project reports (DPRs). As shown in Figure 5.1, these tools are interlinked. Policies are implemented through programmes. Within the framework of a policy, there may be many programmes depending upon the need. Guidelines, within the framework of the policy, provide working details at each step of the redevelopment process. Within the framework of guidelines, schemes are framed with the help of spatial planning tools such as land use plan, thematic maps, norms and standards. For implementation, a DPR is made for each identified project. It is reiterated here that we are planning for the people and their participation at all stages of the decision-making process is essential and desirable.

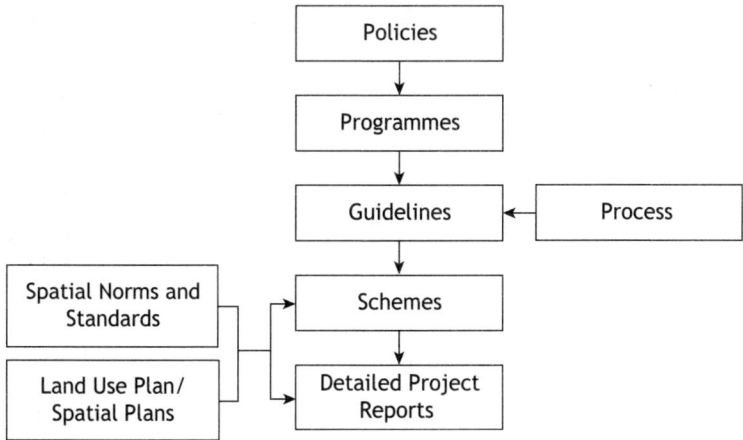

Figure 5.1 *Interrelationship Among Various Tools*

The policies and programmes of the urban renewal have already been discussed in detail in Chapters 2 and 3. This chapter, therefore, covers area redevelopment process, guidelines and schemes, spatial planning norms and standards and public participation.

Area Redevelopment Process

The SRA has evolved a process to be followed for all area redevelopment projects in Mumbai (Annexure 5.1). It presents a very good example of people's participation from mobilisation of majority (70%) support in stage 1 to draw of lots for allotment of tenements in stages 3 and 4 and land management from stage 5. This process promotes gender equality as—in the stage 5—the allotment of the tenement is given in the joint name of the head of the household and the spouse. Since it is practical, participatory, gender-sensitive and effective, the same may be adopted, with variations, if necessary, by the other urban renewal agencies as well. It is a five-stage process as shown in Figure 5.2 and summarised as under.

First Stage

It is the initial stage of the redevelopment process. Right from the word go, people participate in the process and mobilise support of at least 70% of the eligible (based upon the cut-off date as specified) slum dwellers to unite for the purpose of area redevelopment and form slum dwellers' cooperative housing society following the procedure and requirements as per Sections 1.1 and 1.2 of Annexure 5.1. The function of this society, in the first stage, is to (a) document the title of the land, get physical survey of the area with all structures measured, demarcated and numbered on the plan and also prepare a table showing house numbers, as per the plan, and the name of the occupant and (b) appoint a suitable developer by a general body resolution of the cooperative housing society.

The developer, during this first stage, performs two tasks: (a) enters into individual agreements with all the slum dwellers agreeing to participate in the scheme and (b) appoints professionals such as

Tools and Techniques of Urban Renewal 165

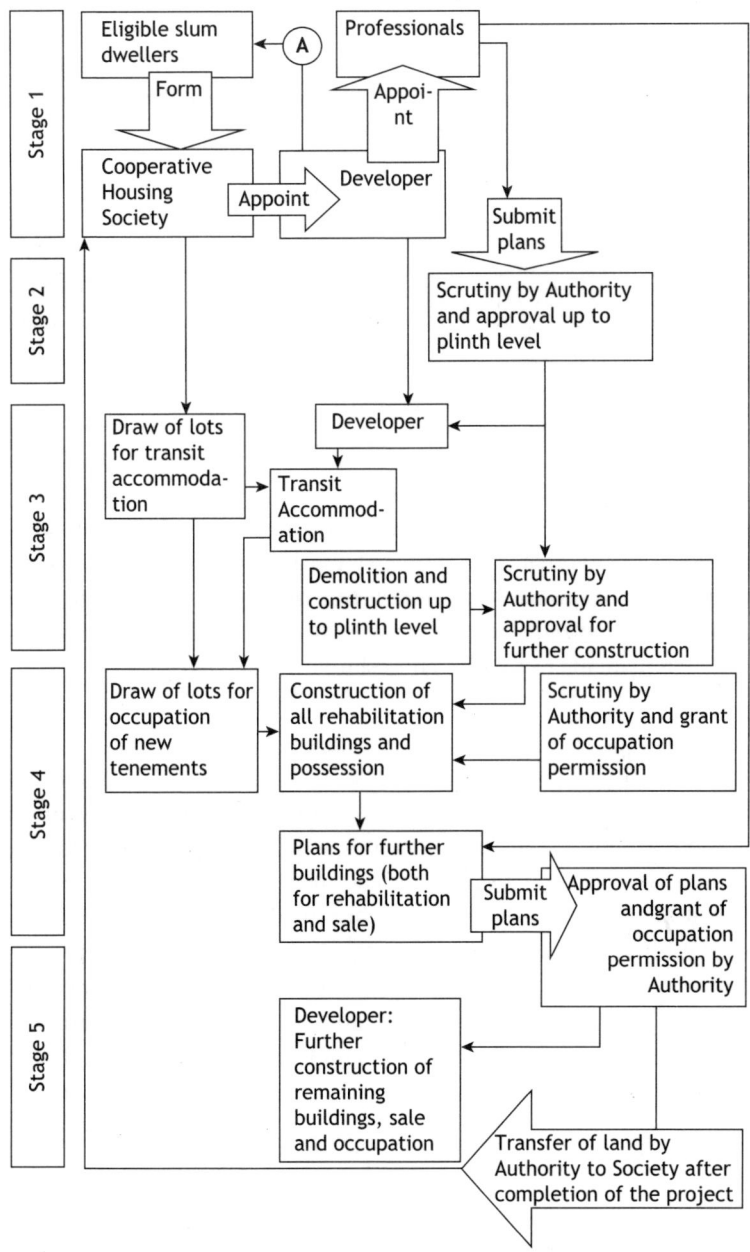

Figure 5.2 Steps in the Process of Redevelopment
Source: Based on Annexure 5.1.

architect/planner/licensed surveyor, structural engineer, etc., and gets all the required technical drawings and documents prepared from the appointed architect/planner who then, submits a proposal, enclosing requisite plans, annexure and documents to SRA.

Second Stage

This stage involves only SRA and the developer. During this stage, the SRA carries out initial scrutiny, as per procedure (Sections 2.1, 2.2 of Annexure 5.1), of the proposal submitted by the architect/planner and, if the proposal is in order, works out the amount of scrutiny fee to be paid by the developer.

The developer pays the scrutiny fee. The SRA, following the laid down process and getting certification from the competent authorities (Sections 2.4 to 2.7 of Annexure 5.1), grants the approvals and commencement certificates to the first rehabilitation building for work up to plinth. It should be noted here that the intention of this process at this stage is to *ensure* the construction of the rehabilitation buildings having tenements to be allotted to slum dwellers first.

Third Stage

During this stage, all the three players in the process—the cooperative housing society, the builder and the SRA—are active. The cooperative housing society (a) draws lots for allotment of the tenements in the transit accommodation to the members who are ready to participate in the scheme and (b) also draws lots for the non-participating members for the remaining tenements. This draw is to indicate to the non-participating members the intention of the cooperative housing society to allot tenements to them if they join the society by becoming members.

The slum dwellers who do not agree to participate in the scheme are given notice by the cooperative housing society, stating the tenement allotment details and requesting them to participate in the scheme. If these members do not agree to participate within 15 days of the approval of the proposal, they are physically evicted from the site under the provisions of Sections 33 and 38 of Maharashtra Slum Areas (Improvement, Clearance and Redevelopment) Act, 1971, to ensure that there is no obstruction to the scheme.

The developer (a) arranges for transit accommodation to the slum dwellers, which can be either on-site or off-site, as mutually agreed between the slum dwellers and the developers (in case of difficulty, the developer may be helped by SRA as per Section 3.3 of Annexure 5.1), (b) based upon the draw of lots for allotment of transit tenements, shifts the slum dwellers to the transit accommodation, (c) demolishes the vacated hutments and (d) completes construction work up to plinth level. After checking the plinth dimensions, further permission to carry out construction beyond plinth is granted by SRA.

Fourth Stage

During this fourth stage also, all the three players in the process—the cooperative housing society, the builder and the SRA—participate and play their respective role.

The cooperative housing society (a) draws lots for occupation in the new tenements and (b) allots tenement in the joint name of the head of the household and the spouse. The developer (a) completes the rehabilitation building/wing (b) through architect/planner submits to SRA building completion certificate and (c) gets plans for the further buildings, for both sale and rehabilitation prepared from the architect/planner and submit them to the SRA. The SRA in this stage (a) scrutinises and approves plans, and grants building permissions for the sale of buildings (b) after checking of the building and compliance of conditions, grants occupation permission and gives possession of the tenements to the slum dwellers, as per the allotment list and (c) issues identity cards to the slum dwellers.

Fifth Stage

During this stage, the developer constructs the remaining buildings. The SRA, at this last stage, (a) grants further building permissions as well as occupation permissions to all the buildings, (b) upon completion of all the buildings in the layout, transfers the underlying land on lease to cooperative housing society of slum dwellers for management and (c) prepares separate property cards for the rehabilitation-building plot and the sale-building plot as well as for the reservation plots to be handed over.

Guidelines

As mentioned earlier in this chapter, guidelines prepared within the framework of the respective policy/Master Plan provide working details at each step of the urban renewal process. The nature and contents of guidelines vary according to the task and strategy adopted for renewal. Accordingly, guidelines for redevelopment will be different from the ones for regularisation of unauthorised colonies or conservation of heritage buildings and sites.

Since, in practice, spatial planners and other professionals are engaged in drafting urban renewal guidelines, an attempt is made here to analyse five existing guidelines for their contents and variations depending upon their renewal strategy. Further, we will discuss the guidelines for area redevelopment in the case of Mumbai and Delhi.

Guidelines for Cluster Redevelopment: Case of Mumbai

These guidelines follow the spatial planning strategy of redevelopment requiring demolition of the existing structures followed by reconstruction (Chapter 3). An analysis of the guidelines for area redevelopment in Mumbai and Delhi (Annexures 5.2 and 5.3) and guideline for cluster redevelopment, Mumbai (Annexure 5.4) indicates that the contents of such guidelines, generally, include the following:

1. Reference to legal provision under which the guideline has been made
2. Implementing agency
3. Cut-off date and eligibility criteria for resettlement
4. Spatial planning norms to be followed include

    i. Area of site
    ii. Size of tenement

iii. Permissible FAR/FSI
   iv. Density
   v. Amenities
5. Land use regulations
6. People participation
7. Resource mobilisation incorporating
   i. Incentive FAR/FSI and/or
   ii. Corpus fund
8. Plan approval

The following paragraphs will provide a brief description of the need and related issues pertaining to contents of the guidelines. The actual details may be seen from the relevant Annexure.

Reference to legal provision is generally given in the preamble to the guidelines. It is important to give this information for any reference in case of litigation, if any. This reference could be from the relevant DCRs, master plan or policy or both, as the case may be. In the case of Mumbai, it is DCR; in the case of Delhi, it is MPD-2021; and in the case of cluster redevelopment in Mumbai, it is a combination of housing policy and DCR.

The implementing agency can be a development authority, municipality, landowner, cooperative society of landowners or private developer. Landowners or agencies may appoint a developer to implement the project. The implementing agency provides ownership to the project and is responsible for (a) the preparation of the layout plans, following the spatial norms and standards and getting their approval from the local body; (b) all demolition, site development and construction works and (c) other administrative and legal matters as required.

Since slum redevelopment involves relocation/resettlement, where a plot of land or built space is given to each landowner, it is very important to decide the eligibility criterion. One of the ways is to announce a cut-off date as the eligibility criteria. As slum areas keep on growing on a daily basis, and when such a scheme is announced, the rate of growth is even faster. This is often a cause of tension as those who do not qualify under the set criterion try to politicise the issue or take legal course which delays project implementation and, sometimes, causes social tension and law and order problems. It should be noted that this date is local area specific and may vary for each scheme. It is also highlighted that this cut-off date may change several times, under political pressure or legal orders, for the same scheme.

Since spatial planning norms, land use regulations and people's participation are overlapping and are common under separate heads (discussed later in this chapter). For resource mobilisation, readers can refer to Chapter 6.

The plan approval process is guided by the local regulations. For example, in Delhi, the approval of redevelopment plan is not required if the area is a part of any existing approved layout/redevelopment/ regulation plan. Approval of the concerned authority is, however, required for the redevelopment plan of cluster block of a minimum area of 3,000 sq. m, where the owners pool together and reorganise their individual properties so as to provide a minimum of 30% of area as common green/soft parking, besides circulation areas and common facilities (see Annexure 5.4). It follows the sanction of individual buildings by the concerned authority.

Guidelines for Regularisation of Unauthorised Colonies Case of Delhi

As mentioned in Chapter 3, a colony or development comprising contiguous area is termed as unauthorised if no permission/approval of the concerned authority/agency has been obtained for layout plan and/or building plans. The objective of regularisation of such colonies is to provide legal status and basic infrastructure and amenities to improve the living conditions of the people. The guidelines for regularisation of unauthorised colonies in Delhi issued by the MoUD in 2007 (Annexure 5.5) provide criteria and procedure for regularisation.

The criteria for regularisation include the cut-off date and other conditions such as development in *lal dora* (boundary of a village settlement area) of urban village. This also gives conditions when an unauthorised colony will NOT be regularised. These include colonies or part thereof

1. falling in notified or reserved forest areas;
2. which pose hindrances in the provision of infrastructure facilities or fall in the area of right of way (ROW) of existing/proposed railway lines, master plan roads and major/trunk water supply and sewerage lines;
3. where more than 50% plots are unbuilt on the date of formal announcement of regularisation scheme and
4. located on public land, if it violates the provisions of Ancient Monuments and Archaeological Sites and Remains Act, 1958.

The process of regularisation of unauthorised colonies includes registration of residents' society, preparation of existing layout plan showing the existing situation and any proposal for improvement and its sanction by the local body. It also includes an undertaking from the residents' society that they shall

1. abide by the layout plans as may be approved with or without conditions and
2. transfer the land available, if any, for social infrastructure in the name of the DDA or MCD/NDMC, free of cost, in order to provide such social infrastructure.

The parameters for regularisation will include (a) title of land, (b) spatial norms as per Para 4.2.2.2 (B) of MPD-2021, (c) mixed land uses as per provisions of MPD-2021 and (d) the recovery of cost.

On receipt of the applications from the societies for regularisation, the local body/DDA completes the process of scrutiny within two months. Simultaneously, the Government of National Capital Territory of Delhi (GNCTD) finalises boundaries of each colony using aerial photography of satellite images, marks the finalised boundary on the scrutinised layout plan and forwards the layout plan to the local body for approval. A competent authority in the local body approves the layout plans and sends them to GNCTD for regularisation and DDA for change of land use. The formal order of regularisation of unauthorised colony is issued by the GNCTD after completing all formalities, including land use change and payment of all costs and charges by the society.

The implementing agencies include local bodies/DDA and GNCTD. The work relating to the regularisation of unauthorised colonies is carried out by the local bodies/DDA/GNCTD, within their respective area of jurisdiction, through a separate cell created for this purpose. Preparation and implementation of development works, involving agencies concerned, is undertaken, coordinated, monitored and supervised by GNCTD.

These guidelines appear to be week as indicated from the following two provisions (note the heighted portion):

1. The construction on each individual plot is to be brought within the prescribed development control norms by the individual owner/resident society. 'However, it will not be a pre-condition for regularisation of colony' (Annexure 5.5, Section 2.4).
2. While preparing existing layout plan, the residents' society shall identify plots/location for social infrastructure facilities. This land would be transferred in the name of the local body/DDA. 'In such colonies where land cannot be made available by the Residents Society, the colony would have to manage without provisions of such facilities' (Annexure 5.5, Section 2.2).

Considering these provisions the main focus, probably, it appears that the regularisation of unauthorised colonies is only to attract people's political support (votes) rather than improving the facilities and services in the area.

Guidelines for Conservation of Heritage Buildings

An area for redevelopment may have heritage buildings, sites and precincts that need conservation. According to the *Central Public Works Department (CPWD) Guide* (CPWD, 2013), the first step for conservation is to list the heritage buildings and then grade them into three categories according to their heritage value to people from national to local levels. Grade I heritage buildings are of national importance due to their historical significance. Grade II buildings are of historical significance and interest to the people of a particular region where these buildings are located. Grade III buildings have local importance and heritage value to people of a specific place only.

The Grade I heritage buildings, sites or precincts need to be preserved. No changes in the interior or exterior and natural features, attached to the heritage buildings, are permitted. Development of the surrounding areas is guided by the Ancient Monument and Archaeological Sites and Remains (Amendment and Validation) Act, 2010. According to provisions of this Act, the surrounding area is divided into two zones: (a) 100 m wide zone around the monument known as prohibited area and (b) 200 m wide zone around the ancient monument and archaeological sites and remains, designated as regulated area. In the prohibited zone, no construction is allowed except repairs and renovation to the building, if permitted by the competent authority. In the regulated area, construction, reconstruction, repair and renovation of building and land is permitted on approval from the competent authority. According to the Act, the extent of both prohibited and regulated areas cover not only horizontally but also vertically and even below the ground.

In Grade II heritage buildings, no external changes are permitted. Changes in the interiors may, however, be permitted for adaptive reuse, if approved by the competent authority. The extension of the same plot is also permitted, provided it is in harmony with the heritage building in respect to height and facade.

In Grade III heritage buildings, sites and precincts, the approach is similar to Grade II buildings where the unique building, feature or attribute is to be conserved and interiors changed for adaptive reuse. The objective of the adaptive reuse of buildings, in the context of conservation, is to retain the embodied energy of the heritage buildings and make them environmentally sustainable, ensuring their survival and significance to the community (CPWD, 2013).

While planning a heritage precinct, care is to be taken to maintain skyline and harmony with architecture style. All new buildings, signs, outdoor display structures and street furniture should be in harmony without obliterating the visual quality and heritage-value of the precinct.

Spatial Planning Norms and Standards

Spatial norms are one of the basic tools of planning. These norms depend upon the spatial planning strategy adopted for urban renewal. The norms for the redevelopment, relocation and regularisation of unauthorised colonies are presented in Tables 5.2–5.4, respectively. It is also emphasised here that these norms vary from place to place

Table 5.2 *Spatial Norms for Slum Redevelopment in Mumbai and Delhi*

		Spatial Norms	
S. No.	Description	Mumbai[1]	Delhi[2]
1.	Minimum Site Area (sq. m)		
	a. General schemes	4,000	4,000
	b. Scheme on government/ semi-government or municipal corporation land (sq. m)	2,000	—
	c. Schemes in slum/JJ areas (sq. m)	—	2,000
	d. Cluster blocks (sq. m)	—	3,000
2.	FAR/FSI		
	a. Maximum permissible FAR/FSI*	4	4
	b. Incentive FAR/FSI over and above the existing permissible FAR/FSI on individual plot	—	50%
	c. Incentive in FSI as percentage of rehabilitation component with the size of cluster ranging from 4,000 sq. m to more than 20,000 sq. m	55–80%	—
3.	Tenement Size	—	—
	a. Minimum size in sq. ft (sq. m) carpet area	300 (27.88)	—
	b. Maximum size in sq. ft (sq. m) carpet area	750 (70)	—

		Spatial Norms	
S. No.	Description	Mumbai[1]	Delhi[2]
4.	**Social Facilities (Reduced Standards)**		
	a. Area, in sq. m, for each primary school per 5,000 population		800
	b. Area, in sq. m, for each senior secondary school per 10,000 population		2,000
	c. Area in sq. m for a composite facilities centre comprising multipurpose community hall, health centre, religious site, police post, open space, milk booth, shop and place for informal trade		500–1,000
5.	**Building Norms**		
	a. Maximum ground coverage		33.3%
	b. Height		No restriction
	c. Parking ECS/100 sq. m built up area		2
	d. Density in DU/ha	DU size up to 40 sq. m	400
		DU size 40 to 80 sq. m	250
		DU size above 80 sq. m	175

Sources: [1] Annexure 5.2.

[2] Annexure 5.3 and MPD-2021, Para 3.3.2; 4.2.2.2 (b); 4.2.3.4; and 4.4.3 (B).

Notes: In addition to the ones mentioned in the table, the physical infrastructure to be provided includes the following:

i. Underground tank, sewage pumping system
ii. RWH system
iii. Protection of natural drainage system
iv. System of recycling of used water
v. System of solid waste management
vi. Electricity supply system and use of solar energy in public places
vii. Provision of decentralised sewage treatment plant

* FAR in this row is presented as ratio.

depending upon the applicable Acts, DCRs, master plan regulations, building bye-laws, etc. These norms and standards, therefore, are indicative and, in practice, the norms applicable to the area should be used.

Table 5.3 *Spatial Norms for Relocation of JJ Clusters in Delhi*

S. No.	Description	Spatial Norms
1.	Minimum Plot Area (sq. m)	
	a. JJ dwellers who were eligible before 31 January 1990	20
	b. JJ dwellers who became eligible between 1 February 1990 and 30 December 1998	15
2.	Plot Coverage	100%
3.	Density in DU/ha	
	a. For 16. sq. m plots	300
	b. For 20 sq. m plots	250
4.	Land Use of Gross Area	
	a. Residential plots	50%
	b. Services	30%
	c. Other social infrastructure	20%
	Total	100%

Source: Annexure 5.6.

The norms presented here are based upon the current DCR of Mumbai and MPD-2021. It should also be noted that as per policy of MPD-2021 (Para 4.2.3.1), relocation on plotted development is to be progressively abandoned because of non-availability of land in the Delhi and substituted by alternative approach such as in situ upgradation or relocation on built-up accommodation of around 25 sq. m with common facilities.

Spatial Plans

Spatial plans are scale-drawings that depict the past, present and future activities, situations, networks and pattern of land uses. With the use of remote sensing technology—Global Positioning System (GPS) and Geographic Information System (GIS)—in the preparation of spatial plans, transfer of such plans on the ground is more effective, accurate and time-saving. Spatial plans are more communicative and with a little explanation, they are easily comprehendible to all stakeholders including common people. They are very useful tools for spatial

Table 5.4 *Spatial Norms for the Regularisation of Unauthorised Colonies in Delhi*

S. No.	Description	Spatial Norms
1.	Social facilities (reduced standards) a. Area in sq. m for each primary school per 5,000 population b. Area in sq. m for each senior secondary school per 10,000 population	800 2,000
2.	Area in sq. m for a composite facilities centre comprising facilities under serial no. 3	500–1,000
3.	Area in sq. m for multipurpose community hall	100
	Area in sq. m for health centre	100
	Area in sq. m for religious site	100
	Area in sq. m for police post	100
	Area in sq. m for park shishu vatika (children park)	200
	Area in sq. m for basti vikas kendra	100
	milk booth, fair price shop, kerosene shop, retail shops and place for informal trade in mixed land use streets	*
4.	Minimum ROW of mixed land use street (m.)	9
	ROW of pedestrian only mixed land use street (m)	6

Source: Annexure 5.5 and MPD-2021 (Para 15.3.3).
As available on the site depending upon space.

planners for analysis, presentation of ideas, issues and proposals and translating them on ground for planned development.

In the context of urban renewal, it is suggested that there should be a set of three spatial plans: (a) urban renewal sub-plan, (b) action plan for each urban renewal zone and (c) DPR for each project.

Urban Renewal Sub-plan

With a view to integrate urban renewal with the urban development, each master plan should have an urban renewal sub-plan for the entire city. This plan should be prepared with active community participation and spatially indicate the following supported by written and graphic material as required:

1. Various urban renewal zones identified in the city (Chapter 1)
2. The population holding capacity of and extent of activity concentration in each of the urban renewal zone as identified in (1)
3. The urban renewal strategy or a set of strategies to be followed for each zone (Chapters 3 and 4)
4. The guidelines for various strategies, specifying community participation mechanism, spatial norms/standards/development control regulations to be followed (Chapter 5), resource mobilisation approach (Chapter 6), institutional framework for implementation
5. Such other details as required

Urban Renewal Action Plan

There should be an action plan for each urban renewal zone as identified under first point of 'urban renewal sub-plan'. This may contain any or all of the following:

1. Location of the renewal zone and its surroundings
2. Analysis of existing
   - land uses
   - road network
   - areas with unique urban design characteristics/built environment/heritage buildings
   - the traffic characteristics and transport network
   - system of open spaces, water bodies
   - distribution and efficacy of social infrastructure (education, health and recreation)
3. Assessment of existing holding capacity of services network—water supply, sewerage, drainage, solid waste management, electricity distribution and communication network

4. Identification of various policy zones, depending upon the renewal strategy to be followed
5. Identification of issues and potentials for urban renewal of each policy zone
6. Identification of vision, development priorities
7. The proposed layout plan of the urban renewal zone indicating any or all of the following:
    - land uses
    - road network, pedestrian and cycle tracks
    - system of open spaces and public spaces
    - urban design
    - transport network
    - provision of facilities—education, health, recreation
    - services network—water supply, sewerage, drainage, solid waste management, electricity distribution
8. Identification of projects, implementation actions and priority of development
9. Identification of implementation agencies
10. Financing mechanism/investment plan
11. Evaluation and outcome mechanism

The assessment of holding capacity of a zone as required under (3) of the urban renewal action plan depends upon a thorough analysis and identification of potential to hold additional population and/or built space by land use in areas that are

- dilapidated and require renewal and can accommodate additional land uses as required;
- low-density residential which can be redeveloped with higher density;
- underutilised and can be developed with their full potential (FAR/FSI);
- available for redevelopment due to shifting of industries, wholesale markets, bus stand and such other activities and can accommodate additional population or land uses; and
- transformed to hold more population due to augmentation of accessibility by road, services (water and sewerage) and transport network (MRT/BRT corridor).

The urban renewal action plan should be prepared with active and effective stakeholder consultation/community participation.

Detailed Project Report (DPR)

Urban renewal action plan should be followed by a DPR of each project as identified under (h) of the urban renewal action plan. This should be prepared with active and effective stakeholder consultation and community participation. It may contain any or all of the following:

1. Location of the project area and its surroundings
2. Ownership of land and buildings
3. Condition of buildings in the area
4. Detailed analysis of existing
   - land uses
   - road network
   - areas with unique urban design, built environment, heritage buildings
   - the traffic characteristics and transport network
   - system of open spaces, water bodies
   - services network—water supply, sewerage, drainage, solid waste management, electricity distribution and communication network
   - distribution and efficacy of social infrastructure—education, health and recreation
5. Identification of various policy zones depending upon the renewal strategy to be followed
6. Identification of issues and potentials of the urban renewal of the area
7. Identification of development objectives
8. Schedule of future requirements including transit accommodation (if needed)
9. Proposed layout plan of the project area indicating
   - land uses
   - road network, pedestrian and cycle tracks

- system of open spaces and public spaces
- urban design
- transport network
- provision of facilities—education, health, recreation
- services network—water supply, sewerage, drainage, solid waste management, electricity distribution
- plan for allotment of transit accommodation
- plan for allotment of built spaces/tenements
- plan for sale of other built spaces
- others as required

10. Cost estimation and financing mechanism
11. Plan for marketing and publicity
12. Mechanism for management of assets created and public spaces provided
13. Outcome assessment

Community Participation

In the context of urban renewal, the community may be defined as the people affected by the project and include both the beneficiaries and the aggrieved, if any. These people tend to unite as they have a common cause and thus, form a community. Participation, on the other hand, refers to the involvement of people in the process of decision-making. In the context of urban renewal, the community participation, therefore, refers to the involvement of affected people in the process and take decisions at its various stages.

For example, in the slum redevelopment process, active participation of the community is envisaged at various stages. It is reiterated here that in Stage 1 (Figure 5.2), the slum dwellers mobilise the support of a majority (more than 70%) of people for the redevelopment of their area and constitute the Slum Dwellers' Cooperative Housing Society (referred as the Society hereafter), and manage its functions and responsibilities. During the same stage, the Society gets physical survey of the area done and prepares a table showing house number, name of the owner and details of the property owned. This Society also takes decision regarding appointment of a suitable developer to implement the project. It should be noted that at this stage, there are two groups—those who support the redevelopment and are members of the Society and the rest who have not yet accorded their support and are not members of the Society.

In the third stage, the Society members participate in the process of draw of lots for the allotment of the transit accommodation. To mobilise support of the non-members, the Society draws lot for the allotment of transit accommodation for them as well. The Society also participates in discussion with the developer for choice of location of transit accommodation which could be on the site itself or outside. On the completion of the transit accommodation, the members shift to their allotted accommodation. At this stage, the Society issues a notice to all non-members to become members and shift to the allotted transit accommodation failing which they will be physically evicted as per law.

On the completion of the tenements in the fourth stage, the community again participates in the draw of lots for the allotment of tenements. On the completion of the project, in the fifth stage, the land is leased to the Society by the authority. In this way, the members of the beneficiary community participate in the redevelopment of their area and also own the land, individual tenements and the project as a whole.

In other strategies such as in situ upgradation, revitalisation, restoration, retrofitting, etc., the knowledge of existing conditions, issues and priorities is of paramount importance which requires community participation for the following:

- Assessment of the existing physical, social, economic and environmental conditions of the area
- Assessment of existing quality of services in the area
- Identification of the physical, social, economic and environmental issues, potential and priorities
- Identification of alternative solutions to address the priority issues
- Resolution of conflicts, if any
- Setting up of the vision of development
- Participation in social audit

- Participation in operation and maintenance of assets created and public spaces provided

Community participation is effective if the following are present in it:

- Empowerment of people to participate and take decisions
- Political support from the local politician (Ward Committee Member, Corporator, MLA, MP)
- Opportunity provided to all social groups (men, women, senior citizens, poorer sections of the community, youth groups, occupational groups, professionals and others affected by the project) to express views
- Ample publicity to make people aware of the nature and contents of the project, the procedure of the consultation and the expected role the people
- Continuity of community participation at different stages of the project which could be initial stage for support; planning stage for identification of issues and priorities; implementation stage for monitoring, draw of lots and social audit; and on completion for outcome assessment and maintenance of community assets created by the project
- Opportunity provided for evolution of social capital in the form of local leadership, informal institutional mechanism for discharging different community responsibilities
- Sufficient fiscal and administrative support for organising community participation

The current practice of community participation in urban renewal projects, generally, appears to be half-hearted that fulfils only the procedural/legal requirements. The suggestions given by the community, in many cases, remain unattended. It is noted that the people's hopes are raised when they participate in the planning process and, when nothing substantial or tangible comes out of the process, they tend to lose hope and confidence in the process. As a result of such conditions, the general experience of community participation in spatial planning programmes is discouraging. Participation and conflict resolution through discussion and negotiations has been criticised in literature (Gualini and Bianchi, 2015a, 2015b, p. 94) on the grounds that the decision taken is by the stakeholders present at the time of meeting represents a compromise solution which may not be acceptable to those who were not present. Such situations may lead to organised resistance through demonstration or legal action and cause long delays in project implementation.

The basic objective of community participation is to gain trust of people and seek their support and involvement in and commitment to the renewal project. Community participation is necessary because of the fact that urban renewal affects people and the quality of their life directly. For success of the project, a large majority of people must be satisfied with its process, outcome and impact. Urban renewal work may be unsustainable without the active involvement of the community. Execution of the project becomes smooth when it is evolved through the participation of people. Community participation generates a sense of belonging to the project and people feel that they are partners in the project and own it as their project.

Urban renewal plans, therefore, should be participatory and communicative so that it (a) makes people aware of its objectives, approach, cost and benefits and (b) communicates to them and other stakeholders the process to be followed and the extent and nature of their participation required at various stages.

As mentioned in Chapter 4, to empower the community to participate in the JNNURM, the central government introduced mandatory state-level reform to constitute Community Participation Law (CPL) for creating a three-tier structure at city level—municipal corporation, wards committee and area sabha. In this structure, the area sabha, comprising all registered voters in the area as members, is conceived at the grassroots level legal institution empowered, among other functions, to generate proposals and determine the priority of developmental programmes in the area, and identify the most eligible persons and prepare a list of beneficiaries in order of priority. Most of the states have passed such an act. Nine states/UTs, including Arunachal Pradesh, Bihar, Delhi, Goa, Meghalaya, Puducherry, Punjab, Odisha and Uttarakhand, have yet to take any action. In some states, such as Maharashtra, empowerment to slum dwellers is provided in the redevelopment process through guidelines, as discussed earlier as well.

The process of participation and manner of consultation may include awareness building; consultation, the presentation of the outcome of the consultation, the identification of points where there is full agreement and also the areas of disagreement; the discussion and negotiations on the resolution of conflicts and finalisation of the outcome.

The consultation could be through well-publicised meetings and workshops. These meetings and workshops should be structured in such a manner that the participants can be divided into smaller groups for further free, fair and intense discussion and, later on, each group can present its specific observations in the joint meeting for further deliberations and taking decisions. The various groups could either be focused and/or social groups. The focused group may include politicians, government officials of line departments, technical experts, legal experts, etc., and social groups may comprise male members of the community, senior citizens, women groups, poorer sections of the community, youth groups and others, as required by the project.

The job of a spatial planner is to follow the participatory process of preparation and implementation of urban renewal plans. It is also his professional duty to always keep people informed about various aspects related to the project, including good practices, alternative possible solutions, approaches, policies, programmes and availability of funds, so that they may take appropriate decision. Always keep in the mind that it is the people who are taking decisions and they should feel as such. This ensures grassroots-up approach to urban renewal, which is essential, as the so far practised top-down approach often results in conflicts, social unrest, law and order problems, litigations and long delays in implementation.

Implementation and Monitoring

The starting point for implementation is the availability of an approved urban renewal plan and DPR of project, which is being implemented.

It requires the identification of a suitable implementation actions and initiators.

Implementation Actions

Depending upon the prevailing local conditions guided by the political climate, community awareness and support, legal status, delays, uncertainty and flow of funds, the actions for implementation can be (a) comprehensive, (b) strategic or (c) tactical.

Comprehensive Action

Comprehensive action could be considered at two levels: (a) city level and (b) project level. At city level, it covers the entire city and all aspects, taking all of them together. This action will require large investment and may result in large-scale displacement of people, causing social tension, unrest and risk which may not be favourable among political and administrative decision-makers. In actual practice, most of the plans suggested are taking comprehensive action and probably, this is the reason for their non-implementation or very poor performance.

At the selected project level, the comprehensive action for the implementation of urban renewal plans refers to a complete action covering the entire project in totality. It is successful in projects where fund flow is ensured and there are no litigations or social resistance by those who are not getting benefits of the particular renewal project. In cases of large redevelopment projects, requiring huge investment and large-scale temporary resettlement, such initiative may not be practical. In such cases, the project is divided into sizable phases and, depending upon the resource availability and priorities, project level comprehensive action is taken for phase-wise implementation. Redevelopment projects generally fall in this category of actions. Redevelopment of East Kidwai Nagar is an ongoing current example of comprehensive action for the urban renewal of government employees' housing in Delhi (see Chapter 2). Examples of comprehensive action, in phases, are also seen in the redevelopment of Bhendi

Bazaar, Mumbai, where the total cost is ₹4,000 crore which, for implementation the project, is divided into nine clusters. Work on clusters 1 and 3 has started and is likely to be completed by 2019 (*Business Standard*, 2016).

Strategic Action

Strategic action is one that creates momentum for change (Dutton and Duncan, 1987). In case of urban renewal, therefore, strategic action refers to the implementation of a selected proposal that will trigger the transformation process and generate a momentum for further change in the surrounding areas. The implementation of such a proposal may be termed as the strategic action. The steps to be taken for strategic action for implementation of the approved urban renewal plan include the following:

1. Depending upon the objectives, availability of resources and expected outcome, identify a few proposals with stakeholders' participation and select one project for strategic action.
2. Prepare DPR, if not already available, of the selected proposal for implementation.
3. Implement the proposal.
4. Evaluate the outcome of the strategic action against the expectations, as mentioned in (1), and take further action as under:

    i. If result is positive, indicating the success of the strategic action, then

        a. to harness the momentum for change created by the strategic action, take further action and implement the other proposals of the renewal plan, as applicable to the surrounding areas and
        b. identify another strategic project and follow steps 2, 3 and 4.

    ii. If result is negative, examine the causes of failure, identify another strategic project considering lessons learned from the review in (4) and follow steps 2, 3, and 4.

It should be noted that the strategic implementation action is more acceptable to people as it addresses the existing problems and issues faced by the community. It also provides to spatial planners and other stakeholders the opportunities for learning lessons about issues, problems and conflicts in the implementation process and also the manner to tackle them.

Development of Metro Rail transport project, under JNNURM, qualifies as a strategic action that has generated momentum for urban transformation in many cities where such a project has been implemented. As given in Chapter 2, MRTS has been successfully implemented in Bengaluru, Jaipur, Chennai, Hyderabad and Kochi. In Delhi and NCR, it covers 213 km which is operational, and it is being further extended to cover another 115 km. Sharma (2014) has shown from a study in Delhi that along the MRTS corridor, property value of buildings has increased, residential land use is getting converted to commercial and the traffic congestion on roads has reduced. To introduce planned transformation, MPD-2021 (DDA, 2007, p. 116) has provided for the preparation of the redevelopment scheme of the influence area of metro stations in Delhi.

Tactical Action

Getting inspiration from literature on tactical urbanism (Charlie, 2015; Lyndon et al., n.d.; Simpson, 2015), an effort is made to adapt the idea for the implementation of urban renewal plans. In this context, tactical action can be defined as the engagement of the community to identify and implement low-cost projects/schemes that are expected to demonstrate immediate positive results and fulfil current needs and aspirations of the people. On successful implementation, it is likely to inspire them and others to participate in such efforts in future. This effort is also likely to introduce social transformation of community in support of urban renewal. Taking into account the huge expenses and risks involved in urban renewal, tactical actions appear to be practical and need to be promoted for urban transformation efforts.

Schemes/projects for tactical action could be those that are low-cost, short-term and where fund are already available. They may, for example, include improvements in the provision of basic services; improvement in accessibility by road; declaring pedestrian-only streets; provision of cycle track and pathway connecting to public transport station, local market and facilities such as school, clinic and parks; environmental improvement through solid waste management; regulating and designating zones for informal commercial activities to reduce congestion on roads; providing and managing parking and such other initiatives.

The various steps for taking tactical actions could be as follows:

1. **Initiation**
   To make the community aware of

   i. the urban renewal plan for the area and the various approved schemes where fund are available;
   ii. the manner in which the people, social groups, NGOs and CBOs can participate and
   iii. invite community members to identify schemes they would like to participate in.

2. **Selection**
   Community organisation and selection of scheme involves

   i. assisting the community to identify their current need and aspirations and to select the scheme/project from 1(i) for implementation;
   ii. assisting the community to form a core committee having composition as decided by the community members for the implementation of scheme/project and
   iii. designate a contact person serving as a liaison between the community and administration.

3. **Implementation and post project management**
   This step involves assisting the community to

   i. implement the scheme and
   ii. form committees, as required, for post project management including maintenance of public spaces and assets created.

4. **Evaluation**
It assesses the outcome of the action and takes further action, such as,
   i. if assessment is positive indicating successful implementation and fulfilment of the community aspirations, identify and implement another project for tactical action following steps 2, 3 and 4 and
   ii. if result is negative indicating failure, examine the causes of failure, improve the action and if it is not practical, abandon the project and identify another scheme following steps 2, 3 and 4.

The benefits of tactical action for implementation of urban renewal projects include the following:

- It is cost-effective and less risky.
- It addresses local issues and provides short-term solutions that attract people.
- It promotes a grassroots-up action and is participatory in nature, hence there is a better acceptability to the renewal plan by the community.
- It creates a sense of ownership to the project by the community, and hence it is more satisfying to the members of the community.
- It promotes community leadership and evolution of social capital in the form of community organisations and groups.
- It inspires people to participate in urban renewal process and be partner to long-term change.

Raahgiri Day introduced in Gurugram, Haryana, in 2013 could be an example quite close to tactical action. It was first car-free initiative taken by citizens. It was a weekly event when a selected portion of a road will be declared as car-free zone for 4–5 hours in the morning for the use of people with their friends and family in any manner they like—walking, cycling, playing, singing in groups and other such activities. Later on, this was extended to Connaught Place and Sector 6, Dwarka sub-city, New Delhi. As an event, it was quite successful. It, however, could not bring change in the behaviour of shopkeepers to support for pedestrianisation of the inner circle of Connaught Place which is one of the key proposals of New Delhi Smart City Plan. The proposal was approved by the MoUD in February 2017 as a pilot project. However, it could not commence due to stiff resistance of the shopkeepers of the area in spite of Raahgiri Day experience.

Another possible tactical action could be car rationing, using odd–even rule of traffic management introduced by GNCTD in January 2016 for 15 days. The objective was to reduce air pollution in the city. It did reduce traffic on roads by about 15–20% in general and up to 50% on some congested roads but could not conclusively achieve reduction in air pollution in the city (Kulshrestha, 2016, p. 3).

Initiators of Implementation

The various initiators of the implementation of the urban renewal plans are in fact the agents of urban transformation and can be

1. individual property owners;
2. property owners' cooperative housing societies;
3. politicians;
4. central, state and local government agencies;
5. public–private joint entities and
6. private developers.

A large part of the urban renewal efforts are generally implemented by individual property owners. In initiative, the property owner takes all actions, including planning, financing and implementation. These actions are authorised if taken within the framework of existing policies, master plan, DCR and building bye-laws and approved by the authorities.

Some DCRs and slum redevelopment guidelines (Annexures 5.1, 5.2 and 5.3) provide for the amalgamation of plots for planning purposes. This provides opportunity to the owners of properties located in such clusters to join hands, form a registered cooperative group housing society and pool their land and redevelop following the process as shown in Figure 5.1. In this manner, the cooperative societies become agents to initiate urban renewal.

For local area development, each Member of Legislative Assembly (MLA) is allocated ₹3 crore per year and each Member of Parliament (MP) is entitled to spend ₹5 crore annually which can be used for the in situ upgradation of slum areas in their respective constituency. In this manner, MLAs and MPs become the agents of urban transformation. Such fund flow is very common during election periods and the slum areas also get some improvement in the form of paving of pathways, provision of drains or street lights.

Large-scale urban renewal missions/programmes/schemes are mostly initiated and state and central governments and implemented by local government (ULBs) and state government agencies such as housing boards, development authorities, slum boards, etc. Some of such current schemes include PMAY, Smart Cities Mission, AMRUT, HRIDAY and UIDSSMT (see Chapter 2 for details and Chapter 6 for available funds).

A joint entity is one that is an outcome of PPP where the government may join hands with a private developer and jointly execute an urban redevelopment plan and share the expenses, risks, built spaces and other assets as per agreement. Need for such an arrangement in urban slum renewal programmes is felt because the budgetary allocations of ULBs and other service providing agencies are grossly insufficient to meet the investment requirement. On the other hand, the private sector developers have proven capabilities for resource mobilisation. Their business approach is, however, profit oriented. They are reluctant to participate in non-profit social projects. The government, on the other hand, is committed to social housing and slum redevelopment and, therefore, joins hands with private sector on mutually acceptable terms which protects the interests of both the partners. Encouraging PPP is one of the reforms committed by ULBs. With such reforms, the investment environment is improving and PPP model is being increasingly promoted in urban renewal projects.

Marketing Rejuvenated Areas

The successful implementation of urban renewal efforts also depends upon marketing rejuvenated areas, their new image, ambience and the quality of life they provide or economic opportunities they present to the people or the rejuvenated tourist product they showcase to the tourists. The focus of marketing may be specific areas, projects or the entire rejuvenated city. In Europe and America, marketing cities is a serious business. The slogan 'I love NY', used to market New York, has caught fancy of many cities (Holcomb, 2010). Private developers in India are marketing their estates, and newspapers are full of such advertisements that highlight the specific quality of their products to attract buyers. Some examples are as follows:

1. Advertisement for a township along river in a mid-size religious city:

    Tired of pollution? Fed-up of traffic?
    Welcome to the paradise

2. Advertisement for a high-end township:

    Rise above the ordinary
    Be your own king

3. Advertisement for a township facing large open space:

    Life becomes beautiful in lap of nature
    Presenting Green View Apartments

In a similar way, the rejuvenated walled cities, heritage precincts, traditional markets and in situ slum redevelopment areas may be marketed through media and other methods. The objective of marketing rejuvenated areas is to attract investments, people and tourists to places and similar other areas. This will improve the image of the area and bring recognition to urban renewal efforts. Cities will feel pride and a healthy competition will start among them to attract investment for urban transformation and people to live there and enjoy the improved quality of life, enhanced property value and other benefits.

'Smart City' tag, earned by 20 cities in the City Challenge round, under the Smart Cities Mission, probably, is the first attempt in India for marketing urban renewal and rejuvenated cities. It has generated a process of competitive sub-federalism where each city municipality is competing with other in the process of socio-economic and spatial transformation. There is a need to initiate research in ways of promoting and assessing the impact of marketing rejuvenated areas.

In Delhi, NBCC has already started media campaign for the sale of the commercial area, permitted to recover the investment (see Chapter 6), on the redevelopment of the government colonies in Delhi. An advertisement, covering two full pages, in *The Times of India* (2017) announces:

Feel Exclusive
Freehold Office Space at
Nauroji Nagar
New Delhi
Apply online
E-auction on 30th May 2017

Outcome Assessment

The outcome of changes occurring, due to urban renewal, is not only physical but also socio-cultural, economic, environmental and political. The assessment of outcome of urban renewal project is complex as it interests a large number of stakeholders who participate in the process and effectively contribute to its success. All these stakeholders have their own expectations from the project. For example, the beneficiaries of a slum redevelopment project judge its success by the size of tenement and nature of the other benefits they receive; the developer expects attractive returns on the investment; the wider community living around the transformed area would judge its success from the increase in their property value, reduction in congestion and improvement in quality of life in the area; law and order agencies will assess the success by the drop in crime rates and provision of safety measures for women children and other persons; politician would judge it on the political losses or gains through votes they got from the area; spatial planner will judge the outcome by the smooth implementation with no delays, social unrest, litigations and cost escalations and gaining community support and confidence in the urban renewal process. The outcome assessment, therefore, needs to be comprehensive, covering interest of all groups.

The tools and techniques and indicators of outcome assessment depend upon the goals and objectives of the project, the strategy adopted and the expectation of the beneficiary groups. The tools should be simple but effective. They should be both qualitative and quantitative. Depending upon the nature of the project, they may focus on the accomplishment of vision; improvement in physical, social visual and environmental conditions; increase in property value, economic activities and employment opportunities provided; improvement in the quality of life of urban poor; evolution of innovative approaches in waste management, energy saving, recycling of water, traffic management and others; evolution of local community leadership and establishment of local community groups.

The outcome assessment should not only cover characteristics of change but also highlight the process of change, the forces that affected the change and conflicts that hindered the process and also, the manner to minimise conflicts. This will guide spatial planners, investors and other decision-makers in their future urban renewal efforts.

In case of in situ upgradation by providing services, the outcome may be accessed through its impact on the users covering items such as access to service, supply continuity, time savings, coverage, service quality and cost savings. In case of reforms in urban governance and management, the outcome assessment should focus on the achievement of set goals, and objective to be measured in both qualitative and quantitative terms. The Government of India (2014, p. 8) has set service level benchmarks (Table 5.5) which may be considered to assess the outcome of urban renewal projects. In case of augmentation of services, the outcome assessment should also cover the capacity enhancement to accommodate more population and support further urban renewal.

It will be useful if various schemes include the expected outcome and specify the indicators. The PRASAD has given the outcome

Table 5.5 Service-level Benchmarks

S. No.	Indicators	Benchmark Levels
	Water supply	
1.	Coverage of WS connections (population)	100%
2.	Per capita availability of WS at consumer end	135 lpcd
3.	Extent of metering of WS connections	100%
4.	Extent of non-revenue water	20%
5.	Continuity of water supply	24×7
6.	Efficiency of redressal of customer complaints	80%
7.	Quality of water supplied	100%
8.	Cost recovery of in water supply service	100%
9.	Efficiency in collection of water supply charge	90%
	Sewerage	
1.	Coverage of wastewater network service	100%
2.	Collection efficiency of wastewater network	100%
3.	Adequacy of wastewater treatment capacity	100%
4.	Quality of wastewater treatment	100%
5.	Extent of reuse & recycling of treated wastewater	20%
6.	Extent of cost recovery in wastewater management	100%
7.	Efficiency of redressal of customer complaints 80%	
8.	Efficiency in collection of sewerage charges	90%
9.	Coverage of toilets	100%
	Storm water drainage	
1.	Coverage of storm water drainage network	100%
2.	Incidence of water logging/flooding	0
	Solid waste management	
1.	Household level coverage of solid waste management service	100%
2.	Efficiency of collection of municipal solid waste	100%
3.	Extent of segregation of municipal solid waste	100%
4.	Extent of municipal solid waste recovered/recycled	80%
5.	Extent of scientific disposal of municipal solid waste	100%
6.	Extent of cost recovery in solid waste management service	100%
7.	Efficiency of redressal of customer complaints	80%
8.	Efficiency in collection of user charges	90%

Source: Government of India (2014).

parameters of the scheme (Ministry of Tourism, 2015, p. 11) which include the following:

- Increase in tourist traffic
- Employment generation
- Enhancement of awareness and development of capacities to augment tourism into value added service.
- Increase private sector participation in the identified tourist destination.

Urban renewal, sometimes, leads to negative impacts such as displacement of inhabitants, disruption in livelihood linkages; traffic congestion, shortage of parking spaces, restructuring of city and indiscriminate declaration of mixed land use streets in Delhi. There is a need to assess implications of such cases and identify ways to deal with them.

Annexure 5.1 *Stage-wise Description of Slum Redevelopment Process in Mumbai*

First Stage

All slum dwellers residing on the plot prior to 1 January 2000 and are in use of the structure are eligible for rehabilitation.

1.1	At least 70% of the slum dwellers in a slum unite under a slum dwellers cooperative housing society.
1.2	They appoint a chief promoter. Collect share capital of ₹50 per member and ₹1 as entrance fee. This is then deposited in the name of the proposed housing society in the Mumbai district central cooperative/Maharashtra State Co-operative Bank Ltd.
1.3	Documents regarding the title of the land are collected by the society. The plot is got measured and the slum structures are properly demarcated.
1.4	Survey of structures on the plot is carried out and the structures are numbered on the plan. A table of house number as per plan and the name of the occupant is prepared.
1.5	A suitable developer is appointed by the society by a general body resolution. The developer appoints professionals such as architect/licensed surveyor, structural engineer, etc.

(continued)

(continued)

1.6 The developer enters into individual agreements with all the slum dwellers agreeing to participate in the scheme.

1.7 A proposal enclosing requisite plans; annexures and documents is submitted by the architect to SRA.

Second Stage

2.1 Initial scrutiny of the proposal is carried out by the concerned sub-engineer. It is ensured that all requisite documents are submitted along with the proposal.

2.2 If the proposal is in order, the amount of scrutiny fee to be paid is worked out by the sub-engineer.

2.3 The scrutiny fee is paid by the developer.

2.4 Annexure II is forwarded to the competent authority for certification.

2.5 Annexure III is simultaneously forwarded to the financial wing for scrutiny.

2.6 Annexure I is scrutinised by the engineering wing.

2.7 After Annexure II & III are certified by the competent authorities, approvals to LOI, layout. Intimation of Approval and commencement certificate to the first building for work upto plinth are processed. Endeavour is made to issue all these four approvals at one go, at-least for the first rehabilitation building.

Third Stage

3.1 The society draws lots for allotment of the tenements to the members who are ready to participate in the scheme. Draw for the non- participating members from the remaining tenements is also drawn.

3.2 The developer arranges for transit accommodation to the slum dwellers, which can be either on-site or off site, as mutually agreed between the slum dwellers and the developers.

3.3 In case the developer has difficulty in arranging for suitable transit accommodation, due to site constraints, SRA extends all help to the developers to locate suitable site in the vicinity for construction of transit camps and helps to obtain permissions from concerned authorities for the same. In case no suitable site is available in the vicinity, transit camps of MHADA, MMRDA, etc. can be taken on rental basis by the developers. SRA extends all possible help for obtaining these transit tenements from these authorities.

3.4 Draw of lots for allotment of transit tenements is drawn.

3.5 The slum dwellers are shifted to the transit camps and their hutments demolished. The slum dwellers who do not agree to participate in the scheme are given notice by the society stating the allotment details and requesting them to participate in the scheme.

3.6 If these members do not agree to participate within 15 days of the approval of the proposal, they are physically evicted from the site under the provisions of Sections 33 & 38 of Maharashtra Slum Areas (Improvement, Clearance and Redevelopment) Act, 1971, to ensure that there is no obstruction to the scheme.

3.7 After demolition of the structures, work up to plinth is completed.

3.8 After checking the plinth dimensions, further permission to carry out construction beyond plinth is granted.

Fourth Stage

4.1 Plans for the further buildings both for sale and rehabilitation are then approved.

4.2 Building permissions for the sale buildings are given in the proportion of the permissions given to the rehabilitation buildings.

4.3 Upon completion of rehabilitation building/wing, list of allotment is drawn up. The allotment is done in the joint name of the head of the household and the spouse.

4.4 Building completion certificate is submitted by the architect.

4.5 After checking of the building and compliance of the IOA conditions, occupation permission to the building is granted. The slum dwellers as per the allotment list are given possession of the tenements.

4.6 SRA issues identity cards to the slum dwellers.

Fifth Stage

5.1 Further construction of the remaining building/s is then taken up.

5.2 Further building permissions as well as occupation permissions to the buildings are then granted in due course.

5.3 Upon completion of the last buildings in the layout, the underlying land is transferred on lease to the society of slum dwellers. In case of government lands, the lease rent is nominal.

5.4 Separate property cards for the rehabilitation-building plot and the sale-building plot as well as for the reservation plots to be handed over are prepared. SRA acts as facilitating agency in case of any difficulty with the revenue authorities.

Source: SRA (2016).

Annexure 5.2 Guideline for Area Redevelopment in Mumbai

In the Municipal Corporation of Greater Mumbai (MCGM) area Redevelopment is guided by the Regulation No 33(9) which was sanctioned in 1991. It was modified in 2009 and further modified in 2012 to include redevelopment of Dharavi. The following are the salient features of this Guideline for Urban Renewal applicable in Mumbai:

Minimum area cut-off dates

1. Urban renewal scheme can be prepared on a minimum area of 4,000 sq. m which consists of a mix of structures of different categories such as:
   - Cessed building.
   - Building erected before 30 August 1969 and acquired by MHADA.
   - Building of government and semi-government and MCGM erected before 30 August 1969 having built-up area up to 2,000 sq. m.
   - Other buildings erected before 30 August 1969 which are unfit for human habitation by reason of disrepair or structural/sanitary defects or dangerous/injurious to health of the inhabitant by reason of their bad configuration or narrowness of streets.
   - Slum areas declared as slums under section 4 of Maharashtra Slum Areas Act, 1971, or slums on private lands prior to 1 January 1995 restricting 25% of total area of project.

Implementing agency

2. The scheme can be undertaken by
   i. The MHADA or MCGM, either departmentally or through suitable agency.
   ii. MHADA/MCGM jointly with land owners and/or cooperative housing societies of hutment dwellers therein.
   iii. Independently by land owners and/or cooperative housing societies of tenants/occupiers or developer.

Maximum permissible FSI and incentive FSI

3. The maximum FSI shall be 4 or required for rehabilitation of existing tenants/occupiers plus incentive FSI (55% to 80% according to total area of project) whichever is more.

Community participation through consent of tenants/occupiers

4. Consent of 70% eligible tenants/occupiers is a necessary condition (consent is not required if scheme is being undertaken by MHADA/MCGM) and the project shall ensure that all eligible tenants/occupiers are rehabilitated in new building.

Size of tenement

5. The minimum size of tenement in new building shall be 27.88 sq. m (300 sq. ft) and the maximum shall be equivalent to the area occupied in the old building. However, for carpet area exceeding 70 sq. m, the cost of construction shall be paid by occupier/tenants and this area shall not be considered for incentive FSI.

Use of incentive FSI

6. To make the project viable, 30% of Incentive FSI can be used for non-residential purposes.

Transit camp

7. Transit camp may be permitted on the same land or elsewhere as the situation demands.

Transfer of tenement

8. Restriction on transfer of tenement shall be governed by Rent Control Act, until society is formed.
9. Slum tenements shall not be allowed to be transferred within a period of 10 year.

Corpus fund for maintenance

10. A corpus fund for maintenance of the buildings for a period of 10 years to be decided by High Power Committee (HPC).
11. A HPC will be constituted.

Approval of the schemes

12. The HPC will approve the schemes with the previous sanction of the government under DCR 33(9).
13. After approval by this committee, the proposal will be submitted to MCGM.

Source: SRA (2016).

Annexure 5.3 Guideline for Area Redevelopment in Delhi

The basic objective of redevelopment scheme, as per Para 3.3 of MPD-2021, is to accommodate more population in a planned manner in all use zones for efficient and optimum utilisation of existing urban land, both in planned and unplanned areas of Delhi. Para 3.3.2 provides the format of guidelines, under which the redevelopment schemes can be prepared, which includes the following:

1. Influence zones along MRTS corridors and the sub-zones for redevelopment and renewal are required to be identified. The Master Plan further states that with the development and introduction of MRTS, need is felt to connect these scattered CBD/district centres/community centres with more imageable components, and with enhanced built-up areas and activities so as to become a part of continued urban experience (Para 11.4.2).

   Layout plan

2. The residents/cooperative societies/private developers have to prepare layout and services plan in consultation with the concerned authorities for approval.

   Plan approval

3. The overall redevelopment plan would require approval at the following two stages:

    i. Planning permission for an area of 4 ha in case any approved layout/redevelopment/regulation plan exists for the area, such permission may not be required.

    ii. Clusterblock for a minimum area of 3,000 sq. m is required where the owners should pool together and reorganise their individual properties so as to provide a minimum of 30% of area as common green/soft parking besides circulation areas and common facilities. Subsequent to cluster block approval, individual building shall be given sanction by the concerned authority within the framework of cluster block approval.

   Amalgamation and reconstitution of plots

4. Amalgamation and reconstitution of plots for planning purpose will be permitted.

Norms

5. For all development envisaged under such provision, the norms of group housing with respect to ground coverage, basement, parking, setback, etc. shall be applicable except FAR which is incentivised as maximum over all FAR of 50% over and above the existing permissible FAR on individual plots subject to a maximum of 400. Appropriate levies for increased FAR and land use conversion shall be payable. Lutyens Bungalow Zone, Civil Lines Bungalows Area and regulated monuments are not allowed for redevelopment for enhanced FAR.

Community facilities

6. For community facilities provision/social infrastructure, reduced spaces standard may be adopted. Moreover, the land require for any public purpose may be acquired with the consent of the owner through issue of development rights, certificates in lieu of payment toward, cost of land, further the concept of AR, that is, allowing construction of community facilities without counting in FAR may also utilised.

FAR for commercial use

7. The redevelopment scheme can help provision of parking and services and up to 10% of FAR may be allowed for commercial use and 10% of FAR for community facilities so as to trigger the process of self-generating redevelopment.

Land use regulations

8. The land use of redevelopment scheme is to be governed as per the master plan/zonal development plan and the non-residential use will be permitted as per provisions of mixed use regulations and Special Area Regulations.

Source: MPD-2021, Para 2.3.2.

Annexure 5.4 *Cluster Redevelopment Scheme, Mumbai*

The following are the salient features of the Urban Renewal Scheme through cluster redevelopment approach as per Maharashtra Housing Policy in 2007 as applicable to urban renewal in island city of Mumbai with specific regulatory provisions in DCR for Greater Mumbai:

Basic objective

1. The scheme is introduced with composite aim of redevelopment of a cluster of existing old structures by amalgamating various plots under different ownership and creating space for development of infrastructures and public amenities in and around such cluster.

(continued)

(continued)

Minimum size of cluster
2. The minimum size of such cluster is stipulated as 4,000 sq. m and additional incentives are provided for formation of bigger size cluster.

Rehabilitation of all occupants
3. The focus is for the redevelopment of old buildings and rehabilitation of all occupants in new buildings on ownership basis.

Government and semi-government lands
4. For enabling cluster formation, even government and semi-government lands falling within the proposed cluster, either vacant or built with office buildings or tenanted residential buildings are allowed to be included in the cluster.

Cut-off date
5. The mix categories of structures considered eligible for inclusion in Urban Renewal Scheme are old and dilapidated buildings existing prior to 1969; buildings in dangerous condition even subsequent to 1969; declared slum area and buildings under construction.

Minimum size of rehabilitation tenement
6. The criteria of minimum 300 sq. ft carpet area for rehabilitation tenement is prescribed.

Implementing agency
7. The scheme is to be implemented through private participation or by local authorities through appointment of agencies.

Consent of tenants/occupants and plot owners
8. The promoter/developer of cluster redevelopment scheme is required to obtain irrevocable consent of 70% of tenants/occupants of structures and consents of 100% owners of plots falling in the proposed cluster.

The promoter/developer to bear all costs
9. The promoter/developer to implement the Urban Renewal Scheme by reconstructing the existing structures at his own cost and rehousing the tenants/occupants free of cost in reconstructed building.

Incentive FSI
10. For implementing the scheme, promoter/developer to get compensation in the form of incentive.

FAR/FSI in stipulated proportion of rehabilitation component.

11. The proportion of incentive FSI increases from 55% to 80% of rehabilitation component with the size of cluster ranging from 4,000 sq. m to more than 20,000 sq. m, respectively. Hence, scheme has inherent stimulation for forming bigger size cluster for better urban renewal.

12. The FSI permissible for the scheme is 4.0 on gross plot area or that required for the rehabilitation of existing tenants/occupants plus incentive FSI (55–80% as the case may be) whichever is more.

Provision of public amenities and their handing over to planning authorities

13. The promoter/developer to develop reservations imposed for public amenities as per Sanctioned Development Plan for Greater Mumbai on plots included in cluster and hand it over to planning authority free of cost; provision of onsite infrastructure—the onsite infrastructure—is to be renewed, developed by promoter/developer as per the remarks and suggestions by respective infrastructure departments of planning authority MCGM.

Provision of offsite infrastructure and collection of cess

14. For offsite infrastructure facilities to be developed by MCGM, development cess is collected in proportion to proposed construction area in the urban renewal cluster from the developer.

Formation of cooperative housing society

15. After the completion of the Urban Renewal Scheme, the land with new buildings to be conveyed to cooperative housing society of rehabilitated tenants/occupants and new members purchasing flats from sale portion.

Source: Based upon Isore (2014, pp. 150–151).

Annexure 5.5 *Guidelines for Regularisation of Unauthorised Colonies in Delhi*

MoUD, the Government of India, from time to time, have notified guidelines for the regularisation and extending legal status of unauthorised colonies in Delhi. Taking into account the order of the Supreme Court dated 14 February 2006, MoUD issued (vide letter dated 05 October 2007) the Revised Guidelines for Regularisation of Unauthorised Colonies in Delhi 2007.

(continued)

(continued)

1. **Criteria for regularisation**
   Cut-off date

   These guidelines are for the regularisation of unauthorised colonies (except those inhabited by affluent sections of society) as existed as per aerial survey of 2002 and 'habitations' existing as on 1 March 2002 that have come up as extension to village *abadi* would be eligible for regularisation on the same lines as unauthorised colonies.

   Habitations existing as on 31 March 2002 that have come up as an extension to village *abadi* and have not been notified as *lal dora* Extension to village *abadi* would be eligible for regularisation on the same lines as unauthorised colonies subjects to meeting the requirements of regulation framed pursuant to these guidelines.

   Colonies excluded from regularisation.

   As per these guidelines, the following types of colonies or parts thereof would not be considered for regularisation:

   1.1 Colonies/parts of colonies falling in notified or reserved forest areas.
   1.2 Colonies/parts of colonies which pose hindrances in the provision of infrastructure facilities or fall in the area of ROW of existing/proposed railway; master plan roads and major/trunk water supply and sewerage lines.
   1.3 Colonies where more than 50% plots are un-built on the date of formal announcement of regularisation scheme. However, plots, which have been built-up in the above-mentioned colonies, even after 31 March 2002 and until the date of formal announcement of regularisation scheme, will be taken into consideration for deciding the eligibility of the colony for regularisation.
   1.4 No regularisation would be done, of colonies or parts of colonies, whether on private or public land, if it violates the provisions of Ancient Monuments and Archaeological Sites and Remains Act, 1958.

2. **Procedure for regularisation**
   2.1 Registration of residents society

   The registration of residents society in each unauthorised colony to liaison with the concerned local body/DDA/GNCTD in various matters would be a precondition for considering the case for regularisation.

   2.2 Preparation of existing layout plan and sanction

   The residents society shall prepare the existing layout plan. However, the residents society may voluntarily submit proposals of improved layout plan for respective colony.

There would be no objection to several associations in a colony, but they would have to be federated into one registered residents society. The local bodies/GNCTD would only interact with such residents societies which have a least 75% of residents of that colony as their members.

While preparing existing layout plan, the residents society shall identify plots/location for social infrastructure facilities. This land would be transferred in the name of the local body/DDA. 'In such colonies where land cannot be made available by the residents society, the colony would have to manage without provisions of such facilities'.

There would be no obligation on the part of the government/GNCTD/DDA the local body allot alternate sites or flats to residents who are displaced on account of the provision of land for roads, civic amenities and community facilities.

2.3 Parameters for regularisation

The parameters for regularisation will include (a) title of land, (b) spatial norms as per Para 4.2.2.2 (B) of MPD-2021, (c) mixed land uses as per provisions of MPD-2021 (Para 15.3.3) and (d) recovery of cost.

2.4 Undertakings

The resident society shall furnish the following undertakings at the time of submission of the layout plan:

Government of NCT of Delhi will issue provisional regularisation certificate to the unauthorised colonies which fulfils the conditions laid down in the Clause 4 of the regulation to be completed by the resident societies as per the notification dated 24 March 2008 for the regularisation of unauthorised colonies in Delhi.

The construction on each individual plot is to be brought within the prescribed development control norms by the individual owner/resident society. 'However, it will not be a pre-condition for regularisation of colony'.

The cost of land will be collected by the concerned local body/DDA on behalf of land owning department/agency. The amount so recovered will be credited to the account of respective land owning department/agency.

The penalties as per Para 2 will be collected by the concerned local body/DDA and credited into a separated fund. From this fund and its own resources, DDA under the guidance of the MoUD, construct houses for EWS or carry out any other developmental works such as development of parks, etc.

(continued)

(continued)

The 1639 applications received by UD department have already been sent to MCD/DDA for the scrutiny of the documents/layout plans as per the procedure laid down in the notification dated 24 March 2008.

The Government of NCT of Delhi has been entrusted with the task of demarcation of boundaries of unauthorised colonies as on 31 March 2002. This work has been entrusted to Guru Gobind Singh Indraprastha University, Kashmiri Gate (New Delhi), and the exercise is to be completed within three months by the University.

As per the notification 16 June 2008, the local body/DDA and GNCTD would complete the prescribed formalities before the formal regularisation of the unauthorised colony as prescribed under Clause 5 of the regulations within a period of 12 months from the date of issue of provisional certificate. Lt. Governor, Delhi, may relax the time limit in respect of individual colonies as provided in Clause 5.11 of the regulations.

3. **Other provisions**
   3.1 In respect of unauthorised colonies to be regularised, suitable modifications, including land use in the master plan/zonal plan, shall be made, as may be necessary.
   3.2 The provision of incentivised redevelopment in the MPD-2021 for unauthorised regularised colonies will also be applicable to these colonies once regularised.
   3.3 To ensure early resolution of issues related to tenure right to promote incentivised redevelopment, a committee may be constituted by GNCTD with the representatives of DDA to evolve suitable guidelines in this regard, preferably within a timeframe of two months.

4. **Implementing agencies**
   4.1 A separate cell will be created in the planning division of local bodies/DDA to carry out the work relating to regularisation of unauthorised colonies.
   4.2 The work related to regularisation, including preparation and implementation of development works involving agencies concerned, would be undertaken, coordinated, monitored and supervised by GNCTD.

5. **Miscellaneous**
   5.1 Within the overall framework of these guidelines, if any clarification is required, instructions/advice of the MoUD, Government of India, shall be obtained.

5.2 Regularisation of unauthorised colonies shall be subject to order of Supreme Court dated 14 February 2006 in which regularisation shall be subject to clearance of local agencies.

5.3 Action against unauthorised construction, which do not fulfil the conditions for regularisation, will be taken by the concerned local body/DDA which is subject to provisions contained in MPD, including those in Para 16.2.3.

Source: Chakraborty (2014, pp. 33–36) and Government of India (2008).

Annexure 5.6 Policy Guidelines for the Scheme for Relocation of JJ Clusters in Delhi

The Delhi Government, vide Cabinet Decision No. 510, dated 10 May 2000, framed Policy Guidelines for implementation of the Scheme for relocation of JJ Clusters, which, *inter alia*, reads as follows:

Relocation from project sites only

1. Jhuggis will be relocated only from project sites where specific requests have been received from the land owning agencies for cleaning of the project lands. No large-scale removal of jhuggis should be resorted to without any specific use for the cleared site.

Land for relocation

2. Land for relocation of jhuggis will be identified in Delhi and NCR in consultation with the DDA and NCRPB so that it is in conformity with the land use policy laid down under the Master Plan, and the NCR Plan. Land pockets in NCR well connected with the transport system should also be utilised for relocation of JJ dwellers in Delhi.
3. Land will be acquired at the sites identified by the DDA / NCR in small pockets not exceeding 10 acre (4 hectare) near existing residential areas so that cost of provision of peripheral services is minimised.
4. A target of shifting 10,000 jhuggis in 2000–2001 is laid down. This target will be reviewed each year in April by Delhi Govt. based on requests received from land owning agencies.
5. Land will be acquired under the scheme of 'large Scale Acquisition for Planned Development of Delhi'. Its development and disposal will also be governed by the conditions laid down under Government of India Orders No. F.37/16/50-Delhi (1) dated 2.5.1961 read with GOI's Order No. J-20011/12/77-L.II dated 14.2.92 making it compulsory for

(continued)

(continued)

conversion of plots below 50 sq. m from leasehold to freehold. After acquisition, the land will be placed at the disposal of the Executing Agency by the Lands Department of Delhi Government. The ownership of the land acquired for relocation will vest with the Delhi Government. Requests for acquisition will be routed by the Executing Agency through the Urban Development Department of Delhi Government.

Cut-off date and eligibility criteria

6. Cut-off date for beneficiaries would be 30.11.98. To verify eligibility, ration cards issued prior to 30.11.98 will be taken into account. The name of the allottee must also figure in the notified Voters' List as on 30.11.98. Jhuggis who come up after 30.11.98 will be removed without any alternative allotment by the project Executing Agency.

Size of plot

7. Keeping in view the scarcity and high cost of land, the plot size now approved for JJ dwellers will be as under:

Size of Plot	*JJ Dwellers Who Were Eligible Before 31 January 1990*	*JJ Dwellers Who Have Become Eligible Between 1 February 1990 and 30 December 1998*
Size of plot for a single dwelling unit with WC	20 sq. m	15 sq. m
Ground coverage	100%	100%

Layout plans

8. The layout plans for the relocation settlement will be prepared by the Executing Agency and proper approval taken from the concerned local body/DDA as the case may be. Executing Agency will follow the ISI Code 8888 for preparing the layout. Land use of gross area will be as under:

Land Use	*Per cent*
Residential plots	50%
Services	30%

Other social infrastructure such as schools, dispensary, community hall and local shopping area and other utility sites	20%

Building plans

9. The Executing Agency will also prepare standard building plans for each relocation settlement which are duly approved by the local bodies/DDA. The sanction shall be given to the beneficiary along with the allotment letters/conveyance deed.

Construction of dwelling units

10. The construction of dwelling units on the plots will be carried out by the allottee in accordance with the sanctioned lay out plans/building plans, within a period of one year from the actual date of shifting. Till completion of the project and handing over of the services to the concerned local bodies, the Executing Agency will exercise the necessary building controls and ensure that the construction activities go on as per the approved plans and building plans. In case, the allottee fails to build even a single floor with WC within a period of one year the allotment be cancelled and plot resumed by the Executing Agency.

Handing of the services for maintenance to the local bodies

11. After two years from the date of actual shifting of the cluster to the re-settlement site, the settlement shall stand transferred to the concerned local body for maintaining services, and for exercising of building controls.

Cost of land and development

12. Cost of land at ₹16 lakh per acre or ₹400 per sq. m; cost of internal development at ₹600 sq. m; total land and development cost: ₹1,000 per sq. m of gross area, or ₹2,000 per sq. m of net area.
13. ......*

Recovery of electricity and water

14. Charges for consumption of electricity and water will be recovered from allottees for community toilets and common water hydrants. Fixed charges shall be recovered by the Executing Agency from each allottee to cover the cost of maintenance and consumption of water for the first two years, during which period metered supply will be provided by DVB/DJB.

(continued)

(continued)

Water supply/water harvesting

15. Individual metered water connections will be given to each allottee within a period of two years of shifting. The reduced norm for supply of water as in the case of unauthorised colonies will be adopted. The work of laying of internal water and sewer lines at the resettlement site shall be executed by the DJB from funds to be provided by the Executing Agency. No departmental charges will however be liveable by DJB for such works. Peripheral and trunk services will be provided by DJB as in the case of other settlement at its own cost.

    The DJB will adopt innovative technology for water harvesting and ground water recharge at the relocation site.

Electricity

16. Individual metered connections will be provided to each allottee. The work of internal electrification as in the case of unauthorised colonies will be carried out by DVB. No departmental charges will be levied by DVB for executing the work. Peripheral and trunk services will be provided by DVB at its own cost as in the case of unauthorised colonies.

Other developmental works

17. Other developmental works like laying of roads, drains, developmental of parks, etc. will be carried out by the Executing Agency. The services shall be transferred to the local bodies/DDA after a period of 2 years from the date of shifting, for maintenance.

Density and size of each dwelling unit

18. Keeping in view the high cost of land in Delhi and the reducing availability, density shall be as follows:

Size	Density
15 sq. m plot	300 dwelling units per hectare
20 sq. m plot	250 dwelling units per hectare

Terms of allotment

19. The grant of freehold plots to JJ dwellers at the relocation site has been agreed to, in principle by Delhi Government subject to clearance by Government of India. Separate instructions with regard to nature and tenure shall be issued shortly.

Public utility sites

20. Sites for putting up sub-stations by DVB, tube wells and other water related infrastructure as also for primary school, community hall and dispensary will be transferred on a token charge of ₹1 to the concerned government agency, since cost of such land has already been paid for by other departments of the Government/Delhi Government.

Survey of clusters

21. Prior to relocation and payment of subside by the land owning agency and Delhi Government, a joint survey of the slum cluster will be carried out by the DC of the revenue district, jointly with the land owning agency and Executing Agency. The figure of jhuggis to be relocated should be determined on the basis of this survey keeping in view the eligibility criteria.

Issue of laser cards

22. Each allottee of a site and services plot shall be issued a Laser Card by the DC of the revenue district. This card will carry all relevant details of the allottee and his family members. This Laser Card will be used by the District authorities to check allotment of more than one plot to a family.

Source: Delhi High Court.[1]

Note: *The judgement of Delhi High Court Order, the basic source of these guidelines, does not give any text under serial number 13 and has left it blank as shown.

References

Business Standard. (2016, 18 May). Bhendi Bazaar redevelopment kicks off. *Business Standard*, Mumbai.

Chakraborty, N. K. (2014, January). *Redevelopment and regeneration of unauthorised colonies in Delhi: Challenges and participatory approach*. Paper presented in the 62nd NTCP Congress at Pune, ITPI, New Delhi.

Chotani, M. L., & Mallick, J. B. (2014, January). *Urban renewal in India: A regulatory mechanism*. Paper presented in the 62nd NTCP Congress at Pune, ITPI, New Delhi.

---

[1] Delhi High Court Judgement on combined writ petitions WP(C) Nos. 8904/2009, 7735/2007, 7317/2009 and 9246/2009, delivered on 11 February 2010 at Delhi, pp. 41–46. http://www.hrln.org/hrln/Order%20Mukundi%20lal.pdf

CPWD. (2013). *A handbook of conservation of heritage buildings: A guide.* New Delhi: Directorate General of Central Public Works Department.

DDA. (2007). *Master Plan for Delhi, 2021.* New Delhi: Author.

Dutton, J. E., & Duncan, R. B. (1987). The creation of momentum for change through the process of strategic issue diagnosis. *Strategic Management Journal, 8*(3), 279–295.

Government of India. (2014). *Handbook of service level benchmarking.* New Delhi: Ministry of Urban Development.

Gualini, E., & Bianchi, I. (2015a). Space, politics and conflicts: A review of contemporary research in urban research and planning theory. In *Planning and Conflict: Critical Perspectives on Contentious Urban Developments* (pp. 37–55). New York, NY: Routledge.

———. (Eds). (2015b). *Planning and conflict, critical perspective on contentious urban development.* New York, NY: Routledge.

Holcomb, B. (2010). Provisioning place, de- and re-constructing image of industrial city. In Tallon (Ed). *Urban regeneration and renewal.* London: Routledge.

Isore, S. N. (2014, January). *Urban renewal scheme through cluster redevelopment approach: Case study Bhendi Bazaar, Mumbai.* Paper presented in the 62nd NTCP Congress at Pune, ITPI, New Delhi.

Kulshrestha, S. K. (2016). Air pollution control through traffic management: The Delhi experiment. *Spatio-economic Development Record, 23*(1, January–February), 3.

Lyndon, M., Bratman, D., Woudstra, R., & Khawarzad, A. (n.d.). *Tactical urbanism vol. 1: Short-term action, long-term change.* Miami: Street Plans Collaborative.

Mehra, S. K. (2014, January). *Regulatory and institutional mechanism for redevelopment in Delhi: The vision of master plan-2021 and further possibilities.* Paper presented in the 62nd NTCP Congress at Pune, ITPI, New Delhi.

Ministry of Tourism. (2015). *PRASAD: Scheme guidelines.* New Delhi: Government of India.

MoUD. (2005). *Guidelines for basic services to the urban poor.* New Delhi: Government of India.

———. (2006). *Jawaharlal Nehru National Urban Renewal Mission: Guidelines for project preparation 3.* New Delhi: Government of India.

———. (n.d.). *Detailed project report: Preparation toolkit.* New Delhi: Government of India.

Nangnure, S. B. (2014, January). *Urban renewal policies: Consequences and implications.* Paper presented in the 62nd NTCP Congress at Pune, ITPI, New Delhi.

Planning Commission. (2008). *Manual of integrated district planning.* New Delhi: Government of India.

Simpson, C. (2015). *An overview and analysis of Tactical Urbanism in Los Angeles.* Occidental College, Los Angeles.

SRA. (2016). *Stagewise description, Slum Rehabilitation Authority (SRA).* Mumbai. Retrieved 23 July 2017, from http://www.sra.gov.in/pgeDescriptionStage.aspx

The Times of India. (2017, May 1). Feel exclusive. *The Times of India,* New Delhi.

CHAPTER 6

Resource Mobilisation for Urban Renewal

Introduction

Resources, normally, refer to money, material and manpower needed for accomplishing the objectives of any business, firm, plan or project. In the context of spatial development, including renewal, the resources include land, finance and institutions. Information and time, as resources, are also needed for the renewal exercises to build awareness and mobilise support of the community/stakeholders. The scope of this chapter is limited to covering three resources—land, finance and institutions.

In spatial planning and development, land is the prime resource for locating various activities and services as well as generating fiscal resources through innovative use of spatial planning tools (land use and FAR/FSI). Before proceeding further in this chapter, it is desirable to understand the land and its potential and the manner it generates funds.

Understanding Land and Its Potential

Land is a geographical entity. As shown in Figure 6.1, land has two attributes: (a) land as a physical entity and (b) land potential. Land as

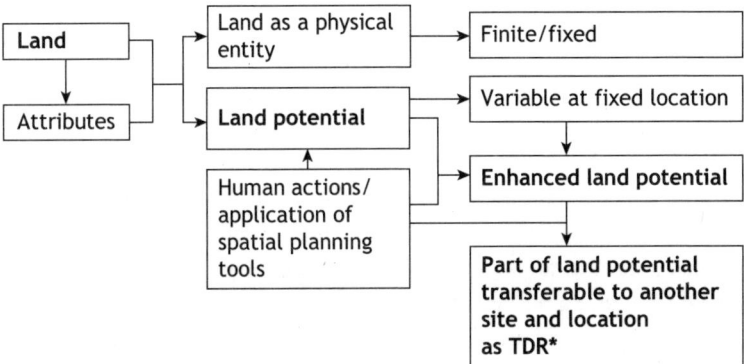

Figure 6.1 *Concept of Land, Its Potential and Transfer of Land Potential*

Note: *TDR: Transferable development right.

a physical entity is defined by location and area. It is finite. The location and area of a specific site are fixed and cannot be changed. Land potential, on the other hand, is the value of returns derived from land for a variety of purposes. The potential of land is not fixed and can be modified through human actions and spatial planning tools that improve the quality of land or decide its use, and hence affect the returns.

For example, returns from land used for agriculture may be enhanced through human actions such as use of fertilisers or improved high-yielding variety of seeds which improve its productivity, and hence returns. With the additional provision of irrigation, the same parcel of land may be used for producing two or more crops in a year which increases the actual sown area and we have net sown area (the physical land area) and gross sown area (the sum of net sown area plus the additional area under two or more crops). Here, gross sown area is always more than net sown area. A double-cropped land has higher value than single cropped hence, increase in potential of land due to human actions.

Application of spatial planning tools (Figure 6.1) in human settlements in the form of a master plan changes the use of land from agriculture to non-agriculture use which modifies the potential of land immensely before and after the plan. Non-agriculture area always gives higher returns than agriculture area. Again, the potential of different parcels of land varies with its designated land use which may be open space, amenities space, residential, industrial or commercial. The comparative returns from land keep on increasing in the same order, where potential of returns from land used for open space is lowest and commercial is highest. Once again, on different parcels of land, having the same land use, the comparative potential can be changed through spatial planning tools such as density (number of persons or number of DU/ha) and FAR/FSI which control the intensity of use. Among different plots of land, having same area and land use, a plot with higher permissible FAR will have more potential than the one which has lower FAR. This is not the end. Though land cannot be moved from one place to another, its potential can be transferred from one site to another through innovative spatial planning tool of TDR (see Figure 6.1). The following sections explain the FAR/FSI and TDR further.

Understanding FAR/FSI

FAR and FSI are one and the same tools. The difference is that FAR is expressed as percentage of the total permissible built-up area to the site area, while FSI is the ratio of total permissible built-up area and the site area. An FAR of 100 means 100% of the site area is permitted as built-up area distributed on different floors of the building. Its FSI equivalent is 1. Similarly, an FSI of 4 is same as FAR of 400. This FAR/FSI of 4 also indicates that on a plot of say 1,000 sq. m, the built-up area permissible is 4,000 sq. m It shows that the plot area remaining the same, the potential of the plot (permissible built-up area) has been increased by four times. This supports the observation that the land area of a specific plot cannot be changed, however, its potential, defined as the permissible built-up area, can be altered through application of spatial planning tools. FAR/FSI defines the potential of land in terms of built space that can be constructed on a site. Higher FAR/FSI means more built space, hence better property value and greater returns. In Delhi and some other states, the term FAR is used and in other states such as Maharashtra and Gujarat, FSI is used.

FAR/FSI is assigned to an area by the master plan and DCRs. It should be noted that

1. the FAR/FSI is given on a specified use zone in a master plan/ DCRs;
2. the FAR/FSI can be different for different use zones;
3. the FAR/FSI can be different for same use zone located in different areas like city core and city periphery or along different hierarchies of roads;
4. the FAR/FSI can be classified as
    i. master plan/overall/gross FAR/FSI,
    ii. additional/compensatory FAR/FSI,
    iii. incentive FAR/FSI,
    iv. floating FAR/FSI and
    v. spot FAR/FSI.

The need for the classification of FAR/FSI is felt because the facts that several documents (master plans, notifications and technical articles) have used them as interchangeable terms or as indicative term without defining or giving their method of calculation. An attempt is being made, here, to define each one of them.

The master plan FAR/FSI is one that has been specified in the DCR of a master plan. It is also termed as overall or gross FAR/FSI.

In slum area redevelopment programmes, sometimes, the given norms and policies stipulate that all eligible slum dwellers have to be accommodated on the same site in tenements of an agreed size. If, in a given redevelopment area, the total built-up area so needed is not feasible as per DCR, an additional FAR/FSI, over and above the master plan FAR/FSI, may be granted. Additional FAR/FSI may therefore be defined as the ratio of the additional built space and the plot area required implementing the redevelopment norm and policy.

To mobilise fiscal resources through the instrument of FAR/FSI (discussed later in this chapter), an incentive FAR/FSI is granted to the developer to recover his cost. Incentive FAR/FSI is, therefore, defined as the ratio of the additional built space and the plot area required for recovering the cost of development with reasonable profit by builder/developer by commercially selling the built space so made available.

If in case the augmentation of infrastructure and improvement in accessibility, through urban renewal efforts in an area, allows densification and increase in FAR/FSI, the same may be used to generate resources. There can be three options for this increased FAR/FSI: (a) distribute equally on all plots and collect higher house tax, (b) distribute a part of the FAR/FSI on all plots to ensure equity and auction the rest of the FAR/FSI and allocated to the highest bidders from the area and (c) auction the entire increased FAR/FSI and allocate to the highest bidders from the area. In options (b) and (c), the FAR/FSI is not fixed to an area or building, and hence it is termed as floating FAR/FSI. Floating FAR/FSI, therefore, can be defined as the ratio of the increased built space and the plot area made available due to augmentation of infrastructure and accessibility.

There are conditions when a specific FAR/FSI is granted for a specific spot due to master policies. For example, in a policy of high-rise-high-density (HRHD) development, the designated HRHD zone may be granted specific FAR/FSI as required by the policy. Such FAR/FSI is termed as Spot FAR/FSI which is applicable to the specific spot only. Spot FAR/FSI can be defined as FAR/FSI assigned to a specific spot in the master plan/approved scheme being developed due to a policy/scheme or guideline.

Understanding TDR

TDR can be defined as a compensation, in the form of FAR/FSI or development rights, which entitle the owner for construction of built-up area in lieu of built-up area surrendered to authorities for a public purpose.

As mentioned earlier in this chapter and indicated in Figure 6.1, TDR is a tool that allows transfer of the land potential of a particular plot to another plot located in another designated area. The owner of the land used for constructing a building for public purposes is awarded TDR, as per DCRs, in the form of FAR/FSI equivalent and the Development Rights Certificate (DRC) is issued. The area where the TDR is raised is termed as 'the generating area' and area where it is to be consumed is termed as 'the receiving area'. The TDR can be used by the owner on their own plot located in the designated receiving area. If they do not have a plot in the receiving area, they can transfer the TDR to any other person owning land in the receiving area. Thus, TDR is a flexible tool and, like shares, it can be traded and transferred to any other person.

TDR can also be granted in lieu of the cost of land required for reservations in the development plan for facilities and roads. It can also be given against the cost of built space provided for housing urban poor in a redevelopment scheme. For example, TDR may be given to the builder in a slum redevelopment scheme where all occupants are to be housed in new tenements, free of cost, and where an incentive FAR/FSI has been granted to recover the cost with reasonable profit, incurred in construction of new tenements.

For the purpose of clarity in understanding and application, TDR can be divided into three categories: (a) General TDR, (b) Heritage TDR and (c) Slum TDR. In Maharashtra, General TDR is normally generated from land reservations for public purposes such as widening the roads and provision for amenities, including open spaces shown in redevelopment plan, and this can be used in the designated receiving zones only.

The Heritage TDR is generated due to the loss of development potential under heritage buildings and precincts. This is granted only on the part of the heritage land parcel or structure that is not developable or used. To boost conservation of heritage, this TDR may be used in non-receiving zones of high potential areas also.

A TDR generated from redevelopment or rehabilitation of eligible slum areas is termed as the Slum TDR, and it is granted to the developer and may be used in the designated receiving zone.

TDR is being applied in Maharashtra, Gujarat, Tamil Nadu, Rajasthan and Karnataka for public purposes such as slum redevelopment, provision of affordable housing, widening the roads and provision of open spaces, playfields, public parking lots and other civic amenities (MoUD, 2014, p. 82).

This understanding of land, which is finite and immovable, and its potential which is changeable and transferable from one site to another, has been used for innovative approaches for land assembly and fiscal resource generation as discussed in the following sections.

Land Assembly for Urban Renewal

Urban renewal schemes, especially, provision of facilities, services, roads and other infrastructure, require land. Assembly of land has always been an important component of spatial development efforts. Urban renewal is no exception. The land acquisition requires huge investment as compensation paid to land owners by the redevelopment agency. In most of the cases, the fiscal resources of these agencies or ULBs are insufficient. The urban redevelopment areas, invariably, have a large number of individual owners which further complicate the problem. As a result, urban renewal projects are delayed or placed on a very low priority. The current land law, known as Right to Fare Compensation and Transparency in Land Acquisition, Rehabilitation and Resettlement (RFCTLARR) Act, 2013, has made the land acquisition complex, costly and time consuming. It requires social impact assessment and establishment of public purpose as essential precondition. In addition, it requires (a) rehabilitation and resettlement of each affected family and (b) consent of 70% landowners in PPP projects or 80% landowners in case of projects of private companies. The rate of compensation in the earlier Land Acquisition Act, 1894, which has been replaced by the new Act of 2013, was fixed on the basis of the date when the intention to acquire land was made public and now it is the market rate on the date of acquisition (Government of India, 2013).

Under the present legal regime, acquisition of land has, thus, become more complex, time consuming and costly. Considering the practical problems faced in the implementation of RFCTLARR Act, 2013, an amendment has been passed by the Lok Sabha, known as RFCTLARR (Amendment) Act, 2015. The upper house, Rajya Sabha, has yet to pass this Amendment. According to this amendment, as far as urban renewal is concerned, the conditions of social impact assessment and establishment of public purpose as well as consent clause will not be applicable for affordable housing and infrastructure projects. All other conditions will remain as the same.

The land acquisition process is still expensive and there is a need to evolve innovative approaches to land assembly. To implement urban renewal programmes, Maharashtra Governments have evolved innovative approaches for land assembly which are being replicated by other states as well.

Innovative Approaches to Land Assembly

Accommodation Reservation for Provision of Amenities

Using the concept of potential of land, as discussed earlier in this chapter, Maharashtra has pioneered an innovative concept, known as Accommodation Reservation, for getting land for the provision of amenities in a development or redevelopment plan. According to this concept,

- The owner of the site, reserved for an amenity in an approved redevelopment plan, is allowed to develop the site using full potential in the form of permissible FSI/FAR on the plot subject to agreeing to entrust and hand over the built-up area of such amenity to the local authority free of all encumbrances and accept full FAR/FSI as compensation in lieu thereof.
- The area utilised for the amenity shall not form part of FAR/FSI calculation.
- In case the owner is unable to utilise the permissible FAR/FSI, in full or in part, they will be entitled to the option of award of TDR.

In this manner, all the stakeholders, the owner, local authority and the public, are benefited as:

- Owner gets full potential of his site and locational advantages.
- The local authority gets the amenity, free of all encumbrances, without acquiring land and incurring expenditure on payment of compensation.
- The people get the required amenity.

In Maharashtra, all municipal corporations have incorporated the provisions of accommodation reservation in their DCR. DDA has also incorporated this concept in the Development Code Clause 3(7) (DDA, 2010, p. 195).

This method of land assembly is applicable in areas where the cost of building construction is lower than the price of land. Accordingly, this technique will be successful in large cities and may not work in small cites where land price is lower than the construction cost.

Award of TDR as Compensation for Land for Provision of Amenities

For the assembly of land for certain amenities such as parks, playgrounds, schools or reserved zones around heritage buildings, as shown in a redevelopment plan of the area, the landowners can be granted TDR in the form of FAR/FSI, if they agree to surrender and handover land, free of all encumbrances, to the development authority/local body.

Land Amalgamation for Cluster Redevelopment

In this innovative approach to land assembly, the provisions, guidelines and regulations of master plans are utilised. This approach, in nutshell, is based upon an amalgamation of plots to form a cluster. It may also require additional FAR to rehabilitate all occupants and also provide all facilities and services as per DCRs and incentive FAR to developer for recovering his investment with reasonable profit.

For example, the Guidelines for Redevelopment Schemes, given in MPD-2021 (DDA, 2010, p. 29), provides for the amalgamation of plots and reconstruction for planning purposes (Annexure 5.3). Regulations for the Rehabilitation and Redevelopment of Slums, 2010, in Gujarat also provide for clubbing of plots for the redevelopment of slums and also for other uses. SRA, Mumbai, has given a practical process for such land assembly by constituting a slum dwellers' cooperative housing society as explained in Chapter 5 (see Figure 5.2 and Annexure 5.1). The Cluster Redevelopment Scheme, Mumbai

(Chapter 5, Annexure 5.4) provides for the redevelopment of a cluster (at least 4,000 sq. m) of existing old structures on various plots under different ownership where even government and semi-government lands falling within the proposed cluster either vacant or built with office buildings or tenanted residential buildings are also allowed to be included in the cluster. To ensure public participation and avoid resistance and unrest, the promoter/developer of cluster redevelopment scheme is required to obtain the irrevocable consent of 70% of tenants/occupants of structures and consents of 100% owners of plots falling in the proposed cluster. The promoter/developer provides all reservations imposed for public amenities, as per provisions of sanctioned Development Plan for Greater Mumbai and hands them over to the planning authority free of cost. For implementing the scheme, promoter/developer gets compensation in the form of incentive FSI in stipulated proportion of rehabilitation component. After the completion of the Urban Renewal Scheme, the land with new buildings is conveyed to a cooperative housing society of rehabilitated tenants/occupants and to the new members purchasing flats from sale portion.

DDA Notification dated 1 April 2011 on Regulation and Guidelines for Redevelopment of Existing Planned Industrial Areas has also provided for the amalgamation of plots for effective and functional renewal projects and an incentive FAR.

This manner of land assembly is suitable for the redevelopment of slum areas and old planned low-density underutilised areas and industrial clusters having multiple landowners. There are several advantages of amalgamation of land for cluster redevelopment. It provides more freedom for planning and urban design and ensures provision for public amenities including school, healthcare, onsite infrastructures such as widened road, adequate space for parking of vehicles, resizing and relaying of water mains, drainage lines and storm water drains. The planning authority also gets benefited as the fully developed reservations for public amenities as per development plan are transferred to them at no additional cost, as covered under incentive FSI. Finally, the city gets the amenities and an overall facelift.

Land Assembly for Widening of Roads Through Additional FAR/FSI

The instrument of FAR/FSI can be applied to assemble land for road widening or construction of new roads passing through built-up areas. In this case,

- The local authority can grant additional FAR/FSI on 100% of the area required for road widening or for construction of new road proposed under the development or redevelopment plan.
- The owner surrenders the land for widening or construction of new road to the local authority free of all encumbrances and accepts the compensation in lieu thereof in terms of additional 100% FAR/FSI on area surrendered.

In such cases, land is made available to the local authority for road widening in built-up areas, with owners' participation, without incurring heavy expenses and facing opposition, resistance or unrest. Hyderabad Municipal Corporation has successfully used this method for road widening in the city.

Fiscal Resource Mobilisation for Urban Renewal

Broadly speaking, there could be eight sources for financing the implementation of urban renewal plans/projects. These are (a) government grants, (b) tax-based resources, (c) non-tax base revenue (user charges), (d) land-based resources, (e) financing through loan, (f) funding by bilateral and multilateral agencies, (g) beneficiary's own contribution and (h) PPP.

Government Grants

Government grant is defined as an amount of money given by the central/state/local government to a person, entity or NGO for a specific purpose. This money, given as grant, is not expected to be repaid. Government grants from JNNURM have been the first major source of funds, available during 2006–2013 for the urban renewal

Table 6.1 *Central Government Grants Available for Urban Renewal in India*

Programmes/Missions	Central Government (₹ Crore)
AMRUT	50,000
Smart Cities Mission	48,000
HRIDAY	500
Swachh Bharat Mission	14,623
Total	113,123

Source: Based upon various Mission Guidelines.

in India. The total grant under JNNURM, including the share of the state government, was ₹100,000 crore. In 2017, as indicated in Table 6.1, there were at least four programmes/missions in India which provide grants of about ₹111,123 crore for the urban renewal. These include AMRUT, Smart Cities Mission, HRIDAY and SBM.

Jawaharlal Nehru National Urban Renewal Mission

As mentioned in Chapter 2, a huge grant of ₹50,000 crore was made available, over a period of seven years, by the central government for the urban renewal under JNNURM. As given in Table 6.2, the share of this grant for million-plus cities was limited to 50% of the total project cost, and the balance cost was contributed by the state government/ULB/parastatal agency and beneficiaries. For other cities, the share of grant was 80% and in case of cities and towns located in north-eastern states, it was 90%. This was based upon the fact that the million-plus cities have better capabilities in local mobilisation of resources.

Atal Mission for Rejuvenation and Urban Transformation

Launched in June 2015, AMRUT has earmarked a sum of ₹50,000 crores, over a period of 5 years up to 2020, as a grant for the provision of basic services; increasing the amenity value of cities; and reducing

Table 6.2 The Central Government Share of Grant Under JNNURM as Percentage of the Total Project Cost

Category of Cities	Grant Central Share (%)	State/ULB/Parastatal Share, Including Beneficiary Contribution (%)
Cities with 4 million-plus population as per 2001census	50	50
Cities with million-plus but less than 4 million population, as per 2001 census	50	50
Cities/towns in north-eastern states	90	10
Other cities	80	20

Source: MoHUPA (2005).

pollution in 500 mission cities. The central government grant share will be limited to one-third of the project cost in 10 lakh-plus cities; and one-half of the project cost in cities and towns with the population up to 10 lakh. The balance fund will be the contribution of the state government/ULBs/or through private investment (MoUD, 2015). The fund allocation, as a CSS, has the following four components as the percentage of the annual budgetary allocation (MoUD, 2015):

1. Project fund (80%)
2. Incentives fund for reforms (10%)
3. Administrative and office expenses (A&OE) of state (08%)
4. A&OE of MoUD (02%)

The incentive fund is provided by the MoUD and no matching grant by the state/ULBs is required for this amount. The state A&OE is to be made available for capacity building, hiring of professionals on contract to support implementation of the projects, activities connected to e-Municipality as a Service (E-MAAS) and support to institutions such as Independent Review and Monitoring Agencies (IRMA).

Similarly, the A&OE of MoUD will be available for capacity building and organising national and regional workshops; award for best practices and smart solutions; support for research and applied studies and activities of EMAAS.

Smart Cities Mission

The Smart Cities Mission, launched along with AMRUT on the same day in June 2015, also provides grant for 100 selected smart cities for smart infrastructure provision with a view to improving liveability of the whole city. A sum of ₹48,000 crore is available, under this CSS, over a period of five years (up to 2020). The state governments/ULBs are to provide matching contribution. Each selected smart city will get ₹200 crore in the first year to create a higher initial corpus. The grant in subsequent years will be ₹100 crore per year for the next three years (MoUD, 2015a). The distribution of this fund is as under:

1. Project fund (93%)
2. A&OE of state/ULBs (05%)
3. A&OE of MoUD (02%)

The total fund, including the matching grant by the state/ULBs, is ₹96,000 crore. This amount is only a small portion of the total project cost and the balance is to be mobilised from own resources of the state or ULBs; additional resources transferred to states as per 14th Finance Commission recommendations; municipal bonds, pooled finance mechanism or tax incentive financing; other central government schemes such as **SBM, AMRUT, HRIDAY**; and borrowing from financial institutions and National Investment and Infrastructure Fund (NIIF).

HRIDAY

HRIDAY, launched by the Government of India in 2015, provides grant of ₹500 crores for 12 cities. This amount is available for the development of physical, institutional, economic and social infrastructure in selected 12 heritage cities in the country (see Chapter 2).

Swachh Bharat Mission

For provision of toilets and solid waste management in cities, a central grant of ₹14,623 crores is available up to 2019, the end of the Mission period. The further distribution of this amount is given in the following table.

Funds	Amount (₹Crores)
1. Project Fund based on Normative Criteria (60%)	8,773.80
2. Performance Fund based on Performance Matrix (20%)	2,924.60
3. Public Awareness & IEC Activities (15%*)	2,193.45
4. Capacity Building & A&OE (3%)	438.69
5. Research, Capacity Building &A&OE (MoUD) (2%)	292.46
Total	14,623.00

Source: Government of India (2014, p. 17).
Note: * 3% of which to be retained by the Ministry of Urban Development.

Government Subsidy/Assistance

Subsidy is usually a cash payment or tax reduction given in an overall public interest by government to a group or individual. To improve housing conditions of EWS/LIG households, various subsidies are given by the government for the PMAY-HFA (U). These include credit-linked interest subsidy and beneficiary-led individual house construction/enhancement assistance. A credit-linked interest subsidy of 6.5% for a tenure of 15 years is available on credits up to ₹6 lakh for new construction (up to 30 sq. m for EWS and up to 60 sq. m for LIG) or addition of rooms, kitchen, toilet, etc., to existing DUs, as incremental housing. In the beneficiary-led individual house construction/enhancement scheme, a central government assistance of ₹1.5 lakh per house for EWS categories is available. In the AHP scheme, a central assistance of ₹1.5 lakh per EWS house is available for such houses provided under an AHP project if, at least, 35% of the total houses are for EWS category and a single project has, at least, 250 DUs. The condition of number of DUs can be reduced if the state government so requests (MoHUPA, 2015, p. 10).

Tax-based Resources

As far as tax-based resource mobilisation for the urban renewal is concerned, a ULB may levy the tax on property value increment due to overall augmentation of infrastructure and physical transformation of an area and recover full or part of the cost of such works. This approach will be successful only where there is a visible and measurable improvement in the physical transformation of the area and level of service delivery. People will be willing to pay additional tax or surcharge on the tax if they see and experience better conditions which have improved their quality of life as well as enhanced the value of their property. To be more effective, there should be a clear-cut distinction of the portion of property tax which is levied for recovering funds spent on renewal. In this context, a surcharge for a limited period until the cost is recovered will be desirable.

With an objective of ensuring a sustained flow of funds for slum redevelopment and poverty alleviation programmes, the Hyderabad Municipal Corporation, in 2001, created the Hyderabad Urban Community Development and Services Fund (Mohanti, 2005) comprising the following:

1. 20% of Property Tax collected annually.
2. 30% of annual per capita grants received from the state government.
3. Funds received from the Government of India/state governments under various ongoing urban poverty alleviation programmes such as SJSRY, National Slum Development Programme (NSDP), Balika Samridhi Yojana (BSY), Chief Minister's Empowerment of Youth (CMEY) Programme, Adarsh Basti scheme, etc.

Non-tax-based Resources (User Charges)

An ULB has power to levy user charges for the provision/augmentation of services such as water supply, sewerage, drainage, municipal solid waste management, entry into redeveloped parks and playfields and such other services which are considered as public goods. Since the beneficiaries of such services pay the charges, these can be effectively levied only when the benefits of the service provided are measurable and the beneficiaries are clearly identifiable. For achieving efficiency, user charges should be levied on those who actually receive the benefits.

Payment of user charges gives feeling of ownership of service and acts as instruments to ensure the accountability of public functionaries. In the cases when benefits are not measurable and the beneficiaries are not clearly identifiable, levying user charges will not be possible and in such a case, a surcharge on property tax may be desirable.

In India, collection and recovery of user charges by the ULBs is very poor due to lack of political will, and these services are generally funded by grants and subsidies. This has resulted into a culture of enjoying free service, as provision of such services is the responsibility of the local government. Collection of user charges was one of the reforms in JNNURM and as shown in Chapter 4 (Table 4.8), only about 35% of ULBs had agreed to collect 100% operation and maintenance (O&M) and only seven ULBs have actually introduced mechanism for the collection of water charges.

Land-based Resource Mobilisation

As discussed earlier in this chapter, the potential of land can be effectively enhanced through spatial planning policies/strategies which guide the pattern of land use and the extent of use as defined by FAR/FSI. Also, through the tool of TDR, the potential of a site, if required, can be transferred to another designated site (Figure 6.1). This has opened immense opportunities for converting land potential into fiscal resource to implement the urban renewal projects in a financially viable manner.

This potential of land has been successfully utilised by Maharashtra in their slum redevelopment schemes such as Bhendi Bazaar (Chapter 2). Housing for All by 2022 Scheme also promotes in situ slum redevelopment with private sector participation, using land as resource (MoHUPA, 2015, p. 2).

There are three ways of using land potential for resource mobilisation. These are through change of land use, grant of additional FAR/FSI and a combination of change in land uses and grant of FAR/FSI. In the change of land use method, the variation in returns on different land uses is utilised to generate funds. It is an established fact that return from property under commercial use is more than one used for residential. Similarly, a high-income housing complex will have a higher return per square metre than a low-income housing area. Utilising this, resources can be mobilised for the implementation of urban renewal projects. For example, in a redevelopment project, if a part of permissible built space is permitted to be used for high-end residential land use or commercial use, the cost of the project can be recovered from the sale of this area. In other words, resource for renewal is mobilised through change in land use of a portion of potential of the site.

In some renewal projects such as the redevelopment of commercial areas being redeveloped by a private builder and the cooperative society of the shop owners, cost of the project may be recovered through a grant of incentive FAR/FSI as the sale component to be sold by the builder and recover the investment with reasonable profit.

There are certain situations where the cost of the project is higher and change of land use using the normal development controls is not recovered, then the next available tool FAR/FSI may be applied and incentive FAR/FSI be granted to recover the cost. In this case, it will be a combination of land use change and grant of FAR/FSI. Housing for All by 2022 (Urban) under PMAY also recommends this method of resource mobilisation by granting additional FAR/FSI and TDR for in situ redevelopment of slums located on central/state government/ULB or private land (MoHUPA, 2015).

The following example illustrates further the method of resource mobilisation using land use change and grant of FAR/FSI. This also indicates the manner of calculating FAR/FSI for resource mobilisation.

It is highlighted here that

- this is just a demonstration of the method of land-based resource mobilisation using FAR/FSI;
- the norms and unit price of built space used in this exercise may change from place to place;

- it does not include the cost of land and it is assumed that a mechanism is legally available to redevelop the area already occupied by people who are required to be accommodated on the same site (in situ);
- the unit price of built space, used for calculation, does not include the cost of land and
- in practice, the actual norms and rates of built spaces, as applicable to the place, should be used.

This exercise is based upon the guidelines given in MPD-2021, which provides the following:

Minimum plot size (sq. m)	2,000
Maximum density DU/ha	600
Maximum (overall) FAR on residential component	400*
Size of DUs (sq. m)	25–30
Land use of site	
Residential (minimum)	60%
Commercial (maximum)	10%
Other uses (open space, roads and facilities)	30%
Total	100%

Source: DDA (2010, Section 4.2.3.4).
Note: *Since this requirement is from MPD-2021, which uses FAR as percentage, the same is used in this exercise.

For demonstrating the use of this method of resource mobilisation, let us consider the MPD-2021 provisions and assume the following:

1.	Site area	10,000 sq. m
2.	Area of one dwelling unit of slum housing	30 sq. m
3.	Average unit cost of construction of slum housing	₹8,000 per sq. m
4.	Average unit cost of construction of affordable housing	₹20,000 per sq. m
5.	Average unit cost of construction of commercial building	₹25,000 per sq. m

6.	Average unit sale price of commercial building	₹100,000 per sq. m
7.	Average unit sale price of affordable housing	₹30,000 per sq. m
8.	Average unit cost of site development	₹60 lakh per hectare

Taking this data into account, the distribution of land use of and built-up area on the site will be as mentioned in the following table:

Description	Area in sq. m	Master Plan FAR	Permitted Built-up Area in sq. m
Total site area	10,000	—	—
Residential (60%)	6,000	200*	12,000
Commercial (10%)	1,000	125**	1,250
Other uses (30%)	3,000	—	—

Notes: * Master Plan FAR on Group Housing (DDA 2010, Section 4.4.3.B, p. 47).
** Master Plan FAR on non-hierarchy commercial centre ((DDA 2010, Table 5.4, p.58).

In this example, the commercial area (10%) with permitted built-up area of 1,250 sq. m is being given to mobilise resources for building the DUs for slum dwellers. Taking these requirements as well as assumptions into account, further calculations are as under:

Built-up area required and additional FAR to be granted

The built-up area of 600 DUs of 30 sq. m each
= 600 × 30 = 18,000 sq. m

Since the permitted built-up area required for residential component is 12,000 sq. m, the additional built-up area needed will be

18,000 − 12,000 = 6,000 sq. m

The requirement of this additional 6,000 sq. m built space to accomplish the task can be fulfilled through allowing additional FAR on residential component (6,000 sq. m) calculated as under:

$$\text{Additional FAR on residential component} = \frac{6,000}{6,000} \times 100 = 100$$

Therefore,

The total FAR used on residential component
= master plan FAR + additional FAR
= 200 + 100 = 300

Cost to be incurred

Cost of building DUs
= 600 × 30 × 8,000 = 144,000,000 = ₹14.4 crores

Cost of site development
= 1 × 60 = 60 lakh = 0.6 crore

Total cost
= 14.4 + 0.6 = 15 crores

Cost recovery
The total cost of ₹15 crore can be recovered through land use change and permitting incentive FAR as required and permissible as per regulations. The calculations are as under:

Cost recovery through commercial component
Taking the requirements as well as assumptions into account, the cost of the construction of 1,250 sq. m permitted commercial area and recovery will be as under:

Cost of commercial building (₹crore)
= 1,250 × 25,000 = 31,250,000 = 3.125 crore

Returns from sale of commercial area (₹crore)
= 1,250 × 100,000 = 125,000,000 = 12.5 crore

Recovery of cost through commercial component (₹crore)
= 12.500 − 3.125 = 9.375

Balance of cost to recover (₹crore)
= 15.000 − 9.375 = 5.625

This means that the commercial component is not enough to recover the cost or mobilise resources to build DUs for slum dwellers. As per the conditions of the Guidelines, commercial components cannot be more than 10% and, therefore, any additional or incentive FAR cannot be granted on this use zone. According to the Guidelines, the overall maximum FAR on residential component is 400, and only 300 is used so far. This balance amount could be recovered if an incentive FAR on residential component is granted for affordable housing.

Balance cost recovery through incentive FAR on residential component
This balance of ₹5.625 crore can be recovered through granting incentive FAR on residential component (for affordable housing). This can be calculated as under:

The residential area needed to recover ₹5.625 crore, if the unit sale price of housing is ₹30,000 per sq. m and unit construction cost is ₹20,000 per sq. m, can be calculated as under:

Money recovered per sq. m (₹)

$$= 30{,}000 - 20{,}000 = 10{,}000 = 0.001 \text{ crore}$$

Since the money recovered per sq. m is ₹0.001 crore, the built-up additional residential area required to recover ₹5.625 crore

$$\frac{5{,}625}{0.001} = 5.625$$

Therefore, the incentive FAR on residential component of 6,000 sq. m will be

$$\frac{5{,}625}{6000} \times 100 = 93.75$$

And, the overall FAR on residential component

= Master plan FAR + Additional FAR + Incentive FAR
= 200 + 100 + 93.75
= 393.75

This is well within the limit of maximum overall FAR of 400. In this way, the total fiscal requirement for the redevelopment of slum area can be mobilised through the use of spatial planning tools—change of land use and grant of additional and incentive FAR.

In case the cost is not recovered from the FAR available on site, the same (balance FAR/FSI) may be granted as TDR to the builder to recover the investment.

A practical example of this method of resource mobilisation (permitting a part of area to be sold as commercial area) is redevelopment of government colonies for the general pool residential accommodation of central government staff in Delhi (Chapter 2). Accordingly, to recover the investment, 806,900 sq. m area has been approved to be sold as freehold commercial, as detailed here (Naqvi, 2016):

Nauroji Nagar	297,000 sq. m
Sarojini Nagar	509,900 sq. m
Total	806,900 sq. m

Financing Through Loans

ULBs and other agencies can finance urban renewal plans through loan from financial institutions or market borrowing. Financial institutions such as Housing and Urban Development Corporation (HUDCO), National Housing Bank (NHB), Infrastructure Leasing and Finance Services (IL&FS) and Infrastructure Development Finance Company (IDFC) are some agencies in India which provide loans for relatively longer durations than banks for financing infrastructure projects.

Financing through market borrowing by issuing bond and debentures has not yet picked up in the country because of inefficiency in financial administration and lack of creditworthiness of ULBs and other agencies. Such agencies, particularly in small- and medium-size cities, find it difficult to raise resources from the market. To enable these local bodies in accessing market funds for their infrastructure projects, the Government of India has launched the Pooled Finance Development Scheme (PFDS). It facilitates these agencies in developing bankable urban infrastructure projects and suggests measures for reducing the cost of borrowing from market.

The Ahmedabad Municipal Corporation (AMC) was the first ULB to issue, in 1998, municipal bonds and access the capital market. Later on, other municipalities and utility organisations issued taxable and tax-free bonds. It was not very successful because, as Vaidya (2009) observes, there were too few creditworthy ULBs and too few financially viable projects. There were varieties of 'administrative and managerial' constraints that inhibited and discouraged potential issuers of municipal bonds.

AMRUT has introduced a new reform in the form of credit rating of ULBs to enable them to issue municipal bonds to raise resources from the financial market (Chapter 4). The process of credit rating has already started in most of the 500 AMRUT cities. In March 2017, credit rating was awarded to 94 ULBs, covering 14 states in the country. The top ranking ULBs were NDMC, Navi Mumbai and Pune with AA+ rating (see Chapter 4, Annexure 4.3). This will transform ULBs as efficient business houses catering to development and redevelopment of cities.

Funding by Bilateral and Multilateral Agencies

Bilateral organisations are government agencies or non-profit organisations of a country that provide aid to other countries. Bilateral organisations receive funding from their national governments, and use the funds to financially assist developing countries. Few bilateral agencies are Department for International Development (DFID, UK), Japan Bank for International Cooperation (JBIC), Japan International Cooperation Agency (JICA) and Australian Agency for International Development (AusAID) Programme.

Multilateral organisations are international organisations whose membership comprises member governments, who collectively govern the organisation and are the primary source of funds while the loans/grants-in-aids are provided for projects in various countries. Some examples of multilateral funding agencies are various UN bodies, World Bank, Organisation for Economic Cooperation and Development (OECD) and Asian Development Bank (ADB). These organisations provide soft loans and grants for infrastructure projects. Central/state government and ULBs can receive external development assistance from bilateral and multilateral sources for projects/programmes following the laid down procedures. Accessing funds from these agencies is relatively a long process, and it requires preparation of various project documents, in-depth planning, and studies to assess compliance of the project with respect to environment, rehabilitation/resettlement and social safeguard policies, and pilot testing of new initiatives (MoUD, 2014).

Bilateral funding has been committed by several counties for the development of Smart Cities Mission. The countries which have offered assistance for the development of smart cities include Japan (for the development of Chennai, Ahmedabad and Varanasi), United States of America (for Visakhapatnam, Ajmer and Allahabad) through US Trade Development Agency (USTDA), United Kingdom (for Pune, Amravati in Andhra Pradesh and Indore), France (for Chandigarh, Puducherry and Nagpur) and Germany (for Bhubaneswar, Coimbatore and Kochi) (*Business Standard*, 2017).

Beneficiary's Own Contribution

A part of the cost of urban renewal can be recovered from a contribution by the beneficiaries of the project. In addition to the recovery of a part of expenses, this contribution has additional value additions. It gives ownership of the project to the people and empowers them to monitor its implementation and social audit.

The slum networking experience of Indore was modified and applied in Vadodara with focus on self-sufficiency and greater community participation and control over the programme. Accordingly, 50% of the resources needed for environmental improvement component of the project were mobilised by stakeholders' contribution. It included the cost of water and sewer connection and construction of dwelling (Ekram, 1989). Under in situ slum redevelopment projects, beneficiary's own contribution is encouraged in PMAY-HFA scheme (MoHUPA, 2015).

Resource Mobilisation through PPP

The public–private partnership (PPP) refers to a working relationship where a public sector agency joins hands with private sector entity, as partner, for a specific purpose and time period, and shares responsibilities as per agreement signed by both the parties. The basic objectives of PPP are as follows:

- To utilise the efficiency of private sector in resource mobilisation and project implementation
- To ensure accomplishment of the social obligations which is the responsibility of public sector
- To share mutually agreed responsibilities and risks attached to and benefits/profits accruing from the project

In the context of urban renewal, the roles and responsibilities of public sector agencies under PPP are generally the following:

- All administrative and regulatory operations
- Land acquisition
- Spatial planning, plan approval
- Development control
- Registration of beneficiaries and allotment of built space (houses) to the beneficiaries
- Sharing of built-space
- Peripheral development
- Impact assessment and learning lessons for future application

On the other hand, the roles and responsibilities of the private sector partner, in urban renewal projects, are as follows:

- Mobilisation of finance and other related operation
- Conducting socio-economic surveys, mobilisation of public support and getting consent for redevelopment
- Spatial planning (if required and agreed upon)
- Site development
- Provision of social and physical infrastructure
- Construction of buildings
- Handing over of social and physical infrastructure to competent authority
- Sharing of built-space with partner public sector agency
- Sale of own share of built-space to recover investment and reasonable profit

PPP mode of resource mobilisation and project implementation is gaining a lot of support in development process. In urban renewal projects, it is increasingly being used for slum redevelopment and infrastructure projects. Some examples of PPP in urban renewal include the redevelopment of Bhendi Bazaar, Mumbai, and Kathputli Colony, Delhi (Chapter 2). The Smart Cities Mission recommends that one of the ways of financing the project should be private sector through PPP (MoUD, 2015b).

Institutional Resources

Institutions are required to make things happen. Due to the lack of institutional support, several urban renewal projects have not seen the light of the day. There is no clear-cut institutional mechanism for urban renewal in the country. The state town planning departments prepare master plans which make provision for urban renewal plans/schemes/guidelines. However, it is not clearly defined who implements these plans. This is one of the main causes of inaction in urban renewal efforts.

According to the provisions of the Twelfth Schedule of the 74th CAA, the functions of municipalities, among other matters, include urban planning including town planning; regulation of land-use and construction of buildings and slum improvement and upgradation (see Chapter 4, Annexure 4.1). However, as discussed in Chapter 4, only some state governments have assigned these functions to ULBs.

In the absence of a clear-cut assignment of functions, urban local bodies are not equipped to perform these functions. On the other hand, all urban renewal programmes such as JNNURM, Smart Cities Mission and AMRUT have made the ULBs as the executing agencies.

In the absence of an existing efficient institutional mechanism, with necessary trained technical manpower, Government of Maharashtra has established SRA, Mumbai, with composition as shown in Annexure 6.1. The functions of SRA include survey and declaration of any area as slum in Greater Mumbai, and formulate and implement the slum rehabilitation schemes. Delhi has constituted Shahjahanabad Redevelopment Corporation and Smart Cities Mission and has promoted the establishment of SPVs for the implementation of each smart city under the Mission. As on February 2017, SPVs of 56 smart cities have been constituted. The functions of SPV include planning, plan appraisal, approval of plans, release of funds and implementation of projects. The functions of SPVs also include management, operation, monitoring and evaluation of the development projects of the smart city (Annexure 6.2).

An SPV known as IRSDC Limited has been set up to implement the redevelopment of railway stations in the country. Constitution of such authorities, corporations or SPVs is not a permanent solution. A permanent solution by strengthening and empowering the existing institutions to perform the full task of urban renewal is needed.

The institutional set-up for various missions generally includes a mechanism at national, state and city levels which may vary from depending upon focus of the mission. The set-up for Smart Cities Mission includes the following (for details of composition and functions, see MoUD, 2015b):

National Level

- Apex committee for the approval of proposals, release of funds, monitoring/review of projects and mid-course correction, if any.
- National Mission Directorate as an overall in-charge to perform all activities related to the Mission.

State Level

- State-level High Power Steering Committee (HPSC) to guide the state-level agencies regarding Smart Cities Mission, oversee the progress and review the SCPs and send them to MoUD.

City Level

- Smart City Advisory Forum to advise and enable collaboration among various stakeholders.
- SPV.

The set-up for AMRUT is slightly different to incorporate more freedom and power to state government and includes (for details of composition and functions, see MoUD, 2015a):

National Level

- Apex committee for approval of SAAP, release of funds, monitoring/review of projects and mid-course correction, if any.
- National Mission Directorate as an overall in-charge to perform all activities related to the Mission.

State Level

- State-level HPSC to prepare SAAP based upon SLIPs of ULBs, approve projects technically appraised by SLTC, manage fund flow, monitor outcome, organise audit and others (see MoUD, 2015).
- State Mission Directorate.
- Programme Management Unit (PMU).
- Project Management and Development Consultant (PMDC).
- SLTC.

City Level

- Urban local bodies for implementation of projects under the Mission.

There is a need to strengthen state town planning departments to prepare urban renewal plan as the sub-plan of the master plan and evolve innovative DCRs to utilise the full potential of the existing cities and their core areas. This requires a strong support of the valuation of property and the assessment of the carrying capacity of the areas to be renewed and the threshold of additional development. Capacity development of town planning institutions, in this respect, needs to be encouraged.

Urban renewal needs teaching and research inputs to focus on and evolve innovative approaches, strategies and techniques of urban renewal, land assembly and resource mobilisation. Research input is required to assess the carrying capacity of an existing area of a city to accommodate additional population, particularly in view of the implementation of programmes such as AMRUT, which focus on the augmentation of services and infrastructure in 500 cities. Schools of Planning and Architecture, IITs and research organisations such as Central Building Research Institute (CBRI) and Central Road Research Institute (CRRI) need to be strengthened in this respect.

There is a need to promote dedicated NGOs and CBOs to serve as a link between the affected people and the implementing agency so that people's participation and support to urban renewal may be mobilised.

Urban renewal will be reduced to only a paper exercise if it is not supported and steered by an efficient and dedicated institutional mechanism run by capable personals to prepare and implement spatial plans, renewal policies and strategies having regard to various challenges.

Annexure 6.1 *Composition of the Slum Rehabilitation Authority, Mumbai*

The full composition of the SRA, Mumbai, as on March 2017 is as given in the following table:

Hon. Chief Minister	Maharashtra State	Chair Person
Hon. Minister (Housing)	Maharashtra State	Member
Hon. Minister of State (UDD)	Maharashtra State	Member
Hon. Minister of State (Housing)	Maharashtra State	Member
Chief Secretary	Government of Maharashtra	Member
Commissioner	BMC, Madhyavarti Karyalaya	Member
Principal Secretary (L&JD)	Mantralaya, Mumbai 400032	Member
Principal Secretary (UDD)	Mantralaya, Mumbai 400032	Member
Secretary (Housing Department)	Mantralaya, Mumbai 400032	Member
Chief Executive Officer	SRA, Prashaskiya Building, Bandra East	Member

Source: http://www.sra.gov.in/pgeConstiandFunction.aspx

Annexure 6.2 Structure and Functions of SPV

1. **Structure of the SPV**

   The city-level SPV will be established as a limited company under the Companies Act, 2013 and will be promoted by the State/UT and the ULB jointly, both having 50:50 equity shareholding. This shareholding pattern has to be maintained at all times. The private sector or financial institutions could be considered for taking equity stake in the SPV, provided the State/UT and the ULB share are equal to each other, and the State/UT and ULB together have majority shareholding and control of the SPV (e.g., State/UT:ULB:Private sector shareholding can be in the ratio 40:40:20 or 30:30:40. Ratios such as 35:45:20 or 40:30:30 are not permitted since State/UT and ULB shares are not equal. Ratios such as 20:20:60 are also not permitted since the State/UT and the ULB together do not have majority shareholding). In addition to equity, the State/UT can provide its contribution to the Smart Cities Mission as grant to fulfil the State Government responsibility for ensuring availability of funds for the mission and for ensuring the financial sustainability of the SPV.

2. **Raising and utilization of funds by the Company (SPV)**

   The funds given by the Central Government to the SPV will be in the shape of tied grants and kept in a separate Grant Fund. These funds will be utilized only for the purposes given in the Mission Statement and Guidelines and subject to the conditions laid down by the Central Government. The ULBs may, through the State Government, request MoUD to permit utilization of GoI grants as ULB's equity contribution to the SPV, subject to the following conditions:

   2.1 The State Government has made adequate contribution to the SPV out of their own funds.

   2.2 The approval will be limited to the GoI grants that have already been released. Since future instalments of Smart City funds are subject to performance and are not guaranteed, the ULB will not be permitted to earmark future instalments to meet its equity contribution.

   2.3 The utilization of GoI grants as equity contributions will not alter the relative shareholding of the State Government and the ULB, which will remain equal as per Mission guidelines.

   2.4 It is clarified that the Government of India contribution to Smart Cities is strictly in the form of grant and the ULB is exercising its own discretion in utilizing these funds as its equity contribution to the SPV.

The SPV will also access funds from other sources such as debt, user charges, taxes, surcharges, etc.

3. **Board of Directors**

   The Board of Directors will have representatives of Central Government, State Government, ULB and Independent Directors, in addition to the CEO and Functional Directors. Additional Directors (such as representative of parastatal) may be taken on the Board, as considered necessary. The Company and shareholders will voluntarily comply with the provision of the Companies Act, 2013, with respect to induction of independent directors. Below, are given the broad terms of appointment and role of the SPV Board:

   3.1 The Chairperson of the SPV will be the Divisional Commissioner/Collector/Municipal Commissioner/Chief Executive of the Urban Development Authority as decided by the State Government.

   3.2 The representative of the Central Government will be a Director on the Board of the SPV and will be appointed by the MoUD.

   3.3 The CEO of the SPV will be appointed with the approval of the MoUD. The CEO will be appointed for a fixed term of three years and will be removed only with the prior approval of MoUD. The functions of the CEO include:

   3.3.1 Overseeing and managing the general conduct of the day-to-day operations of the SPV subject to the supervision and control of the Board.

   3.3.2 Entering into contracts or arrangements for and on behalf of the Company in all matters within the ordinary course of the Company's business.

   3.3.3 To formulate and submit to the Board of Directors for approval a Human Resource Policy that will lay down procedures for creation of staff positions, qualifications of staff, recruitment procedures, compensation and termination procedures.

   3.3.4 Recruitment and removal of the senior management of the Company and the creation of new positions in accordance with the Company's approved budget and the recruitment or increase of employees in accordance with the Human Resource Policy laid down by the Board.

   3.3.5 Supervising the work of all employees and managers of the Company and the determination of their duties, responsibilities and authority.

(continued)

(continued)

3.4 The Independent Directors will be selected from the data bank(s) maintained by the Ministry of Corporate Affairs and preference will be given to those who have served as independent directors in the Board of Companies fulfilling Clause 49 of the listing agreement of Securities and Exchange Board of India (SEBI).

4. **Delegation of powers to the SPV**

    4.1 One of the primary reasons for the creation of an SPV for the Smart City Mission is to ensure operational independence and autonomy in decision-making and mission implementation. The Smart Cities Mission encourages the State Government and the ULB to adopt the following best practices to create empowered SPVs to the extent and as provided under the municipal act.

    4.1.1 Delegating the rights and obligations of the municipal council with respect to the Smart City project to the SPV.

    4.1.2 Delegating the decision-making powers available to the ULB under the municipal act/Government rules to the Chief Executive Officer of the SPV.

    4.1.3 Delegating the approval or decision-making powers available to the Urban Development Department/Local Self Government department/Municipal Administration department to the Board of Directors of the SPV in which the State and ULB are represented.

    4.2 Delegating the matters that require the approval of the State Government to the State Level High Powered Steering Committee (HPSC) for Smart Cities.

5. **The key functions and responsibilities of the SPV are to:**

    5.1 Approve and sanction the projects including their technical appraisal.

    5.2 Execute the SCP with complete operational freedom.

    5.3 Take measures to comply with the requirements of MoUD with respect to the implementation of the Smart Cities programme.

    5.4 Mobilize resources within timelines and take measures necessary for the mobilisation of resources.

    5.5 Approve and act upon the reports of a third party Review and Monitoring Agency

    5.6 Overview Capacity Building activities.

    5.7 Develop and benefit from inter-linkages of academic institutions and organizations.

5.8 Ensure timely completion of projects according to set timelines.

5.9 Undertake review of activities of the Mission including budget, implementation of projects, and preparation of SCP and co-ordination with other missions/schemes and activities of various ministries.

5.10 Monitor and review quality control related matters and act upon issues arising thereof.

5.11 Incorporate joint ventures and subsidiaries and enter into Public Private Partnerships as may be required for the implementation of the Smart Cities programme.

5.12 Enter into contracts, partnerships and service delivery arrangements as may be required for the implementation of the Smart Cities Mission.

5.13 Determine and collect user charges as authorised by the ULB.

5.14 Collect taxes, surcharges etc. as authorised by the ULB.

The above provisions will be included in the Articles of Association of the SPV.

Source: http://smartcities.gov.in/content/innerpage/guidelines.php

References

Business Standard. (2017, 5 January). Japan to assist India with development of three smart cities. *Business Standard,* New Delhi.

DDA. (2010). *Master Plan for Delhi, 2021.* New Delhi: Author.

Ekram, L. N. (1989). *Slum networking of Indore city.* Technical review summary for Aga Khan Award in Architecture. Retrieved 14 April 2014, from www.akdn.org/architecture/pdf/1826_pdf

Government of India. (2013, September 27). *Right to Fare Compensation and Transparency in Land Acquisition, Rehabilitation and Resettlement 2013.* The Gazette of India, Part II, no. 40, Ministry of Law and Justice, New Delhi.

Government of India. (2014). *Guidelines for Swachh Bharat Mission (SBM).* New Delhi: Ministry of Urban Development.

Mohanti, P. K. (2005). *Urban sector reforms agenda: Financing civic services and development.* Hyderabad: Centre for Good Governance.

MoHUPA. (2005). *Guidelines for basic services to urban poor.* New Delhi: Government of India.

———. (2015). *Pradhan Mantri Awas Yojana Housing for All (Urban): Scheme guidelines 2015.* New Delhi: Government of India.

MoUD. (2014). *Urban and Regional Development Plan Formulation and Implementation (URDPFI): Guidelines*. New Delhi: Government of India.

———. (2015a). *Atal Mission for Rejuvenation and Urban Transformation (AMRUT): Mission statement and guidelines*. New Delhi: Government of India.

———. (2015b). Smart cities mission statement and guidelines. New Delhi: Government of India.

Naqvi, S. (2016). *NBCC begins work on three redevelopment projects in Delhi*. New Delhi: Centre for Monitoring Indian Economy.

Vaidya, C. (2009). *Urban issues, reforms and way forward in India*. Department of Economic Affairs, Ministry of Finance, Government of India, New Delhi.

CHAPTER 7

The Future of Urban Renewal

Urbanisation, Spatial Growth and Urban Renewal

India is progressing on the path of urbanisation and by 2050, a majority (55.2%) of the people will be living in urban centres. Urban population will increase 2.4 times from 37.7 crore in 2011 to 91.5 crore in 2050 (Table 7.1). To harness the benefits of urbanisation as well as to sustain their role as generators of economic momentum, providers of employment opportunities, centres of knowledge and innovations and places of hope for the people, cities need to be equipped with integrated spatio-economic planning.

Based upon data from Mumbai, Delhi, Bengaluru, Kolkata, Chennai, Hyderabad, and Ahmedabad and, assuming that a metropolitan core includes an area within a radius of 10 km around the main metropolis and a suburban area covers the belt from 10 to 50 km around the metropolitan core, a study by the World Bank (2013) shows that the percentage change in employment growth, during 1998–2005, in all manufacturing sectors, is negative in the metro-core (Figure 7.1) which indicates closing down of industries due to general industrial dispersal policy of master plans (Chapter 1).

Table 7.1 Projected Urban Population, Decadal Increase and Urbanisation in India (2020–2050)

Year	Urban Population in (Crore)			Urbanisation
	Total	Urban	Decadal Increase in Urban	
2011[1]		37.7	–	31.2
2020[2]	137.9	47.3	9.6	34.4
2030[2]	150.6	61.1	13.8	40.6
2040[2]	159.7	76.4	15.3	47.8
2050[2]	165.8	91.5	15.1	55.2

Source: [1] Census of India 2011; [2] United Nations (2007).

This study (World Bank, 2013) provides recent evidence on the decay of metropolitan core and booming rural suburbs where villages are transforming to provide economically viable locations to high-tech manufacturing sector. Increase in employment in the real estate sector in metro-core, suburban towns as well as suburban villages (Figure 7.1) indicates booming construction activity in and around the metropolitan cities. It also shows the presence of some urban renewal activities taking place in the core areas of such cities as indicated by the increase in employment in real estate.

As discussed in Chapters 2–4, urban renewal efforts and strategies in the country have just not progressed beyond making laws, rules and policies and introducing reforms. Since 2005, with the announcement of the JNNURM, India entered into a mission mode for transforming urban centres. The initial focus was limited to 63 identified cities which has now (after 2015) extended to more than 500 under various schemes such as Smart Cities Mission, AMRUT and HRIDAY. The PMAY-U covers all cities in the country for slum rehabilitation and provision of affordable housing for all.

Ministry of Tourism has initiated PRASAD, which covers 23 sites. The Ministry of Railway is redeveloping 400 railway stations in cities covered under Smart Cities Mission and AMRUT (see Chapter 2).

This is a good beginning. Cities in India have started their journey on the path of transformation. The various missions have just commenced and their implementation will provide very useful insight for urban renewal efforts in future. They will also provide replicable innovative approaches, strategies and good practices in area of planning, financing and management of urban renewal projects.

A quick analysis of plans submitted by the top five smart cities—Bhubaneswar, Pune, Jaipur, Surat and Kochi—indicated that the basic approach appears to be area-based and template-driven, resulting in a fragmented development. This is because of the fact that the guidelines require proposals for four areas—one each for retrofitting, redevelopment, Greenfield development and pan-city development. There is no overall plan that integrates these and such other projects in the city. Convergence with other projects and schemes of both the central and state governments is a welcome requirement of Smart Cities Mission because these projects and schemes have similar goals even though they may follow different path. The approach followed by these five proposals, however, appears to be just an exercise in identifying the source of funding for different schemes proposed.

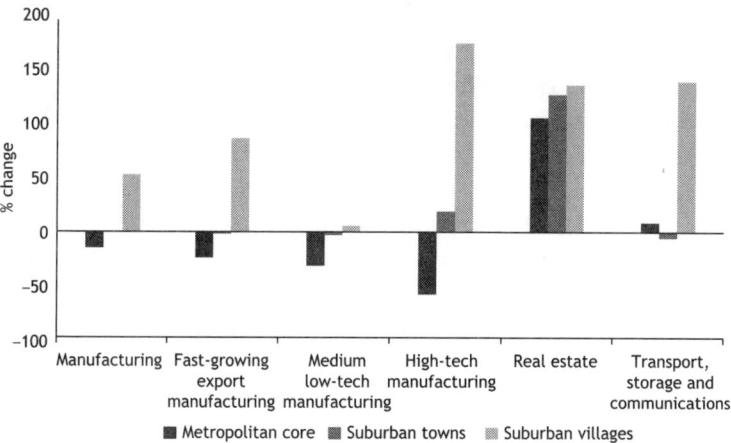

Figure 7.1 *Growth Rate of Employment in Select Metropolitan Core, Suburban Towns and Villages, 1998–2005*

Source: Ministry of Statistics and Programme Implementation 1998 and 2005 quoted from World Bank (2013, p. 3).

In my view, convergence should have an approach to augment the potential of an area through one or more projects/schemes/ programmes and to further utilise this augmented potential for transforming the area through urban renewal. If the spatial planning system, as suggested in Chapter 5, is adopted, it will provide a useful and official source of information about envisaged urban renewal policies and proposals in the city which may form basis for planning by other agencies and convergence of their projects/schemes/ programmes in an integrated manner.

For example, under AMRUT, water supply is augmented to provide 24×7 supply for the *existing population*. This scheme will augment the potential of the area if 24×7 water supply is provided for the *anticipated population* of the area as per carrying capacity of the urban renewal zone given in the proposed Action Plan of Urban Renewal Sub-plan (Chapter 5). Convergence will be better in this manner. The spatial planning agencies need to be equipped to take up this task.

The Way Forward

As discussed in Chapter 1, Indian cities are ageing. Municipal boundaries are being expanded to accommodate population growth. Core areas are dilapidated. Parcels of land are available for urban renewal within cities because of shifting of industries, uneconomical warehousing, poor condition of buildings and loss of business due to congestion and inaccessibility. According to NBCC (2016, p. 20), there are about 30 government housing colonies in Delhi which are 50–60 years old having a combined area of 1,100 ha and require redevelopment. The NBCC has been approached by various organisations and state governments to redevelop government lands under their possession, lying idle, in various cities in India. Such organisations include the Waqf Board (approximately 2,000,000 ha), Indian Institute of Public Administration (IIPA), New Delhi; AIIMS, New Delhi; Indian Railways, Air India and the Governments of Rajasthan and Odisha (NBCC, 2016, p. 20).

There is a need to unlock the potential of the core areas of existing cities (United Nations, 2007, p. 109) and unutilised/underutilised areas located within the municipal limits. This objective can successfully be achieved through urban renewal.

Urbanisation is a great opportunity for socio-economic and spatial development. The spatial planning approach to tackle urbanisation and harness its fruits, therefore, should be a combination of planned urban renewal of core area and infilling of underutilised pockets located within the municipal limit and planned development of new and urban extensions in suburban areas in an integrated manner (Figure 7.2). It is necessary for the sustainability of cities, tackling urban decay and providing a planned suburban expansion. Planned city extension and infilling of available land in the city have also been identified as the seven levers for the New Urban Agenda (UN-Habitat, 2016). Planned city extension is cost-effective and has potential to prevent slum formation and haphazard growth. Planned infilling is a very powerful lever (UN-Habitat, 2016, p. 190) for bringing urban transformation. Well-planned infilling can provide solutions for areas that have low density, poor connectivity, inefficient land uses and inadequate service delivery.

Fast pace of urbanisation, however, has caused indiscriminate expansion and neglect of environment and heritage and resulted in social inequalities in the quality of life of urban poor and the rich as indicated by the growth of number of slum pockets and shortage of housing where 95% pertain to EWS and LIG population (Ministry

	Core area: Urban renewal
	Municipal area: Infilling
	Infilling areas
	Urban renewal areas
	Sub-urban towns
	Sub-urban corridors
	Major roads with TR
	Minor road with TR
	Other roads
S	Suburban area

Figure 7.2 The Spatial Approach for Urban Renewal
Note: TR: Transit Route.

of Urban Employment and Poverty Alleviation, 2005). Urban transformation efforts, therefore, should follow the following four principles of urban renewal (Chapter 1) which state that urban renewal should

1. be humane and provide social justice;
2. strike balance among physical, economic and environmental concerns;
3. conserve socio-cultural values, public spaces, and heritage monuments, buildings and sites and
4. involve stakeholders at all stages of the renewal process.

From Chapters 1, 2 and 6, it is noted that there are five common considerations that, generally, guide the urban renewal efforts. These include the following:

1. Accessibility and connectivity
2. Density, FAR/FSI and infrastructure
3. Mixed uses pattern
4. Inclusion and spatial equity
5. Implementation actions

To lead the way forward, it will be useful to discuss these considerations in a bit more detail.

Accessibility and Connectivity

Accessibility and connectivity are the backbone of all urban renewal plans. In the urban renewal context, accessibility influences the potential of an area in terms of the extent of development, concentration of land use, nature and pattern of public transport system and investment climate. In the same context, connectivity of an area indicates whether it is served by public transport system (bus, BRTS, MRTS and others, as applicable) that connects it with other areas of the city. Connectivity to other places is essential for the success of planned urban renewal. In this context, comprehensive mobility plan (CMP), as a sub-plan of the master plan, is desirable, and it should form the basis for other policy decisions and considerations. Having regard to the network of roads, land uses and urban renewal sub-plan given in the master plan, CMP includes public transport system by various modes as required for the movement of goods and passengers; terminals and transit stations; parking; non-motorised vehicle (pedestrian and bicycle, cycle-rickshaw) zones, that are well integrated with transit stations, markets, various facilities and parking lots. Intelligent traffic management system may also form a part of this plan to make the journey smooth and hassle-free. Mumbai has implemented such a system that optimises the traffic flow with the help of 700 cameras controlling 250 signalised intersections (World Bank, 2015, p. 122). Ahmedabad has introduced BRTS and MRTS. Several other cities—Delhi, Bengaluru, Jaipur, Chennai, Hyderabad, Kolkata, Lucknow and Kochi—have successfully implemented MRTS (Chapter 2). Traffic System Management (TSM) can also be applied to reduce congestion and add efficiency to the transit system.

In the United States of America, over 200 streets were converted to pedestrian streets during 1960s and 1970s. There were three patterns: (a) traditional pedestrian-only (no automobiles) streets, (b) pedestrian streets with limited automobile traffic (vehicles of owners of houses who live there) and (c) pedestrian-only streets served by MRTS stations. In a study (Robertson, 2010, p. 116), it was concluded that pedestrian-only streets have failed to support retail trade in the United States of America. Streets with transit stations have been successful in large cities such as Denver, Portland (Oregon), Philadelphia and Minneapolis. An area having poor parking facilities is considered inaccessible and all renewal exercises should focus on parking issue and provide innovative solutions that reduce car use or provide convenient and sufficient parking spaces. The pedestrian-only commercial streets, served by MRTS stations (pattern c), appear to be applicable in million-plus cities in Indian conditions and may be promoted. The pedestrian-only streets with limited access to automobile traffic (pattern b) during non-shopping hours (say before 11 am and after 9 pm) may be quite successful in medium size cities in India.

Density, FAR/FSI and Infrastructure

As discussed in Chapter 6, potential of an area is defined by the value of returns derived from the land. Returns from land depend upon its location, land use and extent of built-up area (FAR/FSI) permitted as per DCRs. It should be further noted that the FAR/FSI and density can be regulated through DCRs and, therefore, potential of land is variable and also transferable through the mechanism of TDR (see Chapter 6). Currently (2017), the use of land as a resource is not being fully exploited in spatial planning practice. In quite a lot of the recent literature on urban development (UN-Habitat, 2016; World Bank, 2013, 2015), it is highlighted that urban planners in India are following a policy of low-density development which is indicated from the low FAR/FSI and stringent development controls. The justification given by the planners in India for following this approach is lack of infrastructure to support higher densities. In Mumbai, Delhi and Chennai, the FAR/FSI in CBDs varies from 1.2 to 1.35 while in Shanghai, it is 8. In the US cities, it varies from 12 in Chicago to 15 in New York. In Tokyo, it is 20 and in Singapore, it reaches as high as 25 (Table 7.2). The critics argue that low-density development is

Table 7.2 Variation of FSI in CBDs of Selected Cities in the World

City	CBD FSI
São Paulo, Brazil	1:1
Mumbai, India	1:1.33
Chennai, India	1:1.5
Delhi, India	1:1.2–1:3.5
Amsterdam, Netherlands	1:1.9
Venice, Italy	1:2.4
Paris, France	1:3
Shanghai, China	1:8
Vancouver, Canada	1:8
San Francisco, United States	1:9
Chicago, United States	1:12
Hong Kong SAR, China	1:12
Los Angeles, United States	1:13
New York, United States	1:15
Denver, United States	1:17
Tokyo, Japan	1:20
Singapore	1:12–1:25

Source: World Bank (2013, p. 53).

one of the main causes of urban sprawl in Indian cities. Keeping low FAR/FSI suppresses economic growth, housing supply and affordability (World Bank, 2013, p. 48).

The extent of built-up space plays a significant role in urban renewal strategies and financing mechanism. Increasing FAR/FSI, however, cannot be arbitrary. It is emphasised that FAR/FSI is generally guided by factors such as land value, land use, built-up area required, accessibility and infrastructure capacity, urban pattern/form and local characteristics. These factors are closely associated with each other in a cause-and-effect relationship and work simultaneously. Hong Kong and Singapore have high FAR/FSI because of the limited land availability and larger population size to be accommodated there. In the United States of America, only a few cities, such as New York, Chicago, Los Angeles and Denver, have higher FAR/FSI and other cities generally follow the policy of low-rise development. Here the guiding factor for higher FAR/FSI is land value and land use (commercial) as evident from the lowering of FAR/ from 15 to 2 in pockets that are located away from the CBD in New York (see Figure 7.3B).

The impact of policies of FAR/FSI and norms can be illustrated from the following exercise for residential land use. Let us assume that City A has the following characteristics:

Population of city	100,000
Number of households at 5 persons/household	20,000
Overall (city level) density in pph (of developed area)*	100**
Developed area of city (100,000/100) (ha)	1,000
Gross residential area (as residential area of a city is about 50% of total area) (ha)	500
Gross residential density (1,00,000/500) pph	200

Notes: *It should be noted here that the area for density calculation is the 'developed area' of the city, not the total municipal area which is used by the Census of India for density calculation. Since the municipal area is the area under jurisdiction of the local body, it may not be developed fully and may have large vacant lands. In urban planning density is calculated on developed area basis which is defined as the area which is served by access road and basic services. All land use norms are indicated as percentage of developed area indicated in a master plan or existing land use survey.
** Density of 100 pph is based upon the average of 122 urban centres of all sizes, taking developed area as indicated in the respective master plan.

Let us also assume that the composition and distribution of households and built-up area for house is as under:

Composition of HH	Distribution of HH (%)	Number of HH	Built-up area/ DU sq. m	Total Built-up Area sq. m
EWS/LIG	50	10,000	50	500,000
MIG	30	6,000	100	600,000
HIG	15	3,000	150	450,000
VHIG	5	1,000	200	200,000
	100	20,000	–	1,750,000
Average built-up area per household (1,750,000/20,000)				87.5
Average built-up area per person (1,750,000/20,000 × 5)				17.5

Notes: HH: Households; VHIG: very high-income group.

Taking into account the assumptions made in the previous table, the FAR/FSI for different gross residential densities per hectare (10,000 sq. m) will be as follows:

Gross Residential Density (pph)	Built-up Area (sq. m)*	FAR/FSI**
200	3,500	0.35
400	7,000	0.70
600	10,500	1.05
1,000	17,500	1.75

Notes: * Built-up area = gross residential density in persons per ha × average built-up area per person.
** FAR/FSI = Built-up area/gross residential area in sq. m which is 10,000 sq. m in this case.

It shows that the FAR/FSI increases with the increase in gross residential density for a specific household composition. It increases in direct proportion. Accordingly, for gross residential density of 200 pph, the FAR/FSI is 0.35; for 400 pph (overall density of 200 pph), it will be two times that of 200 pph (0.7); and for 600 pph (overall density of 300 pph), it will be three times (1.05). For a high density of 1,000 pph (overall density 500 pph), it will rise to five times (1.75).

It may be noted that, in actual practice, doubling the FAR/FSI may not necessarily result in doubling the density as the increase in built-up area may be utilised by the same household to improve living conditions and quality of life, and hence there may not be an increase in population or density. There may, however, be situations in Indian conditions where many households let out on rent a portion of their house and so add to population increase, and therefore, change the density.

If you change the composition of households in the example mentioned in the previous paragraph, the average built-up area per person will change and hence, for the same density, FAR/FSI will change as well. To illustrate this point, let there be a high-end high-density (1,000 pph or 200 DU/ha) residential cluster accommodating a mix of HIG and VHIG households, with following housing characteristics:

Composition of HH	Distribution of HH (%)	Number of HH	Built-up Area/DU (sq. m)	Total Built-up Area (sq. m)
HIG	60	120	150	18,000
VHIG	40	80	200	16,000
	100	200	–	34,000
Average built-up area per household (34,000/200)				170
Average built-up area per person (170/5)				34

To accommodate this composition of households and gross residential density, the FAR/FSI will be

$$(1{,}000 \times 34)/10{,}000 = 3.4$$

It should be noted that in earlier case of household mix, the FAR/FSI was 1.75 for the same density of 1,000 pph.

Increasing the overall density in cities up to 300 pph (gross density 600 pph), which gives FAR/FSI of 1.05, appears to be rational and desirable in the context of benefits of compact city structures. In MPD-2021 (DDA, 2007), an overall density of 225 pph is used.

There are two questions: Should the FAR/FSI be same throughout the city? Or, should there be designated areas with higher FAR/FSI depending upon the structure of city, land use, urban design considerations, land value, accessibility and infrastructure capacity? In my opinion, the answer to first question is NO and to the second question, it is YES. It will give a variety of urban patterns and forms to the city and provide freedom to urban planners and urban designers while preparing urban renewal plans. As a result, landmarks, public spaces, vistas and street picture will develop, which will give the city a unique image. It will also provide an instrument of achieving affordable housing goals by countering the high land price by increased FAR/FSI in designated affordable housing clusters.

According to a study (ITPI, 2000), a majority of stakeholders, including spatial planners, engineers and officers of fire department, appear to be in favour of HRHD development with a rider that it should be limited to a set of designated clusters strategically located and planned in an integrated manner. It provides support to my argument of a variable FAR/FSI. However, there are two more aspects that require further intervention. These include strategic location and integrated planning. HRHD cluster should be strategically located, having regard for factors such as access by a higher hierarchy of road as well as public transport, high land value, remunerative land use (commercial, high-end residential), overlooking natural landscape areas, large planned open spaces (district park, sports complex), water bodies and such other attributes.

Depending upon the population size, planned cities as well as organically grown urban settlements have a hierarchy of centres for commercial and socio-cultural activities and include CBD, district centres, sector centres and local shopping centres. The land value is generally higher in such areas. To sustain the land value, the extent of built-up space has to be more and depending upon the accessibility, urban design considerations and infrastructure capacity, higher FAR/FSI may be allowed in designated clusters in commercial areas. As noted from Table 7.2, the FAR/FSI in the CBD of Indian cities is very low as compared to other cities of the world. As shown in Figure 7.3A, the FAR/FSI in the CBD of Mumbai, (Bandra Kurla area) is 4 while in case on New York, it varies from 2 to 15 (Figure 7.3B).

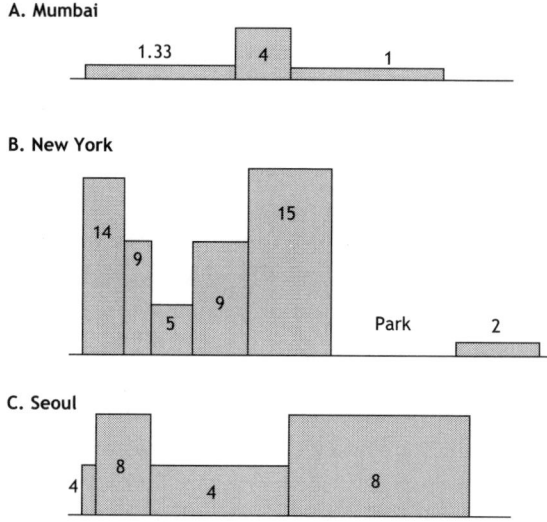

Figure 7.3 FSI Distribution in CBDs of Select Cities
Source: Based upon information from World Bank (2013).
Note: Numbers indicate the FAR/FSI in the zone.

Integrated planning approach is essential for the success of HRHD urban renewal projects. Here integration essentially refers to the convergence of various plans, projects and schemes to achieve the goals of urban renewal. Accordingly, all increase in FAR/FSI must be supported by infrastructure. The efforts pertaining to the augmentation of infrastructure should not be piecemeal, arbitrary and discriminatory where blighted areas are ignored. Under JNNURM, about ₹18,400 crore have been spent on water supply, sewerage, roads and mass transportation, which is 98% of the total amount released (i.e., ₹18,704 crore) in 2012 (Table 2.1, Chapter 2). AMRUT is the current (up to 2020) programme covering 500 cities and focusing on augmenting basic services, open spaces and public transport with fiscal support of ₹50,000 crore. This effort will augment the carrying capacity of the areas and needs to be integrated with urban renewal plan of the city also.

Local area characteristics impact the extent of built-up space and include restrictions due to heritage sites, eco-sensitive areas and socio-economic conditions such as affordability to maintain lifts needed for high-rise development and providing affordable housing to EWS and LIG persons. These issues should be solved with active stakeholder consultation and negotiations.

Use of FAR/FSI for mobilising fiscal resources is also a very practical and potent method and is being increasingly used in India as well (see Chapter 6). While preparing the urban renewal sub-plan, the transit route and nodes may also be identified as higher FAR/FSI areas to promote TOD. In case of residential areas, some pockets strategically located may be designated as HRHD pockets with higher FAR/FSI and such areas may be those that are designed for luxury housing mixed with affordable housing. The urban renewal sub-plan prepared within the framework of approved master plan will provide legal basis for the proposals, including the increase in FAR/FSI, as most of the plans provide that special regulations and DCRs would be framed for 'special areas' identified as urban renewal areas/zones in the master plan.

Mixed Land Use Pattern

Most of the existing urban centres in India have traditionally evolved with mixed land use pattern. It appears desirable to follow the same pattern, particularly in urban renewal programmes. Mixed land use pattern is more convenient to the people than single use zones. Mixed land use pattern provides opportunity for various activities that have close affinity to locate nearby and support each other. In this process, functional linkages are developed which help the business as well as the people. The most common activities found in mixed land use pattern are residential and retail commercial.

Mixed land use pattern becomes undesirable if the uses, in the mix, are of non-conforming nature such as polluting household industries in residential areas or wholesale commercial activity in core areas which attracts goods traffic and cause congestion, pollution, fire hazards and inconvenience to residents. In urban renewal programmes, particularly in core areas, compatible mixing of land uses needs to be promoted. However, care should be taken to ensure safe and convenient circulation pattern, parking and access to public transport network. This nature of mixed land use generally results in maintaining the existing socio-economic linkages, reducing conflicts, minimising displacement of people, attracting people's acceptability to the renewal proposals and adding to the success of implementation efforts. Existing non-conforming mixed uses need to be analysed and only the uses which add to the problem may be shifted to other places as designated in the master plan.

Mixing of land uses could be horizontal or vertical. A mixing of compatible land uses side-by-side on more than one plot or in the front and back portion of the same plot is termed as horizontal mixing. In vertical mixing, the compatible uses are distributed floor-wise in the same building located on the same plot. The common pattern of vertical mixing in commercial areas is shops on ground floor, office on first floor and residence on subsequent floors. Both vertical and horizontal types of mixing of land uses are practical and should be promoted. In HRHD redevelopment, vertical mixing of some social infrastructure may be attempted. For example, in residential towers, community centre may be located on the ground floor of the building and convenient shops may be located next to the lift on ground and upper floors as required. The different terraces and rooftops of the building may be developed as terrace gardens which should be appropriately guarded for children security. In commercial skyscrapers or high-rise office complexes, the uses such as guesthouses, healthcare clinic, gym and restaurants may be permitted in vertical mixed-use pattern.

Open spaces are essential and efforts need to be made in securing all existing and introducing new ones in an urban redevelopment project. A network of open spaces, integrated with pedestrian pathways connecting transit points, school, shops, park or playfield and other public places will be desirable and add convenience to the people of the area.

Mixed land use policy has been misused and diluted for political gains. Delhi is a glaring example of this misuse. There is a rampant conversion of residential areas into commercial areas which has made the area unfit for living. Resident Welfare Associations (RWAs) are resisting the mixed land use policy on account of congestion, encroachment of pedestrian paths and open spaces and lack of parking. MPD-2021 (DDA, 2007, pp. 180–181) has laid very clear conditions for mixed land uses which include no encroachment on streets or public land; front setback should not have boundary wall and be used for parking; and provide parking at the rate of two equivalent car spaces (ECS) per 100 sq. m built-up area. This parking condition has been diluted by providing an option to pay the cost of development for multilevel parking on a common area to be made available by traders' association and developed by local body under PPP mode. The entire Delhi is growing in mixed land use pattern with hardly a few parking structures. There is no land for constructing parking structures where they are needed. The development charges for parking vary from about ₹67,000 to ₹200,000 per ECS which is just a fraction of the actual cost. The shop owners pay the parking charges willingly to the local body which, having collected the money, is unable to find land and construct parking facility at a place where needed. The parking problem remains unattended, reaching to chaotic conditions in some areas.

Mixed land use policy in Delhi has disturbed the existing or planned commercial areas which are losing their business, and MPD-2021 provides higher FAR for the rejuvenation of such areas through redevelopment (DDA, 2007, p. 54). This raises a question: Should the planned hierarchy of commercial centres or land use zoning as city planning technique be discontinued in favour of mixed land uses? The answer to this question has yet to be evolved.

Inclusion and Spatial Equity

To be inclusive, urban renewal should cater to the needs and aspirations of ALL. Here, 'all' refers to all people and sections of the society, including men, women, children, youth, elderly, poor and rich, without any discrimination based on cast, religion or political affinity. It also caters to the needs of pedestrians, cyclists and motorists. As the basic principle, all should be involved in the renewal process, and enjoy its benefits.

Goal 11 of the *Sustainable Development Goals 2016* (United Nations, 2016) focuses on making cities and human settlements inclusive, safe and resilient by 2030. In addition to this, Goal 5 advocates gender equality; Goal 6 focuses on access to water for all and Goal 7 promotes access to energy for all.

To make urban renewal solutions inclusive, they should be evolved in such a manner that

- all shared resources, particularly basic public services, healthcare and education facilities, public open spaces have access to all without any discrimination;
- in case of redevelopment of slum areas, displacement of people is avoided and where necessary, efforts are made to minimise hardships in respect of access to employment opportunities and transportation to the place of work;
- integrated pedestrian pathways and cycle tracks are provided connecting school, shops, parks, playfields, transit stands and public places;
- cycle stands along with car parking lots are also provided near major transit stations;
- designated zones and places are marked in such a manner that they do not obstruct free flow of pedestrian and vehicular traffic, for informal commercial activities, to provide employment for the urban poor, in commercial centres and along access routes, including pedestrian pathways, at strategic and safe places;
- housing should have several choices in terms of size, location and cost to be affordable for all;
- safety of women, children, elderly and differently abled persons is ensured in all public places and
- barrier-free access is provided to facilitate differently abled persons.

Implementation Actions

As discussed in Chapter 5, there could be three actions for the implementation of urban renewal programmes: (a) comprehensive (b) strategic and (c) tactical. Comprehensive action, at city level, covers the entire city for urban transformation and requires large investment and high risks, and it may not find support from political and administrative decision-makers. This action may result in large-scale displacement of people which may cause social tension and unrest. The other two—strategic and tactical—actions, on the other hand, follow area-by-area action and have lesser resource requirements and conflicts and appear to be more practical and acceptable to decision-makers and people. The World Bank (2013, pp. 82–83) also advocates similar approaches and term them 'big bang and gradual' actions where big bang refers to drastic urban transformation (comprehensive action) and the gradual (strategic or tactical) covers a few selected streets and areas around transit stations for renewal at higher FAR/FSI.

The gradual approach allows planners to experiment with different combinations of strategies, rules and regulations and incentives. It also allows the evaluation of the impact of projects on people and the realty market. This evaluation will be very useful for finding the response of the people and the market which will be very useful in mid-course correction, if any, or for the replication of the successful approach to other such areas in future. However, the strategic/tactical/gradual approach results in fragmented and piecemeal development, which may not offer desired result when applied at other places and serve as a step forward in achieving an overall planned redevelopment. Urban renewal is mostly dependent on the extent of built-up space (FAR/FSI) which in turn depends on the basic services, location and land uses. It, therefore, may not be guided only by policy and development controls. Spatial plan plays significant role and there is a need to integrate these actions with the urban renewal sub-plan of the master plan of the city. In New York and Singapore, the extent of built-up space (FAR/FSI) vary by location, land use type and availability of infrastructure (World Bank, 2013, p. 82). I will like to add urban design and land price as two additional criteria to this list for assigning the extent of development. The actions for the implementation of urban renewal plan should be strategic and tactical (see Chapter 5 for details) which must be conceived within the framework of the urban renewal sub-plan of the master plan. This is an approach of total planning and strategic/tactical implementation. Urban renewal provides a win-win situation for all—people, local body/development authority/developer and the city. People get better housing, quality of life and social status. Development authority receives development charges to provide external services. Local body generates revenue as enhanced property tax. Developer earns his due share of profit. And, finally, the city gets the facelift.

Outcome assessment, feedback and research are the three aspects that follow implementation, and there is a need to promote outcome assessment (see Chapter 5) and feedback as a mandatory condition to all urban renewal programmes in future. There is also a need to promote research on urban renewal based upon the outcome assessment and feedback of various urban renewal missions, programmes and projects. The development agencies, teaching and research institutions may be encouraged to take up such research activities.

Marketing of urban renewal is another important action for the success of urban renewal programmes and their acceptance by people. Marketing also assists in promoting the application of good urban renewal approaches to other areas. The success of urban renewal should be judged by the situation when people of different areas come forward by themselves and request the authorities for taking up their area for renewal.

Summing Up

India is transforming. The current (2017–2019) political climate in the country is favourable for this transformation. There appears to be change everywhere. Planning Commission has been reincarnated as NITI Ayog. Demonetisation introduced in November 2016 has initiated fiscal transformation and introduction of cashless system of transaction. Action in 100 cities has started for transforming them to be smart under the Smart Cities Mission. Some 500 cities are being regenerated under the AMRUT in India. The Ministry of Railway is redeveloping 400 railway stations in the country to welcome passengers and improve functional efficiency. To attract tourists to explore India and have unique experience on theme-based tourism, Ministry of Tourism has launched two initiatives (Chapter 2) which include the redevelopment of 13 tourist circuits under Swadesh Darshan and renewal of 23 tourist destinations under PRASAD.

Following the new mantra—reform, perform and transform—advocated by the PM Narendra Modi, urban reforms (Chapter 4) have been introduced various urban renewal missions to equip ULBs to perform better and lead the nation on the path of socio-economic and spatial development. Reforms in urban governance support urban transformation and these are likely to continue in future in the form of e-governance with focus on public information dissemination, redressal of grievances, ease of doing business, citizens' charter, enabling rules and regulations and others. Efficient and transparent urban governance, achieved through reforms, would leverage the process of planned urban transformation. Spatial planning also needs reform to introduce comprehensive planning and strategic/tactical implementation.

Reforms in urban governance will only be successful and effective if the people are made aware of their rights, and they start demanding better services, greater transparency and accountability from the local government. Reform-linked release of fund to urban local bodies for development, as a way to implement the reforms, was adopted by JNNURM but it caused delays. Learning lesson from this, the reforms under AMRUT are not linked to release of funds. Instead, an incentive-driven approach is followed where the ULBs, which implement the reforms and achieve milestones/timeline set for reforms, are entitled to financial incentive (see Chapter 4).

Under Smart Cities Mission, a system of inter-ULBs competition for getting their project selected for funding under the Mission has been successfully implemented. It appears to be acceptable to the ULBs and state governments politically and administratively. It is a new beginning in the direction of competitive sub-federalism and a healthy sign where cities compete with each other on the path of urban transformation.

Starting from 2006, with the introduction of JNNURM (see Chapter 2), urban renewal has become a strong public policy supported with impressive fund allocation by the Government of India. It indicates the political will to transform cities. The present NDA Government is also committed to transform urban India into a vibrant and liveable system of cities and has allocated a combined sum of ₹113,123 crore (see Table 6.1, Chapter 6) up to the year 2020. This will provide the much-required experience in tackling the various situations and evolve success stories which would be the basis for further actions for India's urban transformation.

Urban renewal is the future of Indian cities. With vast political support to urban transformation in India, urban renewal is a reality that will shape urban future in the country. Planned urban extension along with urban renewal will serve as a potent strategy to harness the fruits of urbanisation and equip cities to serve their functions as the centres of immense opportunities and hope. The next 10 years will be the 'decade of urban renewal in India'.

References

DDA. (2007). *Master Plan for Delhi 2021*. New Delhi: Author.
ITPI. (2000). *Low rise high density development versus high rise high density development: Study on cost differentials and public perception*. New Delhi: Development Authority.
Ministry of Urban Employment and Poverty Alleviation. (2005). *National Urban Housing and Habitat Policy 2005*. New Delhi: Government of India.
NBCC. (2016). *NBCC 'Navratna' Enterprise: Market leader*. New Delhi: National Building Construction Corporation.
Robertson, K. A. (2010). Downtown redevelopment strategy in United States: An end-of-century assessment. In A. Tallon (Ed.), *Urban regeneration and renewal*. Oxon, UK: Routledge.
UN-Habitat. (2016). *World cities report*. Nairobi: United Nations.
United Nations. (2007). *World urbanisation prospects: The 2007 revision, population database*. UN Population Division of the Department of Economic and Social Affairs, New York.
———. (2016). *Sustainable development goals report*. New York, NY: Author.
World Bank. (2013). *Urbanization beyond municipal boundaries: Nurturing metropolitan economies and connecting peri-urban areas in India*. Washington, DC: World Bank. doi http://dx.doi.org/10.1596/978-0-8213-9840-1
———. (2015). *Leveraging urbanisation in South Asia, managing spatial transformation for prosperity and livability* (conference edition). Washington, DC: World Bank.

Index

adaptive reuse, 105–106
administrative and office expenses (A&OE), 228
Affordable Housing in Partnership (AHP) Scheme, 230
Ahmadabad Municipal Corporation (AMC), 238
Atal Mission for Rejuvenation and Urban Transformation (AMRUT), 47–51, 227
  reforms under, 136–142

bilateral organisations, 239

cities, 1, 2
  eopolis, 1
  growth and decay, 4–10
  polis, 1
  slums parts of urban fabric, 10
clearance, 100
cluster redevelopment, 101–103
Community Participation Law (CPL), 122
compensation for Land for Provision of Amenities, 224
Comptroller and Auditor General (CAG), 145
conservation, 15, 109–110
contribution by beneficiaries, 240
creation of underground spaces, 111

Delhi
  guidelines
    area redevelopment in, 202–203
    regularisation of unauthorised colonies in, 209
  policy guidelines
    scheme for relocation of JJ clusters in, 209–213
detailed project report (DPR), 180
development control rules (DCRs), 218
dispersal, 104

e-Municipality as a Service (E-MAAS), 228
eopolis, 1
EWS housing-based approach, 18

financing through market borrowing, 238
floor area ratio (FAR), 218
floor space index (FSI), 218

government grant, 226

Heritage City Development and Augmentation Yojana (HRIDAY), 51–52, 229

Implementation of the 74th CAA, 118–119
India
  growth rate of employment in, 1998–2005, 253
  projected urban population, 252
Indian Railway Station Development Corporation Limited, (IRSDC), 243

Innovative Approaches to Urban Renewal, 17–19
in situ upgradation, 108

Jawaharlal Nehru National Urban Renewal Mission (JNNURM), 116, 227
 focus and scope, 33–39
 metrorail in different cities in India, 37
 reforms under, 116–133
 sector-wise committed funds, status of, 35

land, 216
 amalgamation, cluster redevelopment, 224
 assembly, approaches, 223
 based resource mobilisation, 232
 spatial planning tools, application, 217

megapolis, 3
metropolis
 growth of, 2
Ministry of Urban Development (MoUD), 228
multilateral organisations, 239
Mumbai
 Cluster Redevelopment Scheme, 203–205
 guideline for area redevelopment in, 200–201
 slum redevelopment process, 199–201

non tax-based resources, 232

Pilgrimage Rejuvenation and Spiritual Augmentation Drive (PRASAD), 54
 objectives, 54–55
place-based approach, 17–18
polis, 2

Pradhan Mantri Awas Yojana (PMAY), 230
Pradhan Mantri Awas Yojana (Urban) (PMAY), 42–45
 reforms under, 142–143
Public Disclosure Law, 122
public–private partnership, 133, 240

railway ministry
 redevelopment of railway stations, 55
Rajiv Awas Yojana
 affordable housing in partnership, 41–42
 reforms under, 133–136
 slum-free India, 41
redensification, 106
reform-based approach, 19
reforms rationale, 114
regularisation, 107
rehabilitation, 15
relocation, 15, 103–104
Rent Control Act, 7
Rent Control Law
 reform in, 120
restoration, 15
restructuring, 110
retrofitting, 109
Right to Fare Compensation and Transparency in Land Acquisition, Rehabilitation and Resettlement (RFCTLARR) Act, 2013, 222

Slum Clearance Act, 10
Slum Rehabilitation Authority (SRA), 164
slum TDR, 221
Smart City Mission, 45–47, 229
 list of cities, 86–89
 reforms under, 144–145
spatial planning tools and techniques, 163

area redevelopment process, 164–168
  guidelines, 168–174
  norms and standards, 174–177
spatial plans, 176
  urban renewal action plan, 178
  urban renewal sub-plan, 177
Special Purpose Vehicles (SPVs)
  establishment, 243
stamp duty
  reduction in, 121
Swachh Bharat Mission, 56–59, 230
Swadesh Darshan, 52
  new projects sanctioned under, 89–93
  objective, 53–54

tax-based resource, 231
tools
  interrelationship among, 164
tourism-based approach, 18
town planning and development acts in India
  urban renewal, 158
Transferable Development Right (TDR), 220

ULB-level reforms
  implementation of mandatory, 123–133
urban local bodies (ULBs), 115
urban renewal, 11
  accessibility and connectivity, 256
  action plan, 178
  DPR, 180

city-level initiatives, 61–84
community participation, 181–185
conserve socio-cultural values, 24
density, FAR/FSI and infrastructure, 257–264
fiscal resource mobilisation, 227
future, 251–271
humane and social justice, 20–23
implementation and monitoring, 185–194
inclusion and spatial equity, 266–267
innovative approaches, 17–19
land assembly, 222
mixed land uses pattern, 264–266
national-level initiatives, 31–59
outcome assessment, 194–197
post-independence, 30
principles, 19–26
spatial approach, 255
spatial planning strategies, 98–111
stakeholders, 12–14, 25
state-level initiatives, 59–61
strike balance, 23–24
understanding terms associated, 16
urbanisation, spatial growth, 251–256
zones, 16

widening of roads through additional FAR/FSI, 226
world
  FSI in central business districts of selected cities in, variation of, 259

About the Author

S. K. Kulshrestha is a nationally known senior Urban and Regional Planner. His professional qualifications include B Arch (1963), PG Dip.# T&CP (1967) and Ph D (1980). He is a Fellow of the Institute of Town Planners, India (FITP). Dr Kulshrestha has vast experience of five decades in teaching, research and professional practice in India and Nigeria. As an academician, he has taught post graduate students at School of Planning and Architecture, New Delhi (SPA-D) (1967–1973), Ahamadu Bello University (ABU), Zaria, Nigeria (1973–1986) and again at SPA-D until 2016. As a researcher, one of his major contributions has been preparation of Guidelines (1988) for Urban Development Plan Formulation and Implementation (UDPFI) for Ministry of Urban Affairs (now Housing and Urban Affairs), Government of India, which is being widely followed for preparation and implementation of master plans in country. Dr Kulshrestha is currently associated as senior consultant on the research project of Deutsche Gesellschaft fuer Internationale Zusammenarbeit (GIZ), on Land Use Planning and Management for formulation of Land Use Policy for Odisha and Tamil Nadu states. Since 1994, he has been the Founder Editor of *Spatio-economic Development Record*, an academic Journal in spatial planning.

Dr Kulshrestha has contributed to preparation of Master Plans of five cities in India as a part of government service or consultancy (Gangtok, Singrauli, Korba, Lucknow and Kanpur) and four in Nigeria (Bichi, Gaya, Zaria and Kaura Namoda Polytechnic). He also participated in the revision of *Master Plan for Delhi 2001* and the *National Capital Region (NCR) Plan 2001*.

The key positions held by Dr Kulshrestha in the past include: Partner, Satish Jeevan & Associates, New Delhi (1987–1994); Head of the

Department of Urban and Regional Planning, Ahmadu Bello University, Zaria, Nigeria (1980–1985); and Director, Centre for Research Documentation and Training (CRDT), ITPI (1986–2001). He has been Chairman/Member of several committees. One of the most important recent Committees is The National Building Code 2016, Sectional Committee (CED 46) where he was one of the members representing ITPI. He also served on its various panels like Panel on Development Control Rules, Panel on Landscaping and Panel on Sustainability. Currently, he is the Chairman of the Committee on Conditions of Engagement of Professional Services and Scale of Professional Fees and Charges, constituted by ITPI, which will guide the professional practice in urban and regional planning in India.

Dr Kulshrestha has published/presented in national and international journals/conferences, more than 80 papers and written 2 books, including *Urban and Regional Planning in India: A Handbook for Professional Practice*, published by SAGE in 2012.